Prejudices and Antipathies

Without knowing the force of words,
it is impossible to know men.

—Confucian proverb

You with the intentness of your studies
And the elation of your knowledge
Can make the experience of struggle
The property of all.
And transform justice
Into a passion.

—Bertolt Brecht

It is high time to tackle the subject headings.

—Sidney L. Jackson

Prejudices and Antipathies

A Tract on the LC Subject Heads Concerning People

by

SANFORD BERMAN

THE 1993 EDITION,
WITH A FOREWORD BY ERIC MOON

McFarland & Company, Inc., Publishers
Jefferson, North Carolina, and London

Henry Davidoff offers the Confucian proverb on page 472 of his *World Treasury of Proverbs* (London: Cassell, n.d.). Brecht's verse-epigraph derives from a longer poem, "Worker-Actors on the Art of Observation," one of a set of seven originally titled *Gedichte aus dem Messingkauf*. This rendering by John Berger and Anya Bostock, excerpted from their 1961 translated selection, *Poems on the Theatre* (Lowestoft, Suffolk: Scorpion Press, reprint, 1963), appeared in *The Spokesman,* no. 4 (June 1970), p. 19–21. The Brechtian admonition, while addressed to "actors," may equally well be directed to *anyone* who works with the stuff of human experience. Sidney L. Jackson's remark concluded his review of *Requirements Study for Future Catalogs* (Chicago: University of Chicago Graduate Library School, 1968) in the Oct. 1, 1968, *Library Journal* (v. 93, no. 17), p. 3526. This book was originally published in 1971 by Scarecrow Press, Inc., of Metuchen, N.J.

British Library Cataloguing-in-Publication data are available

Alternative Cataloguing-in-Publication Data

Berman, Sanford, 1933–
    Prejudices and antipathies: a tract on the LC subject heads concerning people. 1933 edition, with a foreword by Eric Moon. Jefferson, NC: McFarland, 1993.
    Corrected reprint of the 1971 Scarecrow Press ed., with new foreword, preface, and index.
    Also discusses comparable forms in Sears list of subject headings.
    Some material prepared by Joan K. Marshall and Richard Bottomley.
    PARTIAL CONTENTS: Races, nationalities, faiths, and ethnic groups.
—Chauvinism, the "Bwana Syndrome," and the Third World.
—Politics, peace, labor, law enforcement, etc. —Man/woman/sex.
—Children, Youth, "Idiots," and the "Underground."
    1. Library of Congress subject headings—Criticism and interpretation. 2. Sears list of subject headings—Criticism and interpretation. 3. Subject heading bias. 4. Racism in subject headings. 5. Sexism in subject headings. 6. Ethnocentrism in subject headings. 7. Classism in subject headings. 8. Erotophobia in subject headings. I. Title. II. Title: A tract on the LC subject heads concerning people. III. Title: The LC subject heads concerning people. IV. Marshall, Joan K. V. Bottomley, Richard. VI. Moon, Eric, 1923– Foreword.   025.33 or 025.49

Library of Congress Cataloguing-in-Publication Data

Berman, Sanford, 1933–
    Prejudices and antipathies : a tract on the LC subject heads concerning people / by Sanford Berman.
       p. cm.
    Includes bibliographical references and index.
    ISBN 0-89950-828-6 (sewn softcover : 50# alk. paper) ∞
    1. Subject headings—Social sciences. 2. Subject headings, Library of Congress. 3. Subject headings—Social groups.
    4. Prejudices—United States. I. Title.
    Z695.1.S6B47 1993   025.4'93—dc20   92-50944 CIP

McFarland & Company, Inc., Publishers, Box 611, Jefferson, North Carolina 28640

Again for Samuel and Dorothy Berman,
who made this opus possible
in more ways than one

Table of Contents

Acknowledgments

Heartfelt thanks go to Anthony J. Loveday, librarian, University of Zambia, for his unstinting cooperation;

to Joan K. Marshall, cataloger at Brooklyn College Library and former SRRT Clearinghouse secretary, who contributed a number of excellent comments, substantially authored items 15 through 20 in Section IV, and kindly proofread the 1971 galleys;

to Richard Bottomley, assistant lecturer in sociology at the University of Zambia and a much-prized colleague, for preparing item 7 in Section V;

to Jill and Paul, who at age 9 and 8, expertly sorted the index cards for the first edition;

to Eric Moon and Robert Franklin for "keeping the faith" and taking a chance;

and to Lorraine, my wife, not just for the usually-cited "patience and fortitude," but also for locating much useful material, making valuable criticisms, and furnishing enough of that intangible necessity, inspiration, to power the project through.

Sanford Berman
Lusaka, Zambia, August 1970
and Hennepin County, Minnesota, 1993

Abbreviations

ACS   annual cumulative supplements to *Library of Congress Subject Headings*

API   *Alternative Press Index*

BHI   *British Humanities Index*

IILS   International Institute for Labour Studies

LC   Library of Congress

LJ   *Library Journal*

RG   *Reader's Guide to Periodical Literature*

sa   "see also" reference

SSHI   *Social Science and Humanities Index*

WLB   *Wilson Library Bulletin*

××   "see also from" reference

Foreword

Two decades and a bit ago, as president of Scarecrow Press, I became, through luck and friendship, the proud publisher of *Prejudices and Antipathies,* a small volume bound with unsubtle significance in black, with white lettering. The history of this earthquake of a book, however, began with another publisher, and continues, happily, into the nineties with yet another: one who in a way completes the circle, having been there in Metuchen, N.J., as a member of the Scarecrow family when the Berman book first appeared in 1971.

The real beginning (as my now rather faulty memory has it) was a letter from Sandy Berman which appeared in *Library Journal* in February 1969, just a few months before the end of my editorship of *LJ.* Titled "Chauvinistic headings," the letter reported Berman's conclusion, after a few weeks of using the LC subject-heading list at the University of Zambia Library, that what he had "long suspected" had "now been disgustingly confirmed: Western chauvinism permeates the scheme."

There followed more Berman letters in *LJ* and lesser sources, and gradually subject headings began to emerge as a hot new topic, particularly among the socially conscious who had been making noise in our profession for a number of years by the late sixties. But others, too, began to be aware of a disturbing rumble in the bowels of the normally quiet body of the cataloging world. The Library of Congress of course, but surprisingly also ... ALA.

An enterprising editor in the seldom enterprising publishing department of the American Library Association had his ear to the

1

ground and detected this swell of interest in what surely had not formerly been considered one of the world's most exciting documents, the LC Subject Headings.

Sensing the passion in this new voice in the pages of library literature, the ALA editor dashed off a note to Berman asking him if he'd be interested in developing his thoughts on this curious subject to book length.

The young man at East Huron Street, where things rarely move with the speed of light, must have been shocked. He not only received an enthusiastic response, but in less time than most people would take to develop a sketchy outline there arrived a complete, book-length manuscript. He had his first Berman lesson: here was a man not just of words, but of action.

In the months that followed the tone of the correspondence between Chicago and Africa began to change. Chicago's enthusiasm began to drift into reservations, doubts, then suggested changes, and finally, proposed cuts and deletions. Bureaucracy, with its customary jitters when faced with the new and radical, appeared to be trying to suffocate Berman's baby.

Sandy would have none of it; they could throw out the bathwater, but the baby he wanted back. The manuscript headed for the tropics.

Berman, who must rank high among the world's most energetic correspondents, was at the time in touch with Fay Blake, then on another of her many sojourns abroad, this time in London. Sandy asked her if she knew of a publisher he might be able to trust to publish his manuscript without emaciating it and without the kind of runaround he had just experienced. My good friend Fay said, "Send it to Eric at Scarecrow," a testimonial for which I am ever grateful.

There was, as I remember, only one moment of unease during the correspondence between Sandy and me that followed my joyous acknowledgment of the receipt of *P & A*. It was when I told him that while I had no wish to excise one wonderful word, I wanted to "reorganize" his manuscript. He wanted details, understandably, which I tried to provide, and we agreed that Scarecrow would not proceed until he had approved this latest invasion.

The reason for my proposal was physical, logistical perhaps. You will note as you read this volume that Berman's *text* on each of the subject headings he discusses is very concise and taut as a violin string. But he reinforces his case with a veritable fusillade of notes, drawn from the incredible range of his reading and research. When I received the manuscript these notes were sprinkled throughout the lean text, smothering, almost burying it.

The operation to separate these octopus-like limbs from the body was conducted first with scissors, until the manuscript had been reduced to hundreds of narrow slips of paper, and then with stapler to put these remnants, like Humpty Dumpty, back together again.

I haven't checked the *Guinness Book of Records* but I believe I may be the first person to have developed tennis elbow from editing a manuscript.

A word further about those notes. If you are at all like me you do not swell with ardor at the sight of a footnote. You may, indeed, regard these things as a damn nuisance, a distraction. Prepare for something different within these covers. Good as Berman's text is, it is the notes in this volume that give the book its unique fascination—and its extra zing. Boxers talk about the old one-two. The notes here are the two. Don't miss 'em.

And now Sandy Berman's resounding seminal work is elevated to a new status as a paperback, to be read, one hopes, by many more than have already reveled in the hardbound version. As I browse through its pages once more after all these years, I am amazed to realize how far Sandy has brought us—and cataloging, and LC.

Among all the wonderful quotations that enliven these pages there is one, it seems to me, that speaks of Berman himself. It is the moving Bertolt Brecht quotation which nestles between Confucius and Sidney Jackson at the beginning of the book.

For Berman, indeed, with the intentness of *his* studies and the elation of *his* knowledge, has made the experience of struggle the property of us all. Justice is clearly *his* passion, and one must hope that he so transforms it for all of us. This warm, quiet man has been, during the twenty-odd years I've known him, our leading missionary, revolutionary, irritant, conscience and inspiration. His is one of the great voices among us, and our libraries and our profession are the better for his wisdom and his caring passion. It is a great personal joy to be given this opportunity to welcome his *Prejudices and Antipathies* back into circulation.

Eric Moon
1993

Preface : 1993

It's frankly tempting, some 21 years later, to gloat over the many recommendations that have become reality. JEWISH QUESTION and YELLOW PERIL were both abolished, while RACE RELATIONS and AFRO-AMERICANS rightly replaced RACE QUESTION and NEGROES. The Library of Congress (LC) properly dropped "rogues and vagabonds" as a "see also" reference to GYPSIES, and likewise deleted the prejudicial link from "Sexual perversion" to HOMOSEXUALITY and LESBIANISM. Similarly, LC compacted dozens of WOMEN AS . . . forms—WOMEN AS ACCOUNTANTS for instance becoming simply and nonjudgmentally WOMEN ACCOUNTANTS. And CHILD REARING eventually supplanted the ageist heading CHILDREN—MANAGEMENT.

But these changes, however welcome, are no cause for gloating. It took 13 years for LC to scrap JEWISH QUESTION and 18 to eliminate YELLOW PERIL, hardly examples of swift response and profound sensitivity. GYPSIES, it's true, are no longer tarred as "rogues and vagabonds," but neither are they called by their own, self-preferred name: ROMANIES (or ROMA), and no heading yet denotes their experience during the Third Reich, which directly parallels what happened to Jews. Christocentrism continues to permeate the LC scheme, and most "Primitive" forms persist, despite the fact that anthropologists have renounced the term as unhelpful and "loaded," and an American Library Association committee in 1983 made specific, sensible suggestions for either cancelling or replacing nearly every "Primitive" descriptor. "Oriental" headings still abound, even though what's usually being represented is really "Asian," and the very word, "Orient," seems to be in disfavor among Asian-Americans.

Even more importantly, the original "tract" just didn't go far enough. It should have been at least three times longer, examining not only biased subject headings (including many more inauthentic ethnonyms and scores of slanted, sometimes defamatory, forms concerning seniors, disabled persons, sexual minorities, women, and poor people), but also LC's monumental

- failure to promptly create and begin using headings for people-related topics actually appearing in books and other media;

- failure to helpfully assign headings that are already available: i.e., undercataloging a given work or rendering important aspects of it invisible; and

- failure to compose "public notes" that clarify the scope and meaning of new or unusual topics, perhaps like these done at Hennepin County Library (Minnesota):

SAND CREEK MASSACRE, 1864.
Here are entered materials on the November 29, 1864, massacre of Cheyenne Indians at Sand Creek, Colorado, by United States troops commanded by Colonel John Chivington.

HATE CRIMES.
Here are entered materials on "criminal acts that target individuals or groups because of the victim's sex, race, color, religion, sexual orientation, disability, age or national origin." Such "terrorizing and often violent acts include arson, bombings of homes and businesses, cross burnings, vandalism (like swastika drawings), personal assaults, harassing or obscene phone calls and threatening letters or packages."

ZOUK MUSIC.
Here is entered Caribbean dance music blending West Indian chants, African rhythms, and Western pop.

So this preface concludes not with smugness nor self-satisfaction, but rather with an invitation, a challenge, to help finish the work started in 1971 by copying, signing, circulating, and mailing these petitions:

TO: Chief, Cataloging Policy and Support Office, The Library of Congress, Washington DC 20540

WE, the undersigned, urge the Library of Congress to speedily create and assign the following subject headings for women-related materials:

AFRO-AMERICAN FEMINISM
ANARCHA-FEMINISM
ANTIFEMINISTS
ANTIPORNOGRAPHY MOVEMENT
ARRANGED MARRIAGE
BIOLOGICAL DETERMINISM
CHILD SUPPORT ENFORCEMENT
CHRISTIAN FEMINISM
FAMILY PLANNING
FAMILY PLANNING SERVICES
FEMINIST ART
FEMINIST COLLECTIVES
FEMINIST DRAMA
FEMINIST ESSAYS
FEMINIST ETHICS
FEMINIST FAIRY TALES

FEMINIST FICTION
FEMINIST HUMOR
FEMINIST PERIODICALS
FEMINIST SONGS
FEMINIST SPIRITUALITY
GAY MEN'S WIVES
GYNOCIDE
JEWISH LESBIANS
LESBIAN AUTHORS
LESBIAN BATTERING
LESBIAN FEMINISM
LESBIAN SEPARATISM
LESBIAN TEENAGERS
LESBIANS—COMING OUT
LOOKSISM
NONSEXIST CHILDREN'S LITERATURE

NONSEXIST LITURGY
NONSEXIST PARENTING
NONSEXIST TEENAGE LITERATURE
NONSEXIST WRITING GUIDELINES
PARENTAL NOTIFICATION LAWS
RADICAL FEMINISM
SEX TOURISM
SEXUAL SLAVERY
SOCIALIST FEMINISM
VIOLENCE AGAINST WOMEN
WOMEN-FRIENDSHIP
WOMEN TROUBADOURS
WOMEN'S BOOKSTORES
WOMEN'S MOVEMENT
WOMEN'S MUSIC
WOMEN'S POWER

*Name   *Position   *Library/School/Organization   *Address   *Date

_____

_____

_____

_____

_____

TO: Chief, Cataloging Policy and Support Office, The Library of Congress, Washington DC 20540

WE, the undersigned, ask the Library of Congress to immediately replace the following subject headings with in-clusive terms:

COLLEGE FRESHMEN/suggested: COLLEGE FROSH
COLOR OF MAN/COLOR OF HUMANS
CRO-MAGNON MAN/CRO-MAGNONS
FALL OF MAN/"THE FALL" (BIBLICAL THEME)
FOSSIL MAN/PREHISTORIC HUMANS
FREEDMEN/FREED SLAVES
MAN/HUMANS
MAN-MADE FIBERS INDUSTRY/SYNTHETIC FIBERS INDUSTRY
MAN, PREHISTORIC/PREHISTORIC HUMANS

MANPOWER/HUMAN RESOURCES
MANPOWER PLANNING/HUMAN RESOURCES PLANNING
NORTHMEN/NORTHMEN AND NORTHWOMEN
OMBUDSMAN/OMBUD
SUFFRAGETTES/SUFFRAGISTS
SWORDSMEN/SWORD FIGHTERS
WATCHMEN/GUARDS
WILD MEN/"WILD" HUMANS
WORKMANSHIP/ARTISANSHIP

*Name   *Position   *Library/School/Organization   *Address   *Date

TO: Chief, Cataloging Policy and Support Office, The Library of Congress, Washington DC 20540

WE, the undersigned, urge the Library of Congress to (a) abandon the subject heading GAYS inasmuch as there is no acceptable umbrella-term for both gay men and lesbians; (b) institute a "see"-reference from "Gays" to GAY MEN and LESBIANS; and (c) promptly establish and apply these needed descriptors:

ADOPTION BY GAY MEN AND LESBIANS
DRAG QUEENS
GAY AND LESBIAN RIGHTS
GAY AND LESBIAN STUDIES
GAY ARTISTS
GAY AUTHORS
GAY BATHS
GAY DETECTIVES
GAY HOLOCAUST (1933–1945)
GAY LITERATURE
GAY MEN–COMING OUT

GAY-OWNED BUSINESSES
GAY PERIODICALS
GAY TEACHERS
GAY THEATER
HETEROSEXUALITY
HOMOPHOBIA IN THE ARMED FORCES
JEWISH LESBIANS
LESBIAN ARTISTS
LESBIAN ATHLETES
LESBIAN AUTHORS
LESBIAN BATTERING

LESBIAN DETECTIVES
LESBIAN FEMINISM
LESBIAN LITERATURE
LESBIAN-OWNED BUSINESSES
LESBIAN PERIODICALS
LESBIAN SEPARATISM
LESBIAN TEENAGERS
LESBIANS–COMING OUT
STONEWALL REBELLION, 1969
VIOLENCE AGAINST GAY MEN AND
  LESBIANS

*Name   *Position   *Library/School/Organization   *Address   *Date

TO: Chief, Cataloging Policy and Support Office, The Library of Congress, Washington DC 20540

WE, the undersigned, urge the Library of Congress to (a) replace the present subject heading TRADE-UNIONS with the more familiar and commonly-used form, LABOR UNIONS; and (b) establish and assign these warranted and essential headings:

CALIFORNIA GRAPE BOYCOTT
CHILD LABOR EXPLOITATION
CLASSISM
CLERICAL HOMEWORKERS
COLLECTIVES
COLORADO COAL STRIKE, 1913-1914
CORPORATE CRIME
CORPORATE POWER
COSH GROUPS
EMPIRE ZINC STRIKE, 1950-1952
EMPLOYEE DRUG TESTING
EMPLOYEE LIE DETECTOR TESTING
EMPLOYEE MEDICAL TESTING
EMPLOYEE RESISTANCE AND REVOLTS
EMPLOYEE WELLNESS PROGRAMS
EMPLOYEE WORK MONITORING
EMPLOYEES—PRIVACY RIGHTS
EMPLOYER NEGLIGENCE
EMPLOYMENT PROGRAMS
FRUIT PICKERS

INJURED WORKERS
LABOR CARTOONS
LABOR EDUCATION
LABOR EDUCATION MATERIALS
LABOR EXPLOITATION
LABOR ORGANIZERS
LABOR ORGANIZING
LABOR PERIODICALS
LABOR POSTERS
LABOR REPORTERS
LABOR RIGHTS
LABOR SOLIDARITY
LABOR SONGS
LOWELL TEXTILE WORKERS' STRIKE, 1836
MINNEAPOLIS TRUCK DRIVERS' STRIKE, 1934
OCCUPATIONAL REPRODUCTIVE HAZARDS
PATCO STRIKE, 1981
RACISM IN LABOR UNIONS
SANITATION WORKERS' STRIKE, MEMPHIS, TENNESSEE, 1968

SEXISM IN LABOR UNIONS
VIDEO DISPLAY TERMINAL WORK MONITORING
WEST VIRGINIA MINE WARS, 1912-1922
WORK QUOTAS
WORK SPEEDUPS
WORK STANDARDIZATION
WORK-STUDY PROGRAMS
WORKER COOPERATIVES
WORKER REGIMENTATION
WORKER RIGHT-TO-KNOW LAWS
WORKERS' CONTROL
WORKING CLASS BARS
WORKING CLASS CHILDREN
WORKING CLASS CULTURE
WORKING POOR PEOPLE
WORKPLACE DESIGN
WORKSITE BASIC EDUCATION PROGRAMS
YALE UNIVERSITY CLERICAL AND TECHNICAL WORKERS' STRIKE, 1984

*Name   *Position   *Library/School/Organization   *Address   *Date

TO: Chief, Cataloging Policy and Support Office, The Library of Congress, Washington DC 20540

WE, the undersigned, urge the Library of Congress to (a) replace PUBLIC WELFARE and PUBLIC WELFARE ADMINISTRATION with the more familiar forms WELFARE and WELFARE ADMINISTRATION; (b) humanize the current heading POOR by transforming it into POOR PEOPLE; and (c) swiftly establish and assign these warranted and essential headings related to poverty, hunger, homelessness, and social policy:

ANTI-HUNGER MOVEMENT
CHILD LABOR EXPLOITATION
CHILDREN OF UNEMPLOYED PARENTS
CLASSISM
CLASSISM IN ECONOMIC POLICY
CLASSISM IN EDUCATION
CLASSISM IN LAW
CLASSISM IN LIBRARIANSHIP
CLASSISM IN LITERATURE
CLASSISM IN MEDICAL CARE
CLASSISM IN SOCIAL POLICY
CLASSISM IN TEXTBOOKS
DEMOCRATIC SOCIALISM
ECONOMIC DEMOCRACY
FARM CRISIS

FARM FORECLOSURES
FOOD SHELVES
GRASSROOTS MOVEMENT
HOMELESS AFRO-AMERICAN WOMEN
HOMELESS FAMILIES
HOMELESS FAMILY SERVICES
HOMELESS GIRLS
HOMELESS MENTALLY ILL PERSONS
HOMELESS MENTALLY ILL PERSONS'
    SERVICES
HOMELESS PEOPLE IN ART
HOMELESS PEOPLE'S ADVOCATES
HOMELESS PEOPLE'S ART
HOMELESS TEENAGERS
HUNGER ACTIVISTS

INTERCLASS FRIENDSHIP
LOW-INCOME HOUSING
MARXISM
NONCLASSIST CHILDREN'S LITERATURE
POOR FAMILIES
POOR MEN
POOR PARENTS
POOR PEOPLE – EMPOWERMENT
POOR PEOPLE IN FILMS
POOR SENIORS
POOR SINGLE MOTHERS
RIGHT TO SHELTER
UNEMPLOYED SENIORS
UNEMPLOYED WOMEN WORKERS
URBAN POOR PEOPLE
VIOLENCE AGAINST POOR PEOPLE

*Name   *Position   *Library/School/Organization   *Address   *Date

TO: Chief, Cataloging Policy and Support Office, The Library of Congress, Washington DC 20540

WE, the undersigned, urge the Library of Congress to (a) change the present heading HOLOCAUST, JEWISH (1939–1945) to HOLOCAUST, JEWISH (1933–1945), thus making the Holocaust coincide with the Third Reich instead of appearing to be merely a byproduct of World War II; (b) replace NATIONAL SOCIALISM and NATIONAL SOCIALISTS with the more familiar and commonly-used forms, NAZISM and NAZIS; (c) convert FALASHAS, ESKIMOS, and GYPSIES to these people's self-preferred, authentic names: BETA ISRAEL, INUIT, and ROMANIES (or ROMA); (d) fully implement recommendations made in 1983 by the American Library Association's Ad Hoc Subcommittee on Concepts Denoted by the Term "Primitive" (for details, see *Technical Services Quarterly*, v. 2, nos. 1/2, Fall/Winter 1984, p. 121–53); (e) eliminate "Christian primacy" in all religion-related headings; e.g., assign to works on the Christian deity a new form, GOD (CHRISTIANITY), instead of the unmodified and therefore preeminent GOD; (f) substitute HANSEN'S DISEASE and HANSEN'S DISEASE PATIENTS, both terms sanctioned by the U.S. Public Health Service, for the stigmatizing LEPROSY and LEPERS; (g) abandon PYGMIES, instead use the names of specific "pygmy" groups; e.g., MBUTI (AFRICAN PEOPLE); and (h) establish and assign these warranted and essential headings:

AFROCENTRIC EDUCATION
AFROCENTRIC HISTORIOGRAPHY
AMISTAD REBELLION, 1839
ANTI-ARABISM
ANTI-SEMITES
ANTISEMITISM IN CHRISTIANITY
ANTISEMITISM IN THE ARMED FORCES
ARPILLERAS
BLACK-ON-BLACK CRIME
CULTURAL IMPERIALISM
DISABILITY RIGHTS MOVEMENT
DREADLOCKS
ETHNIC POLICY
ETHNOCENTRISM IN CHILDREN'S LITERATURE
ETHNOCIDE
FOOD AS A WEAPON
HATE GROUPS
HOLOCAUST, ROMANI (1933–1945)

INTERRACIAL FRIENDSHIP
JEWS, SPANISH—HISTORY—EXPULSION, 1492
MAKOSSA MUSIC
MBAQANGA MUSIC
MULTICULTURAL EDUCATION
MULTIETHNIC NEIGHBORHOODS
MUSLIMS—SPAIN—HISTORY—EXPULSION, 1502
NATIONALITY POLICY
NATIVE AMERICAN HOLOCAUST (1492–1900)
NAZI COLLABORATORS
NAZI FUGITIVES
NAZI HUNTERS
NEOCOLONIALISM
NEW INTERNATIONAL ECONOMIC ORDER
NEW WORLD INFORMATION ORDER
NONALIGNED MOVEMENT
NONRACIST CHILDREN'S LITERATURE

NORTH-SOUTH RELATIONS
PA NDAU APPLIQUE
PALESTINIAN STATE (PROPOSED)
POWWOWS
RACISM IN BIOLOGY
RACISM IN CAPITAL PUNISHMENT
RACISM IN CHILDREN'S LITERATURE
RACISM IN CHRISTIANITY
RACISM IN EMPLOYMENT
RACISM IN HOUSING
RACISM IN LAW
RED POWER
SKINHEADS
SOCA MUSIC
SOUKOUS (MUSIC)
TEX-MEX MUSIC
THIRD WORLD SUPPORT GROUPS
VIOLENCE AGAINST GAY MEN & LESBIANS
VIOLENCE AGAINST MINORITIES

TO: Chief, Cataloging Policy and Support Office, The Library of Congress, Washington DC 20540

WE, the undersigned, urge the Library of Congress to assign genre and form headings (e.g., REGENCY NOVELS, ENGLISH ESSAYS, NICARAGUAN POETRY, ISRAELI HUMOR, AMERICAN DRAMA, UNDERGROUND COMIX, FEMINIST FICTION) as well as topical and character headings with form subdivisions (e.g., RAPE—FICTION, AIDS—DRAMA, GAULS—COMIC BOOKS, STRIPS, ETC., HOLMES, SHERLOCK—FICTION, WOMEN WORKERS—POETRY, CHICAGO BEARS—FICTION, OKLAHOMA—MUSICALS) to individual literary, musical, and artistic works, including novels, poetry, essays, letters, humor, plays, librettos, scores, cartoons, comic books, and photography.

*Name	*Position	*Library/School/Organization	*Address	*Date

For further reading:

"Access/Equity," *The Joy of Cataloging: Essays, Letters, Reviews, and Other Explosions* (Oryx Press, 1981), p. 61–155.

"Cataloging Tools and 'Copy': The Myth of Acceptability—A Public Librarian's Viewpoint," *Cataloging Heresy: Challenging the Standard Bibliographic Product* (Learned Information, 1992), p. 31–6.

"Compare and Contrast, or, The Unexamined Cataloguing Record Isn't Worth Inputting," *Alternative Library Literature, 1988/1989* (McFarland, 1990), p. 173–81.

"The 'Fucking' Truth About Library Catalogs," *Progressive Librarian*, no. 5 (Summer 1992), p. 19–25.

"Politics of Cataloging," *National Librarian*, August 1990, p. 2–7.

Subject Cataloging: Critiques and Innovations (Haworth Press, 1984), especially "Two Changed Headings: Documentation" (p. 155–65), "Out of the Kitchen—But Not into the Catalog" (p. 167–71), and "Beyond the Pale: Subject Access to Judaica" (p. 173–89).

"Things Are Seldom What They Seem: Finding Multicultural Materials in Library Catalogs," *Alternative Library Literature, 1990/1991* (McFarland, 1992), p. 132–36.

"Tips on Cataloging and Classification for Library Users: A Generic Handout," *Public Image*, v. 3, no. 1 (Oct. 1990), p. 1–3.

Worth Noting: Editorials, Letters, Essays, an Interview, and Bibliography (McFarland, 1988), especially "Herrenvolk Language" (p. 3–8), "Fiction Access" (p. 9–20), "Where Have All the Moonies Gone?" (p. 23–31), and "The Terrible Truth About Teenlit Cataloging" (p. 38–50).

Sandy Berman
Edina, Minnesota, January 1993

Introduction : 1971

Since the first edition of *Library of Congress Subject Headings* appeared 60 years ago, American and other libraries have increasingly relied on this list as the chief authority—if not the sole basis—for subject cataloging. There can be no quarrel about the practical necessity for such a labor-saving, worry-reducing work, nor—abstractly—about its value as a global standardizing agent, a means for achieving some uniformity in an area that would otherwise be chaotic. Undoubtedly, it is a real boon to scholars, as well as to ordinary readers, to find familiar, fairly constant headings in subject catalogs as far removed geographically as Washington, D.C., and Lusaka, Zambia. Knowledge and scholarship are, after all, universal. And a subject-scheme *should*, ideally, manage to encompass all the facets of what has been printed and subsequently collected in libraries to the satisfaction of the worldwide reading community. *Should*, that is. But in the realm of headings that deal with people and cultures—in short, with humanity—the LC list can only "satisfy" parochial, jingoistic Europeans and North Americans, white-hued, at least nominally Christian (and preferably Protestant) in faith, comfortably situated in the middle- and higher-income brackets, largely domiciled in suburbia, fundamentally loyal to the Established Order, and heavily imbued with the transcendent, incomparable glory of Western civilization.[1] Further, it reflects a host of untenable—indeed, obsolete and arrogant—assumptions with respect to young people and women.[2] And exudes something less than sympathy or even fairness toward organized labor and the sexually unorthodox or "avant-garde."

15

In reply to a brief assault on the "racist/colonialist bias," double-standards, and "self-serving euphemisms" embodied in the LC scheme,[3] A. C. Foskett explained that both the LC and Sears schema "are designed for use in Western libraries" and so "reflect the historical bias of those libraries and their users."[4] Exactly the point! Once recognized, surely the most foolish and wrong-headed aspects of the bias can be corrected. Mr. Foskett admitted, in fact, that the sort of *Baaskap* nonsense limned in that initial attack might be "objectionable" within "the context of a different tradition."[5] Why not "objectionable" *any*where?[6] Just because the scheme germinated, historically, within a Western framework of late Victorianism, rampant industrial expansion, and feverish empire-building (with its "White Man's Burden" rationale)—just because, in short, we were "brought up that way" is no valid reason for perpetuating, either in our crania or catalogues, the humanity-degrading, intellect-constricting rubbish that litters the LC list.[7] Moreover, within the context of a world increasingly polarized between White/Black, rich/poor, West/Tiers-Monde, the burden is fully and immediately upon *us* to at least rectify the worst features of library practice: in cataloging, the selection of "relevant" (even if controversial) material, service to long-bypassed groups, and—with particular reference to Western institutions—employment.[8] "Which side are you on?" asked striking miners years ago in a song that has since become an American folk staple. The question holds with even greater immediacy now.[9]

The cry to "tell it like it is" currently echoes, justifiably, around the globe.[10] Granted, being fallible, we don't always know precisely *what* it is or *how* to "tell it." Still, simple honesty and our own professional commitment to elemental decency require that we *try*.

Mr. Foskett concluded his remarks with the comment that if the fault-finding letter-writer "wants a disinterested scheme, he will have to look elsewhere."[11] Such advice, however well-intentioned, evades the issue. The LC scheme, like it or not, dominates the subject-cataloging scene.[12] It may be somewhat optimistic, yes, to believe it can be wholly metamorphosed into the *disinterested* tool that most American (and other) libraries, presumably democratic and egalitarian in spirit, desire. But on the other hand, it is impossibly utopian, an exercise in fantasy, to expect that even hugely-disgruntled librarians will scrap it completely in favor of another, better scheme that hasn't yet materialized. And probably never will.

What follow, then, are not *dicta* nor *commandments,* but rather probes—hopefully provocative—into what has been a largely unquestioned orthodoxy; a not-so-delicate burrowing into the subject-muck that constitutes an important element of our "professional practice" and which we have cheerfully (if, in most cases, innocently) propagated to our all-too-receptive brethren across the seas. If this be incitement, good. But not to riot, if you please—only to remedy long-standing mistakes and to gain for the profession a genuine, earned respect among people who read and think.

Four final observations:

1. Some, not "bad" people, will make the argument-from-inertia that to correct even the most glaring outrages presently embedded in library catalogs would require too massive an undertaking in time and labor, that it is not easy to at once undo the mess that has accumulated over half a century, that the job is inconvenient.[13] Assuredly, this is no flippant nor meanly inspired objection. Yet the certain "inconvenience" must be weighed against the colossal demands of our revolutionary age and professional integrity alike. Once weighed, we are unquestionably ingenious and energetic enough (not to mention well-enough equipped with electric typewriters and erasers)—whether at LC itself or in our individual institutions—to do what must be done.

2. The profession has lately undergone, in Sidney L. Jackson's opinion, a "ten-year struggle," expending vast amounts of "labor and money," to fashion "a new code for main entries, while neglecting by and large the problems of subject access." His conclusion, based on hard evidence demonstrating a reader preference for the "subject approach," is that the main entry campaign, "in terms of *user* advantage," was a *"monumental blunder."*[14] Although Jackson does not spotlight ingrained bias as one of the problem priorities in subject cataloging, it must certainly rate high in the sort of thorough-going examination and reform he advocates. The cardinal point here is that, from a purely pragmatic view, we have probably been riding backwards on the wrong horse.

3. Questioning the basic philosophy that underpins LC practice, Joan Marshall writes:

> The guiding principles of the establishment of subject headings
> in the LC list are set forth in Haykin's *Subject Headings: A
> Practical Guide* (Washington, D.C.: Library of Congress, 1951).
> The first of the fundamental concepts in the establishment of a
> heading, as stated by Haykin (p. 7), is "that the reader is the
> focus in all cataloging principles and practice." The termi-
> nology, therefore, of an effective and easy-to-approach catalog
> must be determined by the majority of the readers' probable
> psychological approach, rather than a *logical* approach, to the
> subject. References serve the needs of minorities.
>   This "cataloging axiom" has two serious faults. The first is
> the assumption that libraries, keeping "in mind the kind of
> reader the library serves, his social background and intellectual
> level" (p. 9), tailor-make subject headings to suit their patrons.
> This assumption is unfounded. Libraries use lists. The use of
> maintained, up-dated lists is an economic necessity (and has
> the added desirability of creating uniformity of usage from
> library to library). Since the use of lists is the norm, the list-
> makers must accept responsibility for viewing their reader as an
> aggregate who has varied social backgrounds and intellectual
> levels. Since the reader cannot validly be identified, assump-
> tions about his probable psychological approach to a subject
> result in serious lapses in logic.
>   The second fault of the axiom is that it violates the principle,
> constantly defended in regard to our collections, that libraries
> do not exhibit bias. If librarians defend their right as educators
> to present all points of view in their collections, they must ac-
> cept their obligation to provide an approach to their collections
> that is equally without bias, and which does not reinforce the
> psychological, sociological, economic, political, etc. assump-
> tions and prejudices of their readers. Such obvious pandering to
> the "social backgrounds and intellectual levels" of a library's
> clientele as the entry of works under FILTHY BOOKS or NIGGERS
> would be castigated by the profession; it would be recognized
> that such an obviously biased *approach* to the material biased
> the *material,* whatever its content.[15]
>   What we must come to recognize are the more subtle forms
> of the reinforcement of attitudes through a biased subject
> heading approach.
>   The LC list, in its headings referring to persons, reflects the

application of Haykin's axiom (actually, though not logically, Haykin's axiom is a statement of LC subject heading policy—the list came before the guide). The list's bias and illogicality are a reflection of its identification of the majority reader and the extrapolation from that identification that *that* reader is the norm. An examination of the list makes it clear that the "majority reader" (and the norm)—as far as LC is concerned—is white, Christian (usually Protestant), and male.[16]

4. This "tract" has emphatically *not* been conceived as an *ad hominem* attack on the LC editors and staff. They perform, competently, a gargantuan labor, which deserves our appreciation. The following critique ought not to be construed as an insult to them, but instead as an aid and plea for finally grappling with a significant matter—the reexamination of inherited assumptions and underlying values—that in the past has probably seemed too difficult or insufficiently pressing to confront because of the sheer volume of traffic, of other things to do. An aid, then, and a plea—directed to *all* of us—to attend to urgent business.

The cited examples and complaints may well be multiplied, and perhaps even more penetratingly analyzed, by an alert and sensitive profession. Let the dialogue and *action* begin...

Notes

1. In broader perspective, of course, it is not alone in this many-pronged bias. Similar ills beset educational systems and the publishing world itself. For a report, e.g., on stereotyping and racism in British school texts, cf. Ian Stewart, "Readers as a Source of Prejudice?," *Race Today,* v. 2, no. 1 (Jan. 1970), p. 27–8. *Rank and File,* "produced by left-wing teachers within the N.U.T. [National Union of Teachers]," similarly carries incisive, usually firsthand material on racial and religious bias in British classrooms; cf., for instance: Mike Slatter, "Racialism... One Teacher's Experience," no. 6 (June 1969), p. 9–10, and Maurice Hill, "Religious Discrimination in Our Schools," no. 7 (Sept. 1969), p. 20–1. The quarterly bulletin issued by the Council on Interracial Books for Children (9 East 40th Street, New York, N.Y. 10016), together with the bimonthly *Integrated Education: Race and Schools* and *Changing Education,* the American Federation of Teachers' journal, furnish like data on the American scene. And so, frequently, do

"Movement" organs like *Liberation;* cf., e.g., Steve Gold, "Unlearning White Racism," v. 14, no. 1 (March/April 1969), p. 21–9.

Perhaps no one has more compellingly and thoroughly examined the mechanics and effects of cultural "brain-washing" and White-instigated de-racination among people of specifically African descent—in the Caribbean, North America, Europe, and Africa—than Frantz Fanon in *Black Skin, White Masks* (New York: Grove Press, 1967). "He demonstrates," said one reviewer, "how insidiously the problem of race, of color, connects with a whole range of words and images." Robert Coles, *New York Times Book Review,* April 30, 1967, p. 3. His work is thus essential reading for anyone wanting a fuller perspective on the psychosocial impact of "Westernism" upon non–Western and minority peoples.

As another, necessary overview of racist contagion among Western peoples, a slender volume that nonetheless makes a multitude of excellent conceptual distinctions and lucidly defines many terms often misused by laymen and specialists alike, cf. Pierre L. van den Berghe, *Race and Racism; A Comparative Perspective* (New York: John Wiley & Sons, 1967). Granting that "racism" may be found "in a number of societies," the author empha-sizes that "it remains true that the Western strain of the virus has eclipsed all others in importance. Through the colonial expansion of Europe, racism spread widely over the world.

"Apart from its geographical spread, no other brand of racism has developed such a flourishing mythology and ideology. In folklore, as well as in literature and science, racism became a deeply ingrained component of the Western Weltanschauung. Western racism had its poets like Kipling, its philosophers like Gobineau and Chamberlain, its statesmen like Hitler, Theodore Roosevelt, and Verwoerd; this is a record not even remotely ap-proached in either scope or complexity by any other cultural tradition." Cf. "Introduction," p. 13.

2. In this regard, again, it fits into and mirrors a much larger soci-etal pattern. For insightful critiques of "women's subjugation in our soci-ety," cf. the lately-arisen "women's liberation" vehicles like *No More Fun and Games* and *Women: A Journal of Liberation,* both approvingly reviewed by Mary McKenney in the April 15, 1970, *Library Journal* (v. 95, no. 8) p. 1459.

Young people, too, have taken up the cudgels on their own behalf, zestfully and often angrily assailing the hoary shibboleth that youth should "be seen and not heard." Bill Katz, on p. 354 of his *Magazines for Libraries* (New York: Bowker, 1969), cites a number of such "student power" organs, confected wholly by high schoolers. Still more data on the genre can be secured from the Amerikan Press Syndicate, 9426 Santa Monica Boule-vard, Beverly Hills, California 90210.

3. Sanford Berman, "Chauvinistic Headings," *Library Journal,* v. 94,

no. 4 (Feb. 15, 1969), p. 695; subsequently reprinted, with some changes, in the *Zambia Library Association Journal,* v. 1, no. 2 (June 1969), p. 31–3.

4. "Dead Heads?," *Library Journal,* v. 94, no. 8 (April 15, 1969), p. 1559.

5. *Ibid.* "Chauvinistic Headings" originated in a Central African milieu, the writer having discovered, "after three weeks of using the LC subject heading list at the University of Zambia Library," that what he had "long suspected" had "now been disgustingly confirmed: Western chauvinism permeates the scheme." Berman, *op. cit.*

6. Of that ice-breaking *LJ* letter, *ibid.,* Donald B. Engley, librarian, and Mrs. Marian Clarke, curator, at Trinity College Library, Hartford, Connecticut, declared in a statement sent to both LC and the American Library Association: "In it [the writer] makes the point that our major cataloging and classification schemes reflect a western racist/colonial bias. We believe that this is evident not only in an African setting such as his, but also to the sensitive observer anywhere in the world today." Quoted from a carbon copy, dated March 13, 1969.

7. This is not to propound a "magic-wand" thesis that once the LC "prejudices and antipathies" are corrected, Love and Good Feeling will radiate across the planet. But the operation may nevertheless prove a definite, if small, step in the right direction—toward amity and mutual understanding. Henri Tajfel reasonably maintains that "there is no easy way to deal with intergroup prejudice in its manifold varieties, and all one can hope for is that its more vicious and inhuman forms can be made less acute sooner or later. It is patently obvious that beliefs and views about causes of social events which are held by great masses of men are more easily accessible to change than their motives; and that there is at least a chance that a change of beliefs and views may affect in turn the management of conflicts, real or imaginary." He concludes that "it is therefore important and *useful,* for the purposes of science as well as for those of the society at large, that a consideration of prejudice as a phenomenon in the minds rather than in the guts of men should take precedence over views which are, on the whole, not only untestable but also useless in the planning of any form of relevant social change." Cf. "Cognitive Aspects of Prejudice," 1968 winner of the first annual Gordon Allport Intergroup Relations Prize, *Journal of Social Issues,* v. 25, no. 4 (autumn 1969), p. 96.

8. On the employment-promotion imperatives re women, Blacks, Mexican-Americans, etc., cf., as examples: Anita R. Schiller, "Women Employed in Libraries; The Disadvantaged Majority," *American Libraries,* v. 1, no. 4 (April 1970), p. 345–49; "Librarians Must Care," an editorial, *ibid.,* p. 335; "Library Employment of Minority Group Personnel; LAD Report," *ALA Bulletin,* v. 63, no. 7 (July/Aug. 1969), p. 985–87; Fay M. Blake, "What's Happening to the Dream?," *WLB,* v. 43, no. 5 (Jan. 1969),

p. 474–75; E. J. Josey, "Black Aspirations, White Racism, and Libraries," *WLB*, v. 44, no. 1 (Sept. 1969), p. 97–8+; "Black Decision Makers," *LJ*, v. 94, no. 11 (June 1, 1969), p. 2203–06; Phyllis S. Anderson, "Marchant's Misogyny [letter]," *LJ*, v. 95, no. 9 (May 1, 1970), p. 1680; and Janet Freedman, "The Liberated Librarian? — A Look at the 'Second Sex' in the Library Profession," *ibid.,* p. 1709–11.

The principal library periodicals have almost literally exploded over the past two years with guides, checklists, bibliographies, and exhortations designed to promote selection of books, magazines, and audiovisual matter for minority-group readers, young people, "ecophiliacs," radicals, conservatives, "peaceniks," draft-resisters, and the "disadvantaged." As merely a few examples, cf.: Effie Lee Morris, "Blowing in the Wind; Books on Black History and Life in America," *LJ*, v. 94, no. 6 (March 15, 1969), p. 1298–1300; James E. Wright, "Help Change the Pecking Order; A Booklist for Negro History Week," *LJ*, v. 94, no. 2 (Jan. 15, 1969), p. 153–55; four articles on the "underground" and Chicano press, including an extensive bibliography by Ned Kehde, *Missouri Library Association Quarterly*, v. 30, no. 3 (Sept. 1969); Sanford Berman, "Where It's At," *LJ*, v. 93, no. 22 (Dec. 15, 1968), p. 4615–18; Henry P. Durkin, "Where It's *Also* At," *LJ*, v. 94, no. 9 (May 1, 1969), p. 1839–40; Michael J. Spencer, "Why Is Youth So Revolting Nowadays?," *WLB*, v. 43, no. 7 (March 1969), p. 640–47; Daniel Tatko and Carol Brown, "The Underground and New Left Press," *ibid.,* p. 648–52; Sanford Berman, "African Magazines for American Libraries," *LJ*, v. 95, no. 7 (April 1, 1970), p. 1289–93; Carrie Robinson, "Media for the Black Curriculum," *ALA Bulletin*, v. 63, no. 2 (Feb. 1969), p. 242–46; Michael Darvell, "Long Live the Revolution!," *Assistant Librarian*, v. 63, no. 2 (Feb. 1970), plus replies in v. 63, no. 4 (April 1970), p. 58–9; Anne Leibl, "Canada's Underground Press," *Canadian Library Journal*, v. 27, no. 1 (Jan./Feb. 1970), p. 16–23; the symposium on "Who Speaks for Youth?," *LJ*, v. 95, no. 2 (Jan. 15, 1970), p. 205–17; "Books by and About the American Negro," *ibid.,* p. 218–19; Madeline Kirschner, "Puerto Rican Bibliography; Serving the Spanish Community," *RQ*, v. 9, no. 1 (fall 1969), p. 9–19; Binnie Tate, "Integrating Culture: A Credo for Believers," *LJ*, v. 94, no. 10 (May 15, 1969), p. 2053–56; Jane Coffman, "The CO and the Draft," *ibid.,* p. 2059–65; and Sylvia Price, "Books for the Counter-Culture," *LJ*, v. 94, no. 11 (June 1, 1969), p. 2193–2202. Cf. further the "Afro-American," "Dissident," and "Underground Newspapers" sections in Katz, *op cit.; Synergy*'s March/April 1970 "Ecology" issue (no. 26); and *Sipapu,* "a newsletter for librarians, scholars, editors and others concerned with ethnic studies, the counter-culture, and the underground press" (c/o Noel Peattie, ed., Collection Development Section, University Library, University of California, Davis 95616).

For insights into "outreach" and "High John"–type programs as the library response to a demonstrated, escalating need for improved and expanded service to the rural poor, prison and other institutional readers, the ghettoized multitudes, and the elderly, cf.: 12 articles collectively titled "Libraries and the Spanish-Speaking," *WLB*, v. 44, no. 7 (March 1970); Antoine Predock, "Branch Library Permutations, or the Socially Oriented Library," *MLA Quarterly*, v. 30, no. 2 (June 1969), p. 136–40; Carla Stoffle, "Public Library Service to the Disadvantaged; A Bibliography," pt. 1, *LJ*, v. 94, no. 2 (Jan. 15, 1969), pt. 2, v. 94, no. 3 (Feb. 1, 1969); *Public Library Service to the Disadvantaged; Proceedings of an Institute: Dec. 7th and 8th, 1967* (Atlanta: Division of Librarianship, Emory University, 1969); the "Library Outreach" issue of *WLB*, guest-edited by John C. Frantz, v. 43, no. 9 (May 1969), p. 848–904; John M. Cloud, "Why Didn't They Burn the Libraries?," *WLB*, v. 43, no. 8 (April 1969), p. 787+; Major Owens, "A Model Library for Community Action," *LJ*, v. 95, no. 9 (May 1, 1970), p. 1701–04; and Dorothy Romani, "Guidelines for Library Service to the Institutionalized Aging," *American Libraries*, v. 1, no. 3 (March 1970), p. 286–89.

9. Itzhak Epstein, writing in the May 1969 *Jewish Liberation Journal*, candidly relates the old refrain to the modern situation. "A polarization," he notes, "is taking place in the land and it looks like it is sharpening. As the gap widens and the opposing camps become more easily identifiable, it becomes more difficult to be neutral. At such times the question arises— *which side are you on?* Do you stand with the draft board or with the draft resister, with the slumlord or with the slum-dweller, with the student fighting for a meaningful education or with the educational bureaucracy and its corporate allies? Are you on the side of vulgar consumption or with the creators of meaningful life-styles? Will you be a 'good German' while increased oppression is applied around you and in your name or will you put your body on the line in a futile attempt to stop the madness? Will you mouth the pious dogma that assimilation is good for Blacks, Jews, Indians and other minority nations dwelling among the Whites in this land, or will you try to pass and qualify for membership in the DAR? . . ." Cf. "American Jewry: On the Barricades or on the Fence?," v. 1, no. 1, p. 3. Emphasis added. While Epstein apostrophizes American Jewry, the core question may just as well be asked of *everyone.*

10. Although it's not really a "modern" or especially "hip" idea, for much earlier Hans Christian Andersen masterfully conveyed the same message in "The Emperor's New Clothes."

11. *Op. cit.*

12. Says Jay Daily, most poignantly, "We have nothing else." Cf. "Many Changes, No Alternatives," *LJ*, v. 92, no. 19 (Nov. 1, 1967), p. 3961.

13. In Daily's view, this is LC's posture. "In point of fact," he claims, "the Library of Congress needs remarkable urging to change a heading for any reason. . . . The reason is the vast cost of changing all those headings on

all those cards, let alone the work of picking out the heading and its cross-references from the closely knitted fabric of the whole list." *Op. cit.,* p. 3962.

14. *Op. cit.,* p. 3526. Emphasis in original.

15. Unhappily, however, the profession has *not* recognized nor castigated even *these* "obvious" forms of "pandering." Cf., for example, the discussions that follow under LITERATURE, IMMORAL; KAFIRS; and NEGROES.

16. Personal communication, dated June 23, 1970.

Section I

Races, Nationalities, Faiths, and Ethnic Groups

1. *Item:* JEWISH QUESTION (p. 685; Sears, p. 344)[1]

For the image of the Jew to arouse any feelings, pro or con, he had to be generalized, abstracted, depersonalized. It is always possible for the personal, individual case to contradict a general assertion by providing living, concrete proof to the contrary. For the Jews to become the foils of a mass movement, they had to be converted into objectified symbols so as to become other than human beings. Moreover, mass agitation demanded simplicity and consistency, and consequently did not readily countenance subtle distinctions which might have excluded some Jews from condemnation. Hitler followed the path of his Volkish predecessors when he presented the Jewish evil not in its flesh-and-blood aspects, but as an abstracted stereotype.

The growing abstraction of the Jew reflected the growing process of his depersonalization. Once the Jew had been denied a soul and genuine emotions, once his religion had been categorized as a fossil without ethical content, he was well on the way to being dehumanized. And who could feel any sorrow for or commiserate with an entity that had lost all human dimensions? Once a population had accepted this depiction of the Jew, it was possible to regard him as a cipher, as a figure that aroused no human compassion—only the large numbers of the martyred dead would stagger the imagination.[2]

This and its analogues (e.g., "Race question" as a subdivision) qualify as the most odious examples in the whole list of outright

25

racism, WASPish myopia, and marvelous insensitivity to the suffering and legitimate aspirations of minority peoples. What was (and in
many places still *is*) the "Jewish Question"? Who posed the "question"? And what kind of "answer" did they furnish? In Europe, the
"questioners" were (are) the Slavic or "Teutonic" majorities, not the
Jews themselves. They "questioned," in essence, what to do with the
Jewish communities who had lived among them for centuries, but
who had seldom enjoyed full political or social rights. They "an-
swered" with relatively more or less heinous versions of the *End-
lösung* (Final Solution): exterminate; expel; or reduce the "non–
Aryans," the "rootless cosmopolitans," to a subhuman condition.
On the face of it, "Jewish Question" may seem a bland, neutral term.
Yet it is just the opposite, masquerading ruthlessness and in-
humanity—the age-old and altogether vicious practice of scape-
goating—in a deceptive, leisurely abstraction. The phraseology is
that of the oppressor, the ultimate murderer, not the victim.[3] Strong
language? The stench at Auschwitz was stronger. The "question"
facing the soon-to-be-incinerated millions was not one to be calmly
debated. It was fundamental: life or death.[4]

   Remedy: Reconstructions are possible for many other inap-
propriate terms. Not, however, for this. It richly merits deletion.[5]

Notes (Item 1)

   1. This and all succeeding references are to the *Library of Congress Subject Headings,* 7th ed. (Washington, D.C.: Card Division, Library of Congress, 1966). The ensuing study is founded solely on the 7th edition itself,
not on the quarterly supplements, titled *Subject Headings Used in the Dictionary Catalogs of the Library of Congress* (Washington, D.C.: Card Division,
Library of Congress). The presumption here, based on actual experience in
libraries of varying size and kind, is that the public, as well as noncataloging
staff, ordinarily know the list in book-form only and that changes often go
unmarked in the basic volume. Moreover, there may be some comparative
and historic worth to a treatise on the "state of the art" as of 1966, even if—
with luck—it radically changes, or to some extent *has* changed, afterwards.
Relevant modifications, however, that have been made in the annual cumulative supplements (hereafter: ACS), five of which have appeared since the
list itself, will be footnoted. Many such changes are wholly commendable

and should be called to the attention of librarians and others unaware that such alterations have occurred. Others are less praiseworthy and, as will be shown, still require change.

The methodology has been to survey the 7th ed. page-by-page, prepare an itemized analysis based on the book-form edition alone, and then to examine the annual supplements, revising the book-grounded survey as necessary in notes.

Broadly considered, the *Sears List of Subject Headings*, first published in 1923, represents an adaptation or simplification of the LC scheme. Indeed, Barbara M. Westby, editor of the 9th ed. (New York: H. W. Wilson, 1965), states in a Preface that "as in earlier editions of Sears, the Library of Congress forms of subject headings were used, with some modifications to meet the needs of smaller collections or to follow popular terminology." She adds that "several correspondents have expressed the opinion that Sears should follow the Library of Congress form of headings without exception," and — while believing that "further study and discussion is needed" on that proposal — nonetheless observes that "the increase in centralized and cooperative cataloging services may make standardization more desirable" (p. 5).

That Sears commits many of the same errors as LC and incorporates a similar stance toward various elements of humanity should startle no one. Since, however, Sears-using librarians may mistakenly feel that none of the LC problems to be discussed directly affect *them*, page-citations will be made to identical constructions in both the LC 7th ed. and Sears 9th ed., hereafter referred to simply as "Sears."

2. George L. Mosse, *The Crisis of German Ideology; Intellectual Origins of the Third Reich* (London: Weidenfeld and Nicolson, 1966), p. 301–02.

3. "The *Jewish question*," predicted Joseph Goebbels in 1938, "will in a short time find a solution satisfying the sentiment of the German people. *The people want it this way, and we only carry out the people's will.*" Quoted by Ernest K. Bramsted, *Goebbels and National Socialist Propaganda: 1925–1945* (London: Cresset Press, 1965), p. 387. First emphasis added, second in the original.

4. Documentation on the Jewish plight abounds. Cf., e.g., Gerald Reitlinger, *Final Solution* (New York: A. S. Barnes, 1961) and the entries under "Jewry," as well as individual countries, in the Institute of Contemporary History and Wiener Library *Quarterly Select List of Accessions* (London: 4 Devonshire Street, W. 1), plus continuing and retrospective material in both the quarterly *Wiener Library Bulletin* and bimonthly *Patterns of Prejudice* (London: Institute of Jewish Affairs, Ltd., 13–16 Jacob's Well Mews, George Street, W. 1), the latter including a regular feature, "Books to note," which briefly describes new works under heads like "Holocaust," "War Crimes," "Antisemitism," and "Germany."

5. The anxious, meticulous cataloger who finds that this leaves some

titles without *any* subject entry may turn to several existing forms that will do equally well: e.g., GENOCIDE (p. 536), HOLOCAUST, JEWISH (1939–1945), JEWS—PERSECUTIONS (p. 687), JEWS IN GERMANY [ARGENTINA, POLAND, RUSSIA, etc.] (p. 688). The admirable "Holocaust"—form was introduced on p. 203–04 of the 1968 ACS. Inexplicably, however, LC did not take this ready-made opportunity to simultaneously *cancel* JEWISH QUESTION.

2. *Item:* —RACE QUESTION as a subdivision (p. 1063)

This variant of JEWISH QUESTION invites much the same accusations. To American, Rhodesian, and South African Blacks, or to Asians in East Africa, as examples, their status in the larger, White- (or Black-) governed society is no ethereal concern, no matter for rhetorical gamesmanship. It involves *survival* in its every aspect: physical, cultural, social, economic, and political. The "question" is one of maintaining group (or, better, human) integrity and dignity, of ending oppression and the soul-wracking uncertainty that pervades their daily lives; more positively stated: of winning those elemental rights that numberless international conventions and proclamations have promised to everyone on earth, of becoming *free, whole* persons who command their own destinies and contribute fully to the body politic of which they form a part. "Race question" is the overlord's terminology, nicely suggesting that the oppressed—not themselves—represent the "problem." It is a consummate piece of double-think.[1]

Remedy: (a) Assign RACE QUESTION as a subhead to the dustbin, where it belonged from the start, and excise it as a *See* referent to RACE PROBLEMS (p. 1063).

(b) Replace RACE DISCRIMINATION (p. 1063) with the totally new head, RACISM, a broader term encompassing attitudes, as well as deeds, creating extensions and variations as necessary (e.g., RACISM—AFRICA, SOUTH; RACISM—U.S.; RACISM IN EDUCATION; etc.).[2] Additionally, make cross-references from and to GENOCIDE and PREJUDICES AND ANTIPATHIES.

(c) Where required to express the relationship *between* various racial groups, particularly those identified by themselves and or others as "different" on the basis of physical characteristics to which are linked certain nonphysical attributes, employ the subhead—RACE RELATIONS; or, in the case of relationships between *ethnically* differentiated peoples—i.e., groups distinguished by cultural characteristics like language and religion—use the subdivision—INTERETHNIC RELATIONS.[3]

Notes (Item 2)

1. A specific application of the subhead appears on p. 759: LOS ANGELES—RACE QUESTION. Its utter *in*applicability becomes clear when juxtaposed with these honest, if somewhat apocalyptic, remarks by a young Black resident of the Watts ghetto:

> Sometimes living in Watts brings me to the point where I'm just a drop in the ocean, an ocean that is dirty.... And sometimes I feel like I even don't want to live in Watts, because Watts is in the United States, the United States is in the Western Hemisphere, and the Western Hemisphere is part of the Western philosophy, and the Western philosophy is doomed to die. Watts is a container of filth and ignorance, because it was created by the white man. There're containers all over the country, of black people, and they hold and suppress the people that are in them. The filth and ignorance that's in the community is fermenting, to where it's exploding out of the container, and this chemical of filth in the black community is going to emerge and going to destroy itself along with the country, just to prove that black people's minds haven't been robbed, they can't live in this country where they are second, they can't live in a society where they're unhappy....

Paul Williams, quoted by Paul Bullock in his *Watts: The Aftermath; An Inside View of the Ghetto by the People of Watts* (New York: Grove Press, 1969), p. 285.

2. There are ample precedents: Two well-reputed Wilson publications, the *Readers' Guide to Periodical Literature (RG)* and *Social Sciences and Humanities Index (SSHI)*, employ "Racism" as a primary head. So does the newly born *Alternative Press Index (API)*, issued by the Radical Research Center (Carleton College, Northfield, Minnesota 55057; v. 1, nos. 1/2, covering July–Dec. 1969, appeared in early 1970).

For a useful distinction, incidentally, between "Racism" and "Ethno-centrism," cf. van den Berghe, *op. cit.*, p. 12. Taking advantage of his insights, "Race" should be eliminated as an "××" under ETHNOCENTRISM (p. 445).

3. As precedents: The Insitute of Contemporary History and Wiener Library in their *Quarterly Select List of Accessions, op. cit.*, employ "Race rela-tions" as a major category; so do the annual *Index to Periodical Articles by and About Negroes* (Boston: G. K. Hall) and *British Humanities Index* (*BHI*; Lon-don: Library Association), while Sears uses it as a subdivision under coun-tries, cities, etc., having eliminated "Race question" altogether. Moreover, numerous periodicals incorporate the expression into their titles; e.g.: *Race Relations* (London: Race Relations Board), *Race Relations Abstracts* (Lon-don), *Race Relations Law Survey* (Nashville, Tenn.), *Race Relations Bulletin* (London: Institute of Race Relations), and *Race Relations News* (Johan-nesburg: South African Institute of Race Relations).

As a social scientist, van den Berghe opts for a working definition by which "race" signifies "a human group that defines itself and/or is defined by other groups as different from other groups by virtue of innate and im-mutable physical characteristics. These physical characteristics," he adds, "are in turn believed to be intrinsically related to moral, intellectual, and other non-physical attributes or abilities." It is within this framework that he subsequently discusses "race relations," particularly in Mexico, the United States, Brazil, and South Africa. *Op. cit.*, p. 9.

The very first sentence of van den Berghe's chapter on Mexico implicitly makes a strong case for the suggested subhead —INTERETHNIC RELATIONS. "Of all the multiracial societies created by the expansion of Europe since the late fifteenth century," he writes, "those of Spanish America stand out as ex-hibiting only traces of the racist virus. Indeed, most of these countries con-stitute such limiting cases that one may more properly speak of *ethnic rela-tions*." *Ibid.*, p. 42. Emphasis added. The phrase also served as the full title of Julio de la Fuente's 1955 study, *Relaciones interétnicas* (Mexico, D. F.: In-stituto Nacional Indígenista).

3. *Item:* YELLOW PERIL (p. 1427)

Such phraseology is of a piece with gutter epithets like "slope," "gook," and "chink." It is not only an affront to the people so labelled, but also demeans the user. How it has remained with us this long perhaps only the Sphinx can explain. Or a pathologist.[1]

Remedy: Cancel the head and ensure that it does not reappear even as an unused *See* referent to other forms. Abundant heads are already available to handle material hitherto assigned YELLOW PERIL; e.g.: EAST AND WEST (p. 396) and PAN-PACIFIC RELATIONS (p. 940). The innovative form RACISM, recommended above, might also be appropriate.

Note (Item 3)

1. For anyone unfamiliar with the term or skeptical about its debasing quality, *Webster's Third New International Dictionary of the English Language Unabridged* (hereafter: *Webster's Third*) supplies *two* definitions, one as repulsive as the other: "1: a danger to Western civilization held to arise from expansion of the power and influence of Oriental peoples (as the Chinese and Japanese) 2: a threat to Western living standards developed through the incursion into Western countries of Oriental laborers willing to work for very low wages and under inferior working conditions" (Springfield, Mass.: G. & C. Merriam Co., 1961), p. 2650.

4. *Items:* **JAPANESE IN THE U.S. (p. 679; Sears, p. 342); MEXICANS IN THE U.S. (p. 817; Sears, p. 393); CHINESE IN THE U.S. (p. 224; Sears, p. 146); etc.**

The nub here is that these people are described or classed *exclusively* according to racial, national, or ethnic origin, with no regard nor recognition that many, while still "Mexican" or "Japanese" in heritage, if not appearance, are nonetheless *American* in nationality, citizenship, and actual residence. The head, in effect, makes them *permanent aliens.*

Remedy: (a) Determine from the "Americanized" peoples themselves what they wish to be called and add these terms to the scheme (e.g., as appropriate, JAPANESE-AMERICANS, MEXICAN-AMERICANS, etc.).[1] The very titles of scholarly studies produced over the past decade imply a marked preference for the hyphenated form.[2]

So do the organizational and other names created by these various groups.[3] And so does at least one major periodical index, plus one newcomer to the field.[4] Most spectacularly, the LC scheme itself— albeit inconsistently—furnishes several precedents.[5]

(b) The now existing heads could continue to play a role, but much narrower, applying solely to "aliens" (like Mexican seasonal laborers) whose permanent abode is clearly outside the country. Once the "hyphenation" or some similar principle becomes operative for peoples of foreign extraction in the United States, it may also be applied elsewhere, to other countries whose populations developed at least in part through immigration. This might result, e.g., in forms like UKRAINIAN-CANADIANS, ITALO-ARGENTINIANS, ANGLO-AUSTRALIANS, etc. Indeed, when rigorously employed solely within the *United States* context itself, no "people" apart from Amerindians justly qualifies for the *un*-hyphenated AMERICANS. It is thus appropriate that constructions like ANGLO-AMERICANS and DUTCH-AMERICANS should coexist with MEXICAN-AMERICANS and JAPANESE-AMERICANS, however much that may discomfit the Daughters of the American Revolution.

(c) Another serious problem inheres in the scheme's treatment of the Japanese-American experience during World War II. The only pertinent subhead is —DEPORTATION, which less-than-adequately describes the forced interment of over 110,000 Japanese-Americans in concentration camps at Tule Lake and elsewhere entirely on the basis of their "ancestral origins."[6] To do justice, subject-wise, to this wholly shameful episode requires, minimally, a new subhead like —MASS INTERMENT, 1942–1945, with "××'s" for "Civil rights" and "Racism—U.S."[7] Further, the individual "detention" or "relocation" centers deserve specific entries; e.g., TULE LAKE (CONCENTRA-TION CAMP). And at least one of these should be cited as an "also" example under CONCENTRATION CAMPS (p. 286). In this particular in-stance, the profession can modestly contribute to our own national maturity by destroying the illusion that only *other* nations or systems (e.g., the Nazis) have committed grievous crimes like the establish-ment of KZs.

"Know thyself" runs the ancient injunction. It's not yet too late to start.

Notes (Item 4)

1. As an even further refinement, cross-references to JAPANESE-AMERICANS, if selected as a bona fide head, might be introduced from "Issei," "Nisei," and "Sansei" (first, second, and third generation immigrants, respectively), and from "Chicanos" and "La Raza" to MEXICAN-AMERICANS. For completeness, additional *see* or "*sa*" references will be necessary from "Latin-Americans," "Spanish-Americans," "Hispano-Americans," and "Latinos" to all the particular forms representing Spanish-surnamed peoples of Latin-American origin (i.e., Puerto Rican, Mexican, Cuban, etc.).

2. As examples: *De Aztlan a Hoy; Mexican-American Culture and History*, "A Major Bibliography of English and Spanish-Language Materials" (Los Angeles: Los Angeles Public Library, 1970); Abe Arkoff, "Need Patterns in Two Generations of Japanese-Americans in Hawaii," *Journal of Social Psychology*, v. 50, no. 1 (Aug. 1959), p. 75–9; H. L. Kitano, *Japanese-Americans: The Evolution of a Subculture* (Englewood Cliffs, N.J.: Prentice-Hall, 1969); G. M. Meredith, "Observations on the Acculturation of Sansei Japanese-Americans in Hawaii," *Psychologia*, v. 8 (1965), p. 41–9; Gary M. Matsumoto, and others, "Ethnic Identification: Honolulu and Seattle Japanese-Americans," *Journal of Cross-Cultural Psychology*, v. 1, no. 1 (spring 1970), p. 63–76; *Mexican-American Education: A Selected Bibliography* (Las Cruces, N.M.: Clearinghouse on Rural Education and Small Schools, New Mexico State University, 1969); *New Look at the Attributes of the Mexican-American* (Albuquerque, N.M.: Southwestern Cooperative Educational Laboratory, 1969); Robert P. Haro, "How Mexican-Americans View Libraries," *WLB*, v. 44, no. 7 (March 1970), p. 736–42; Clyde Bullion, "Mexican-Americans: A Survey," *Choice*, v. 6, no. 8 (Oct. 1969), p. 985–88; William Madsen, *Mexican-Americans of South Texas* (New York: Holt, 1964); Julian Samora and Richard A. Lamanna, *Mexican-Americans in a Midwest Metropolis: A Study of East Chicago* (Los Angeles: UCLA Graduate School of Business Admin., 1967); Octavio Ignacio Romano, ed., *El Espejo—The Mirror: Selected Mexican-American Literature* (1969); Ernest Kaiser, "American Indians and Mexican Americans: A Selected Bibliography," *Freedomways*, v. 9, no. 4 (4th quarter 1969), p. 298–327; and Keith Revelle, comp., *Chicano! A Selected Bibliography of Materials by and About Mexico and Mexican Americans* (Oakland, Calif.: Latin American Library, 1969).

3. E.g.: Mexican American Student Confederation, Association of Mexican-American Educators, Union of Mexican American Students, Mexican-American Political Association, Mexican-American Youth Organization, Chinese-American Citizens Alliance, Asian Americans for Peace, Finnish-American Historical Society of Michigan, Greek-American

Progressive Association, United Italian-American Labor Council, United Italian American League, Italo-American National Union, Japanese-American Citizens League, Japanese American Service Committee, Lithuanian-American National Alliance, Maltese-American Benevolent Society, Norwegian-American Historical Association, Association of Philippine-American Women, Polish-American Historical Association, German American National Congress, and the Joint Civil Committee of Italian Americans. Sources: William L. Ramirez, "Libraries and the Spanish-Speaking," *WLB*, v. 44, no. 7 (March 1970), p. 714–15; "Fraternal, Foreign Interest, Nationality, and Ethnic Organizations," *Encyclopedia of Associations.* 5th ed. (Detroit: Gale Research Co., 1968), v. 1, p. 713–61; Revelle, *op cit.*, p. 3; *Interracial Books for Children*, v. 2, no. 4 (spring 1970), p. 5; *Los Angeles Free Press*, Jan. 23, 1970, p. 5; and *Circle Library Reporter* (University of Illinois at Chicago Circle), v. 1, no. 2 (summer 1970), p. 2.

   4. *RG* employs both MEXICAN AMERICANS and JAPANESE AMERICANS; cf., for example, v. 69, no 22 (Feb. 10, 1970), p. 159, 193; while *API* uses MEXICAN AMERICANS, together with CHICANO MOVEMENT, *op. cit.*, p. 39, as well as JAPANESE AMERICANS, p. 35.

   5. Cf., for example, CZECH-AMERICAN LITERATURE and CZECH-AMERICAN NEWSPAPERS (p. 346), DANISH-AMERICAN LITERATURE (p. 349), NORWEGIAN-AMERICAN FICTION (p. 899), FRENCH-CANADIANS (p. 516), GERMAN-AMERICAN WIT AND HUMOR (p. 542), IRISH-AMERICAN WIT AND HUMOR (p. 672), SWEDISH-AMERICAN POETRY (p. 1261), and GREEK-AMERICAN WIT AND HUMOR (1966 ACS, p. 67).

   6. For a recent, photo-illustrated retelling of "this story of racist hysteria and abuse of government power," cf. Allan R. Bosworth, *America's Concentration Camps* (New York: W. W. Norton, 1967). The quoted phrase is from the introduction by Roger Baldwin, wartime director of the American Civil Liberties Union, who neatly annuls the "military necessity" argument by noting that "no evacuation was even suggested for the Germans and Italians, aliens or citizens, on the Atlantic Coast where submarines and defense installations were far more numerous, and the dangers of espionage and sabotage apparently greater" (p. 6–7). Bosworth served at the time as a captain in naval intelligence, stationed on the Pacific Coast. Scholars, students, and concerned citizens will particularly appreciate the year-by-year chronology (p. 254–57) and complete bibliography of both primary and secondary sources (p. 258–61).

   7. Works like Paul F. Gerhard's *The Plight of the Japanese Americans During World War II; A Study of Group Prejudice* (Wichita, Kansas: 1963) have, in fact, been assigned by LC catalogers the misleadingly austere head JAPANESE IN THE U.S. Cf. U.S. Library of Congress, *Catalog, Books: Subjects, 1965* (Washington, D.C.), v. 2, p. 845. Indeed, the later Bosworth volume, *op. cit.*, underwent even worse handling. It received two headings: WORLD

WAR, 1939–1945—PRISONERS AND PRISONS, AMERICAN and CONCENTRATION CAMPS—U.S. The latter rubric could hardly be avoided, given the book's title, but the former erroneously implies that the prisoners were *war combatants* and probably *foreigners*, rather than *civilians*, many of them *native-born*. Still more blameworthy is the utter failure to denote just *which* group—what *kind* of people—suffered this long incarceration, although the cataloger could have determined this salient fact without ever opening the volume. It appears on the jacket. Cf. *National Union Catalogue, 1963–1967* (Ann Arbor, Mich.: J. W. Edwards, 1969), v. 7, p. 310.

5. *Items:* JEWISH CRIMINALS (p. 685); NEGRO CRIMINALS (p. 885)

A frankly off-handed squib appeared in the April 1969 *ALA Bulletin:*

> Though it may be more a reflection on publishing and writing than librarianship, the 1966 LC subject-heading list contains entries for JEWISH and NEGRO CRIMINALS, but none for the Italian, Irish, Dutch, English, or German varieties. Curious, hmmm?[1]

It elicited from LC's assistant director for cataloging the retort that:

> As a matter of fact, LC exposes the allegedly protected varieties, along with many others, under the heading CRIME AND CRIMINALS with direct geographical subdivisions, e.g. —ITALY, —IRELAND, —HOLLAND, etc. The form beginning with an adjective is used for books that deal with the criminal elements of groups that cannot be expressed in geographical terms.[2]

The "justification" is at once revealing and tragic. Indeed, it transformed what had been little more than a tongue-in-cheek jibe into a matter of ugly proportions, for it manifested an attitude, a type of moral blindness, that now commonly bears the rubric, "institutionalized racism." The LC defender is no Mississippi redneck. Far from it. He's a responsible, high-ranking, experienced official. And yet he apparently couldn't *see* that his prize subdivisions only pertain to "criminals" *in* Ireland, Italy, etc. These wrongdoers *may* be Irish or Italian. They could equally be Black, Jewish, or Asian. That two ethnic/racial/national groups alone have been accorded "special" treatment seems to have escaped him.[3] Were there any equity or logic to the scheme, heads like ITALIAN-AMERICAN CRIMINALS (has there been *nothing* published on the U.S. Mafia?) or IRISH CRIMINALS IN GREAT BRITAIN would also be included. In fact, MAFIA appears as a discrete head (p. 767) with an "××" for "Crime and criminals," but with no subhead specified for "—Italy" nor any other indication of the Mafiosi's nationality, ethnicity, etc. Curious, hmmm?

Remedy: Perhaps the wisest path would be to abandon adjectival forms altogether in this case. Given, though, that *some* are specified, why not the rest? Appearing as they do in splendid isolation, the two *used* heads impute a distinct if not unique criminal propensity to Jews and Blacks.[4] If it were simply that LC hasn't any books on the others, okay. But that's not the way the LC spokesman explains it. Which, again, is revealing. And tragic.

Notes (Item 5)

1. Sanford Berman, "Did You Look Under WASP: Nests?," v. 63, no. 4, p. 428–29.

2. C. Sumner Spalding, "The WASP Is Out of the Nest," *ALA Bulletin*, v. 63, no. 7 (July-Aug. 1969), p. 892.

3. But not Joan K. Marshall and Nancy Toy, two practicing librarians who effectively rebutted Mr. Spalding's "defense" in the Dec. 1969 *ALA Bulletin*. Cf. "Crime and Life" and "Criminal Green Men," v. 63, no. 11, p. 1516–17.

4. A "propensity," be it noted, once vigorously maintained by Nazi propagandists like Otto Dietrich, who operated the *Deutscher Wochendienst*, an official agency charged with supplying anti–Semitic material to both foreign and domestic journals. Among the emphases urged on journalists by Dietrich was that "Every single Jew, wherever he is and whatever he is doing, shares the guilt. There is no such thing as a 'good Jew,' but only degrees of skill and camouflage. *The Jew is a Notorious Criminal*." Quoted by Bramsted, *op. cit.*, p. 401. Emphasis added.

Joan Marshall correctly points out—in a personal communication, *op. cit.*—that Catholics, too, appear as "a special class of criminals" (p. 197). To conserve searching-time, it may be recorded here that no complementary forms exist for PROTESTANT CRIMINALS, BAPTIST CRIMINALS, EPISCOPALIAN CRIMINALS, etc. Moreover, the list expresses not even one iota of *doubt* about Catholics' criminal proclivities, for it refers directly from the unused "Catholics *as* criminals" to the uncompromising CATHOLIC CRIMINALS. Until members of other religious groups are accorded "equal treatment," the "Catholic" rubric should be abolished.

6. *Items:* MOHAMMEDANISM (p. 839); MOHAMMEDANS (p. 840), and some 16 adjectival forms beginning MOHAMMEDAN ... (e.g., MOHAMMEDAN ANTIQUITIES, p. 839), as well as several phrase forms like MOHAMMEDANISM AND PHILOSOPHY (p. 840) and COMMUNISM AND MOHAMMEDANISM (p. 281)

In legal jargon, this is a virtually open-and-shut case. Even as the *first* edition of the LC came off the press, James Hastings wrote in his *Encyclopaedia of Religion and Ethics* that "Islam is the name peculiar to the religion founded by Muhammad, and embraces all the different sects which are now found among his followers. Thus, a Shi'ite and a Sunnite are both Muslims."[1] The proper terminology, then, for the religion and its professors is "Islam" and "Muslims," respectively. Lest any doubts remain:

- the *New Catholic Encyclopedia* declared that Islam is the name "invariably preferred by its adherents to 'Mohammedanism' ... and its believers call themselves Moslems (more accurately, Muslims, Arabic *muslimun*).... "[2]
- "muhammadan ... *or* mohammedan," according to Webster, is a term "used predominantly by those outside the faith of Islam and *usually taken to be offensive by the Islamic believer*."[3]

Remedy: Replace the long favored LC forms with ISLAM and MUSLIMS (or the adjectival "Islamic" and "Muslim"), making appropriate cross-references from the discarded terms.[4]

Notes (Item 6)

1. (Edinburgh: T. & T. Clark, 1914), v. 7, p. 437.
2. (New York: McGraw-Hill, 1967), v. 7, p. 676.
3. *Op. cit.,* p. 1484. For Webster on "Islam" as the preferred nomenclature for the faith itself, cf. p. 1198.

In an extensive review of the just issued 7th ed., Jay E. Daily wryly observed that "there are new entries, although [it] is [still] too early for the great conversion from Mohammedanism to Islam." *Op. cit.,* p. 3961.

4. For a precedent, cf. the March 1970 *SSHI* (v. 57, no. 4), which uses ISLAM, MUSLIMS, and the adjectival ISLAMIC, p. 82, 111. The *BHI,* however, persists in adhering to the discredited "Mohammedan/Mohammedanism" forms. So, ludicrously, does the *Guide to Indian Periodical Literature* (Guragon, Haryana: Prabhu Book Service), where the searcher will regularly discover titles like "*Islam* and Pakistan," "*Islam* in India's Transition to Modernity," and "*Islamic* Modernism in India and Pakistan" under the heading MOHAMMEDANISM! Cf. v. 6, no. 2 (April-June 1969), p. 101. Emphasis added.

Somewhat strangely—indeed, contradictorily—another precedent appears in LC itself: PAN-ISLAMISM (p. 941).

Though accomplished too late for inclusion in the 7th ed., it is unreservedly to LC's credit that it undertook, by means of the July 1964–Dec. 1965 ACS, perhaps the greatest and longest overdue heading-rectification in many years. Not only has ISLAM replaced MOHAMMEDANISM as the head for material "on the religion of which Muhammad is the prophet," but MUSLIMS is now to be applied to "works on the community of believers in this religion" and the adjectival forms "Islamic" and "Muslim" have been introduced wherever necessary. This conversion, evidenced throughout the cited supplement, but particularly concentrated on p. 107–12, appears to be total, all possible ramifications having been accounted for. The massive revision, which convincingly underscores the technical competence of LC's staff and reveals that large organization's capacity to be flexible, merits hearty congratulations and augurs well for future improvements. It proves in short, that needed changes, however vast, *can* be made, though it is earnestly to be hoped that the "goliath" will henceforth respond somewhat more rapidly to such imperatives than in the past. Fifty years, after all, is rather long to wait.

7. *Item:* MIXED BLOODS as a subdivision under INDIANS (p. 627); INDIANS OF MEXICO (p. 629); INDIANS OF NORTH AMERICA (p. 633); and INDIANS OF SOUTH AMERICA (p. 636)

A colorful, frontier-style term that no doubt appeals to whole generations nourished on Cowboy-and-Indian thrillers, it nevertheless represents shoddy science and the White Man's hauteur: (a) "Blood" is by no means the crucial element in genetic crossing; it is merely one element among many for determining or defining "racial" groups and not in itself a causal factor; (b) It is highly dubious that Indians anywhere in the Americas credit "Mixed bloods" as a proper, acceptable term for persons of White-Indian or Black-Indian parentage. In Mexico, for example, the common designation for the majority of the population descended from Europeans and Indians alike (with some African admixture) is "Mestizos," not "Sangres mixtas."[1]

Remedy: Canvass the principal Amerindian organizations, establishing a substitute head through consensus.[2]

Notes (Item 7)

1. "Over 85% of today's population" in Mexico is so classed. Cf. van den Berghe, *op. cit.,* p. 42. A valuable treatment of "mestizoization" in both its genetic and social aspects appears on p. 45 and 48–9.

Edward T. Price in 1953 estimated the total number of "mixed-bloods" in America, mainly scattered in endogamous groups along the Eastern Seaboard, as between 50,000 and 100,000. He further indicated that their "unusual group names," ranging from Bushwhackers and Jackson Whites to Melungeons and Croatans, *"were applied to them by the country people."* Cf. "A geographic analysis of white-Negro-Indian racial mixtures in Eastern United States," in Association of American Geographers, *Annals,* v. 43, no. 2 (June 1953), p. 138. Emphasis added.

2. For a comprehensive list of such groups, national and—more specifically—California, cf. "Organizations" in the Jan.-Feb. 1970 *Synergy* (No. 25), p. 14–7. It might also be useful to consult the editors of leading

Amerindian magazines and newspapers. A roster of these publications, compiled by Carol Brown and Celeste West, appears in the same "First Americans" issue, p. 4–10.

An analogous head, requiring the same sort of alteration, is GUINEAS (MIXED BLOODS, U.S.), p. 569. According to Webster, the singular form means "one of a group of people of mixed white, Indian and Negro ancestry who live chiefly in West Virginia and Maryland," p. 1010. The lexicographer adds, importantly, that the term is "often used disparagingly." In this case it seems wise to consult not only Amerindian but also Afro-American authorities like John Henrik Clarke, editor of *Freedomways* and president of the African Heritage Studies Association (AHSA).

An objection is also in order here to MULATTOES, presently accorded primary-head status (p. 858), as a designation for persons of mixed African and other descent. Its palpably offensive character is revealed by its very etymology, its derivation: "from *mule*, implying a cross between different biological species." Cf. van den Berghe, *op. cit.*, p. 52. Emphasis added. This, then, is still another form in which a substitute should be devised by Afro-American and perhaps Amerindian experts.

The situation has further deteriorated with the gratuitous appearance of an "×" for "Half-breed Indians" under INDIANS—MIXED BLOODS in the 1969 ACS, p. 108.

8. *Item:* MORAL AND SOCIAL CONDITIONS as a subdivision (uniquely) under NEGROES (p. 896; Sears, p. 426)

The enormous problem surrounding "Negroes" itself will be dealt with later. The difficulty with this subhead centers on the word "Moral." It smacks of paternalism, condescension, and the ubiquitous "White Man's Burden," all the more so since it is *not* applied to any other ethnic/racial group. A concern with Black "morals" can only be attributed to a missionary, warder, or trustee. The very approach reeks of *in*equality. For comparative purposes, note that merely "Social conditions" is shown as a subhead under CONFEDERATE STATES OF AMERICA (p. 299), although it might be reasonably argued that the very system of chattel slavery which the Confederacy so warmly adulated and staunchly defended represented a *moral* problem or condition of impressive dimensions. Why, then, was the same solicitude displayed for "moral" conditions among Black men not also expended on the Confederates?

Remedy: Excise "Moral" from the subhead, thus reducing it to the fully adequate —SOCIAL CONDITIONS.

9. *Items:* PAGANISM (p. 935; Sears, p. 443); PAGANISM IN LITERATURE (p. 935); CIVILIZATION, PAGAN (p. 254)

"Heathenism," mercifully, goes unused. But "Paganism" is bad enough, fully illustrating the Christian chauvinism epidemic to the scheme. A. Babs Fafunwa, dean of the Faculty of Education at the University of Ife in Nigeria, cogently addresses this theme with respect to Africa, but his comments are generally applicable:

> Religious intolerance is another important contributory factor to racial prejudice in Africa. The early Christian missionaries genuinely but naively believed that their mission was to convert the "African pagans and muslims" to Christianity and thus bring light to the "benighted" Africans. The early Christian attitude presumed that the Africans' own religions were inferior and should be ruthlessly eliminated. The missionaries, in collaboration with local colonial administrators, joined forces together in imposing their own religion and culture on the African populace....[1]

Coming directly to "pagan," Fafunwa observes:

> The word "Pagan" is defined as *"one of a nation or community which does not worship the true God."* How any human being can arrogate to himself the power to determine who and who does not worship *the true God* is still one of the mysteries of life and living.[2]

How the wretched heading survived on the pages of the LC subject list through at least 1966 is no less a mystery.[3]

Remedy: Cancel all three heads. The legitimate forms CHRISTIANITY AND OTHER RELIGIONS, RELIGIONS, RELIGION IN LITERATURE, and the many existing permutations of "Civilization" should suffice.

Notes (Item 9)

1. "Recommendations concerning terminology in education on race questions," in the *Final Report* of the Meeting of Experts on Educational Methods Designed to Combat Racial Prejudice that met under UNESCO auspices in Paris from June 24 through 28, 1969 (Paris: UNESCO, 1968), Document ED/MD/4 (hereafter: Meeting of Experts), p. 23–4.

2. *Ibid.,* p. 26. Emphasis in original.

3. Substitute "pagan" for "heathen" in this account of an actual childhood experience in Painesville, Ohio, and the human, flesh-and-blood implications of the term, as well as the haughty, pogrom-generating attitude it embodies, become clear:

> ... This little girl. A nice one, she was. She wanted to help me.
>
> You see, I was a Jew, and that meant that I was one of those who ground up babies to make matzohs for the High Holy Days. She believed that, and she wanted to save me. She followed me for several days, and then one day she caught up with me and tried to help.
>
> "You've got to repent," she said, seriously.
>
> I stared at her. I didn't know what she meant, but I was frightened.
>
> "You're a heathen," she said. "You're damned to hell by God because you aren't baptized."
>
> I wanted to run.
>
> "Please, please"—she was almost crying—"you've got to believe in the Christ child, because you're going to Hell, and you'll be burning, and you'll ask for water on your tongue, and I can't give you any, because you're a heathen...."
>
> I turned and ran, terrified that she was right.

Harlan Ellison, *The Glass Teat* (New York: Ace Publishing Corp., 1970), p. 118. Ellison contributes a stimulating, iconoclast TV-column to the weekly *Los Angeles Free Press;* the first year's crop is reprinted in this volume.

Irmgard Johnson accents the anti-intellectual, education-thwarting effect of the "pagan" posture. An individual, she writes, "seeks approval and fears disapproval; he gains approval and avoids disapproval by making the expected responses. His indoctrination is the core of his self-identity, and he fears the disorientation and insecurity that are the result of threat to or loss of any part of it. His family and church have equipped him with feelings of guilt should he for a moment entertain ideas or facts contrary to the 'right' ones. Such ideas belong to 'pagans,' 'foreigners,' 'others,' the 'unenlightened,' to use the politest terminology, and therefore should not be allowed to contaminate him." Cf. "Religion as a deterrent to learning," *Journal of General Education*, v. 20, no. 4 (Jan. 1969), p. 282–83. The whole essay, founded on concrete classroom experience, is worth serious attention, for the author alleges that powerful, "irrational forces," to whom "fixed beliefs" are sacred, willfully suppress, rationalize, or disparage data that challenge their convictions.

10. *Items:* NEGROES (p. 886; Sears, p. 425); the numerous adjectival forms beginning NEGRO ... (e.g., NEGRO ART, NEGRO LIBRARIANS, p. 885–86; Sears, p. 424–25); all extended phrases commencing with NEGROES (e.g., NEGROES IN LITERATURE, NEGROES IN AFRICA, p. 886–87; Sears, p. 426); and relevant inverted constructions (e.g., LUTHERANS, NEGRO, p. 763)

How do we handle catalogue relevance for blacks? How do we assign subject headings to black material? Do we follow the Library of Congress and put it all under Negroes? This violates the thinking of blacks in this area and might be construed as just another example of white racism at work.[1]

Being a complex matter, it demands systematic unravelling:

(a) Mr. Fafunwa, a Nigerian, states unequivocally that Africans prefer "to be called 'African,' not 'Negro' or 'coloured.'"[2]

(b) Among Black Americans, "Negro" has increasingly become an object of derision, stigmatized as "Whitey's" language, an instrument of *de*-identification.[3]

(c) Its employment by LC is wholly "special" and inconsistent vis-à-vis the two other major "racial" categories, Caucasian and Oriental. No comparable forms, like CAUCASIAN LIBRARIANS or ORIENTALS AS FARMERS, appear anywhere in the list. And the "Oriental" entry, by means of an *sa* note, seems to prefer forms for "individual peoples" (e.g., "Chinese, East Indians, Mongols").[4]

(d) In the sphere of sheer practicality, monumental confusion

arises over the delimitation imposed by the scope note under
NEGROES: that the unqualified term applies solely to "Negroes" in the
United States. African (and other) readers, not to mention overseas
librarians themselves, thus find it difficult to "discriminate" between
"Negroes" who dwell in America and Black Americans ("Negroes"
again) who may reside, for example, in Liberia. Does NEGROES IN
LIBERIA refer to Black Americans there or to black *Liberians*? Or, per-
haps, to Black *Americo*-Liberians? The scheme fails to resolve this
dilemma. If nothing else, such a master guide should promote *clarity*.
Instead, it encourages intellectual anarchy and much frustration.[5]

The remedy must discard the manifestly offensive and racially
mired current term, replacing it with forms chosen on an essentially
ethnic or national basis:

(a) For material on Black Americans, substitute AFRO-
AMERICANS for NEGROES and institute AFRO-AMERICAN as the adjec-
tival form (e.g., AFRO-AMERICAN ART; AFRO-AMERICAN AUTHORS;
LUTHERANS, AFRO-AMERICAN, etc.). Similarly: replace NEGROES IN
LITERATURE with AFRO-AMERICANS IN LITERATURE, etc.[6]

(b) As a corollary, abolish altogether phrases beginning NEGROES
IN. . . . If a work treats with Black people *in* Canada or Brazil, as examples, it would be assigned AFRO-CANADIANS or AFRO-BRAZILIANS.
Together with the recommendations advanced earlier regarding, e.g., JAPANESE-AMERICANS and MEXICAN-AMERICANS, this should
achieve both fairness and consistency.[7]

(c) Completely delete such monstrosities as NEGROES IN AFRICA
and NEGROES IN LIBERIA. Material on *Black* Africans, Liberians,
Nigerians, etc., since they constitute the majorities on that continent
and in nearly all of its lands, can be adequately handled by a number
of already-available heads (e.g., LIBERIA—SOCIAL CONDITIONS;
AFRICA—POPULATION) or the proposed subdivisions —PEOPLES.[8]

(d) If necessary to specify Black Americans, Africans (in general), or Liberians, et al., who are temporarily outside their home
continent or country, use forms like AFRO-AMERICANS IN SWEDEN,
LIBERIANS IN THE U.S., or AFRICAN STUDENTS IN RUSSIA.[9]

(e) The much greater sophistication among library users today,
plus overwhelming hostility to the antiquated word "colored"
among people of African descent, compellingly dictate that the nine

"Colored" *See* references on p. 274 be deleted. Why pamper the troglodytes?[10]

(f) FOLKLORE, NEGRO (p. 496) should be split into two new heads: FOLKLORE, AFRICAN and FOLKLORE, AFRO-AMERICAN.

(g) Consistent application of the "Afro-" principle will alter forms like NEGRO POETRY (AMERICAN), NEGRO POETRY (FRENCH), NEGRO POETRY (PORTUGUESE), and NEGRO POETRY (SPANISH-AMERICAN)[11] to AFRO-AMERICAN POETRY, AFRO-FRENCH POETRY, AFRO-PORTUGUESE POETRY, and AFRO-SPANISH POETRY, with glosses added as necessary to indicate location; e.g., AFRO-SPANISH POETRY (LATIN AMERICA), AFRO-SPANISH POETRY (EQUATORIAL GUINEA).[12]

(h) The heading and note for FREEMASONS, NEGRO (p. 515) may be revamped as:

> FREEMASONS, AFRO-AMERICAN
> *Only general works are entered here. Works relating to individual Afro-American lodges, as well as the literature of Afro-American freemasonry in any given locality, are entered under* Freemasons. [local subdivision], *e.g.,* Freemasons. U.S. Scottish Rite. National Supreme Council (Afro-American).
> ×× Afro-Americans

Notes

1. Amy S. Doherty, "Black Studies: A Report for Librarians," *College and Research Libraries,* v. 31, no. 6 (Nov. 1970), p. 384.

2. *Op. cit.,* p. 26. He further scores the term as "derogatory," p. 24.

3. As indirect evidence: the venerable, widely-read *Negro Digest* this year changed its title to *Black World.* For a powerful, convincing assault on "Negro" by a Black American, cf. Adelaide Cromwell Hill, "What Is Africa to Us?," in Floyd B. Barbour, ed., *The Black Power Revolt* (Boston: Porter Sargent, 1968), p. 127–35. Also: *The Name "Negro"—Its Origin and Evil Use,* by Harlem bookstore-owner Richard B. Moore (New York: Afroamerican Publishers, 1960). Lerone Bennett, Jr., in a cogent exploration of the "name" controversy, notes that "a large and vocal group . . . charges that the word 'Negro' is an inaccurate epithet which perpetuates the master-slave mentality in the minds of both black and white Americans." From his discussion the irrefutable fact emerges that "Negro" as a term derived from the *slavers* who forcibly transported Africans to the New World. Adds Bennett, it "fused not only humanity, nationality and place of origin, but also certain

white judgments about the inherent and irredeemable inferiority of the persons so designated." Cf. "What's in a Name," *Ebony*, v. 23, no. 1 (Nov. 1967), p. 46+. Echoing this view, the editor of the 10-year-old *Liberator* in the April 1970 number stated: "We prefer to designate ourselves, as a whole people, as 'Black,' or 'Afro-American,' rather than by the objectionable slave term 'negro.'" V. 10, no. 4, p. 22. Van den Berghe further substantiates the odious nature of "Negro" in his contention that Spaniards, who figured among the earliest slavers and slave-owners, regarded Africans as a "vile, immoral race possessing unclean blood and low intelligence." *Op. cit.*, p. 52. The word itself is Iberian in origin.

4. P. 928.

5. The *BHI*, for example, finds it necessary to specify NEGROES IN UNITED STATES. Cf., e.g., no. 4 (Oct.-Dec. 1969), p. 78.

6. The "Afro" form is hardly a startling innovation. A national *Afro-American* Council existed in the 19th century; a well-known Baltimore weekly has borne the term on its masthead since 1982; "Black Power" advocates Robert F. Williams, Ron Karenga, LeRoi Jones, and Lawrence P. Neal have freely used it; likewise Black Panther Minister of Information Eldridge Cleaver. Representatives of the Student *Afro-American* Society attended the 1967 National Conference on Black Power; at the 1967 Racism in Education conference of the American Federation of Teachers (according to Bennett, *op. cit.*, p. 47), "the delegates unanimously endorsed a resolution which called on all educators, persons, and organizations to abandon the slavery imposed name 'Negro' for the terms 'African-American' or 'Afro-American.'" A Brooklyn-based organization called Brothers and Sisters for *Afro-American* Unity publishes the quarterly *Habari Barua*, "a new experience in black magazines." The *Amsterdam News*, an important Black paper in New York, regularly identifies Americans of African descent as "Afro-Americans," and within the last year or two it has become common currency among Blacks and Whites alike, entirely free of opprobrium or "bad vibes." In fact, *RG* has lately incorporated AFRO AMERICAN STUDIES as a primary head, but curiously continues to refer from "Afro-American culture" and "Afro-American students" to "Negro" forms. Cf., e.g., v. 70, no. 4 (April 10, 1970), p. 2. For another precedent in professional literature, cf. the "Afro-American" listings in Katz, *op. cit.*, p. 7–11.

For an LC precedent, cf. p. 4 of the 1969 ACS, which instituted AFRO-AMERICAN STUDIES as a primary head. The same supplement, however, perhaps as a belated and surely heavy-handed concession to the new mood among American Blacks, instead of pursuing the logic of AFRO-AMERICAN STUDIES to its obvious consequences elsewhere in the scheme, simply and feebly manufactured a series of *See* references to NEGROES from "African-Americans," "Afro-Americans," "Black people (U.S.)," and "Black Americans" (p. 4 and 25). Such "tokenism" will *not* do.

7. Keith Baird's opinion, quoted by Bennett, is apropos: "The unwillingness of the dominant group to recognize the humanity of the African is evidenced by the fact that when it is necessary or desired to identify Americans in terms of the land of their origin, terms such as Italian-American, Polish-American, Spanish-American, Jewish-American..., etc., are employed. In the American mind there is no connection of the black American with 'land, history and culture'—factors which proclaim the humanity of an individual." *Op. cit.*, p. 52. Baird is coordinator of the Afro-American History and Cultural Center of the New York City Board of Education.

8. See below under NATIVE RACES, Section II, item 1.

9. "Nationalist" militants, in particular, may argue strenuously for "Blacks" in preference to "Afro-Americans." Indeed, the *API* opted for such terminology, and so has at least one perhaps hyper-responsive public library. But "Blacks," however emotionally satisfying to some, perpetuates the old "racial" hang-up and could well wreak havoc subject-wise. BLACKS IN SOUTH AFRICA really affords little improvement over NEGROES IN SOUTH AFRICA, both wrongfully implying that black South Africans somehow constitute a minority in their own land. And BLACK WIT AND HUMOR, as another instance, could mean something radically and undesirably different from AFRO-AMERICAN WIT AND HUMOR.

The LC, acknowledging the imprecision and consequent misunderstanding that would result from a phrase like NEGRO STUDENTS IN THE U.S. applied to students who were in fact from an *African* country, permits: AFRICAN STUDENTS IN THE U.S. [etc.], p. 23.

10. As another instance of retrogession (or simply continuity), the 1967 ACS on p. 59 *added* "Colored people (U.S.)" to the previous "Colored people (American)" as a *See* reference to NEGROES.

11. P. 885.

12. In fact, the 1966 ACS altered these basic forms to AMERICAN POETRY—NEGRO AUTHORS, PORTUGUESE POETRY—NEGRO AUTHORS, etc. (p. 106), which still does not meet the objection to "Negro" and—if retained—would only complicate application of the "Afro" forms, producing quasiredundancies like AMERICAN POETRY—AFRO-AMERICAN AUTHORS. The proposed heads can easily be related to the larger language or culture-complex through cross-references; e.g., from "American poetry—Afro-American authors" to AFRO-AMERICAN POETRY.

The 1967 ACS, on p. 179, spewed up an extraordinarily regressive form, albeit as only a cross-reference:

> Negro literature (African)
> *See* African literature

It was unnecessary labor, whose offspring ought to be cancelled, since it may be safely assumed that most *African* literature is in any event authored by *Black writers.*

11. *Items:* CHURCH (p. 238; Sears, p. 150); CHURCH HISTORY (p. 241; Sears, p. 152)

> When I mention religion, I mean the *Christian* religion....
> —Parson Thwackum[1]

There can be no great quarrel with the fact that *Christian* entries preponderate in a scheme based on the actual holdings of a *Western* (i.e., religion-wise: Christian-oriented) library. The problem thus does not revolve about the *number* or *extent* of these entires, but rather with the *manner* of presentation. If the scheme is to be truly disinterested in tone and universal in applicability, there must be a parity in approach toward *all* the various faiths that compose the earth's religious landscape. A Jew, Jain, Shinto believer, or Muslim will *not* find that these heads embrace *his* Church or its history. The scope is restricted to Christianity, as a *See* reference under CHRISTIANITY—HISTORY (p. 235) and the multiple subdivisions like —BIBLICAL TEACHING under CHURCH clearly indicate.

Remedy: (a) Remove CHURCH HISTORY as a primary head, transferring the two columns of subdivisions to CHRISTIANITY—HISTORY.[2]

(b) The unqualified CHURCH, together with all other heads beginning CHURCH ... (p. 238–42), if designed for sole application to the *Christian* Church, should be prefaced by "Christian" (e.g., CHRISTIAN CHURCH ARCHITECTURE, CHRISTIAN CHURCH MUSIC, CHRISTIAN CHURCH GROUP WORK, CHRISTIAN CHURCH WORK WITH PROSTITUTES, CHRISTIAN CHURCH WORK WITH WOMEN).[3]

Notes (Item 11)

1. "Mr. Thwackum, the divine," makes this statement to "Mr. Square" in Henry Fielding's *The History of Tom Jones*, A Foundling (New

York: Signet Classics/New American Library, 1963), p. 105. Emphasis added.

2. This will then conform to already established practice elsewhere in the scheme; e.g., JUDAISM—HISTORY (p. 691–92).

3. The last two unprefaced forms appear, together with several others, in the 1966 ACS, p. 31.

12. *Items:* HERESIES AND HERETICS; HERESY (p. 587)

Another example of *Christian* bias, for the heads are obviously restricted to heretics and heresy vis-à-vis Christian dogma or orthodoxy.

Remedy: As suggested previously, indicate to *which* faith the heresy and heretics relate; e.g., HERESIES AND HERETICS, CHRISTIAN.[1]

Note (Item 12)

1. The scheme itself affords precedents: HERESIES AND HERETICS, JEWISH and HERESIES AND HERETICS, MOHAMMEDAN (p. 587).

13. *Item:* NEGROES AS BUSINESSMEN [CONSUMERS, FARMERS, etc.], p. 886[1]

The "as" necessarily implies that the occupation or activity that follows is somehow odd, uncommon, or unfitting for "Negroes" to engage in. The "proof of the pudding" is that no NEGROES AS SLAVES or NEGROES AS DOMESTIC SERVANTS is thought necessary.

Remedy: Directly precede the occupation or activity with the adjectival form; e.g., AFRO-AMERICAN BUSINESSMEN [CONSUMERS, FARMERS, etc.].[2]

Notes (Item 13)

1. Also, the spanking new form NEGROES AS COWBOYS (1966 ACS, p. 106).

2. The same criticism and rectification apply to JEWS AS FARMERS [SEA-MEN, SOLDIERS, ETC.], p. 688. For a precedent, cf. JEWISH CRIMINALS (p. 685). Apparently the qualms that obviously troubled the list composers regarding a Jew's fitness for farming or soldiering did not afflict them with respect to his capacity for law-breaking.

Not unexpectedly, Amerindians fare little better than Blacks or Jews. Cf. INDIANS OF NORTH AMERICA AS SEAMEN and INDIANS OF NORTH AMERICA AS SOLDIERS (p. 635). Ranganathan has nicely tabbed this construction a "Bias Phrase" in which a subject is treated "from the point of view of a class of users [or doers] whose primary interest lies in another subject." Cf. E. J. Coates, *Subject Catalogues; Headings and Structure* (London: Library Association, 1969), p. 105. To which nations or peoples, then, can a "primary interest" in soldiering be ascribed? Probably none. Yet no heads appear for AMERICANS AS SOLDIERS, CHRISTIANS AS SOLDIERS, or CAUCASIANS AS SOLDIERS.

DEAF AS AUTHORS (p. 352) belongs in the same category. There are no intelligent grounds for assuming that deafness *per se* is likely to blunt anyone's literary or creative potential. The form should be altered to DEAF AUTHORS. The 1967 ACS on p. 71 compounded this foolishness by installing DEAF AS ATHLETES as a new rubric. Perhaps the innovator would be good enough to explain why a deaf person cannot be expected to run, jump, or swim as well as anyone else.

14. *Item:* ANGELS (p. 51)

Now what could be amiss with so patently inoffensive a term? Simply that *these* angels are automatically assumed and understood to be *Christian*, while other varieties require an explanatory gloss; e.g., ANGELS (JUDAISM) and ANGELS (MOHAMMEDANISM).

Remedy: To establish equality among the seraphim of all faiths, add the gloss: (CHRISTIANITY). The unglossed form may be retained to cover material, if any, on Comparative Angelics.

15. *Item:* GOD (p. 552)

Subsequent primary heads on the same page—e.g., GOD (BRAHMANISM), GOD (CHINESE RELIGION), GOD (JUDAISM)—prove conclusively that the *Christian* deity (just, as previously shown, *Christian* angels, the *Christian* Church, etc.) has been allotted an unqualified prominence. For identical reasons, the form should be amended so that the Christian Divinity simply assumes its rightful, yet not over-powering, place alongside Zeus, Shiva, Parvati, Isis, and Allah in the vast panoply of gods.

Remedy: Add the gloss (CHRISTIANITY), and transfer the resultant head to its proper slot in the alphabetical sequence, between GOD (CHINESE RELIGION) and GOD (EGYPTIAN RELIGION).[1]

Note (Item 15)

1. Several more glossed forms have since been added; e.g., GOD (AFRICAN RELIGION), GOD (SIKHISM). Cf. 1967 ACS, p. 114.

16. *Item:* GENOCIDE (p. 536)

(a) An inconspicuous entry, its one *sa*—"Trials (Genocide)"— and four "××'s" occupy barely a column inch. "Race problems," figuring third among the ×× referents, seems starkly incongruous, if not macabre. Signifying mass murder, the deliberate annihilation or degradation of a people, "Genocide" itself represents a *problem* of mammoth dimensions. Only by means of lingual alchemy, pervert-ing the very substance of speech, can it be counted an *aspect* of "Race problems," or vice versa. A "problem" presupposes a "solution." Genocide, once effected, nullifies and liquidates any such antece-dent "problems," whether racial or ethnic. Considered within the framework of a Judaeo-Christian or broadly humanistic ethic, it *solves* nothing. Moreover, "Race problems" intimates a certain minimal distribution of strength among the contestants, no party be-ing *wholly* at a disadvantage, which bears no relationship whatever to a genocidal situation in which *one* side enjoys such a *monopoly* of power that it can eliminate the other. There *is* decidedly a "problem" here; not of "race," but of fathoming the enormity of that "in-conspicuous" eight-letter entry.

(b) Under MASSACRES (p. 789) appears the useful direction to

"sa names of massacres, e.g. St. Bartholomew's Day, Massacre of,"
etc. Referring to specific instances thus amplifies and illustrates the
general head. Yet no such specific referrents amplify or illustrate
GENOCIDE, by any standard a far weightier—and from a strictly moral
viewpoint, immensely more reprehensible—matter.[1] The omission,
in effect, results in a pronounced imbalance of horror, of depravity.

Remedy: (a) Excise "Race problems" from the "××'s."

(b) Expand the *sa* statement to read: *sa* Trials (Genocide) *and
entries for specific victims of Genocide; e.g.,* Armenian Massacres, 1915–
1923[2]; Indians, Treatment Of; Indians of North America—Government Relations; Jews in Europe—History—1933– .[3]

Notes (Item 16)

1. As of Dec. 31, 1965, 68 nations had ratified the UN Convention on
the Prevention and Punishment of the Crime of Genocide, which the
General Assembly had unanimously adopted on 9 Dec. 1948. Cf. *Everyman's United Nations,* 8th ed. (New York: United Nations, 1968), p. 352.

2. Introduced on p. 25 of the 1968 ACS, with an "×" for "Armenian
genocide, 1915–1923." An "××," however, for "Armenian question" (p. 72,
7th ed.) powerfully suggests that this phrase, like "Jewish question," should
be cancelled, relying upon the new form, together with ARMENIANS IN
TURKEY (p. 72), as adequate substitutes.

3. Reporting on the "Alcatraz occupation" undertaken by Amerindians in November 1969, Peter Collier wrote: "The California Indians now
on the Rock know that their people were decimated from a population of
100,000 in 1850 when the goldrush settlers arrived, to about 15,000 thirty
years later, and that whole tribes, languages and cultures were erased from
the face of the earth. There are South Dakota Indians there whose grandparents were alive in 1890 when several hundred Sioux, mostly women and
children leaving the reservation to find food, were caught at Wounded
Knee, killed, and buried in a common grave—the old daguerreotypes still
showing heavily-mustachioed soldiers standing stiffly over the frozen bodies
like hunters with their trophies." If *any* single word properly describes the
Amerindian agony as recounted by Collier and many others, it is Genocide.
Cf. "The Red Man's Burden," *Ramparts,* v. 8, no. 8 (Feb. 1970), p. 26–38.

According to the "President's Message to the Congress on Goals and Programs for the American Indians," presented on March 6, 1968, "There are
about 600,000 Indians in America today." Once, when Columbus arrived,

there were some 850,000 in what is now the U.S., a figure that by 1910 had declined to 220,000. Cf. *Cherokee Examiner,* no. 2 (1969), p. 2, and *Collier's Encyclopedia* (New York: Crowell & Macmillan, 1967), v. 12, p. 643.

Ernest Kaiser maintains that "more than 75 million Indians have been exterminated throughout the Americas. Some tribes," he continues, "have been destroyed completely by the cruel and inhuman treatment of white imperialist Americans. America's colonial Indian policy of destruction of all Indian organizations, denial of all self-rule, constant violations of treaties which were only to trick the Indians, suppression of all Indian cultures including their religions and the theft of almost all Indian lands was really a policy of liquidation of Indian properties and Indian life, that is, genocide." About 1,200,000 Amerindians, he claims, "were massacred in the U.S. alone." *Op. cit.,* p. 298–99. Likewise, van den Berghe, limiting his scope solely to Mexico, declares that the "Indian population declined from an estimated 4.5 million in 1519 to 3.3 million in 1570 to 1.3 million in 1646." As reasons for this staggering decimation he lists: "smallpox and typhus epidemics, wars, forced labor, and mistreatment on mines and plantations, heavy tribute demands, spoliation of land, and the general social and economic disruption which came in the wake of the Conquest." *Op. cit.,* p. 43. Cf. also: Ian T. Peters, "The Non-vanishing American," *International Relations,* v. 3, no. 9 (May 1970), p. 717–25. Peters estimates the pre–Columbian Amerindian population in the U.S. at 1,000,000, which had dropped "at the turn of the century" to an "all-time low of approximately 300,000." p. 717.

It should be noted that the new form, HOLOCAUST, JEWISH (1939–1945), installed by the 1968 ACS (p. 203–04), *does* specify an "××" for "Genocide."

17. *Item:* BANDEIRAS
×× Brazil—History—To 1821
Brazil—History—1549–1762 (p. 109)

This head deserves embellishment, rather than correction. The metal-working, gold-discovering *bandeirantes,* says Gilberto Freyre, were "an active, creative, and one might almost add, a noble element in the colonization of Brazil."[1] A "frontier folk," remarks Basil Davidson, "of unusual daring and accomplishment," they were also, for the most part, runaway slaves, Africans who fled the tyranny of coastal plantations. And they may well qualify, in addition, as the first

Republicans in the Western Hemisphere.[2] Were library catalogues to show their origin, it would render a distinct bibliographic service to programs of Black and African Studies.

Remedy: Establish AFRO-BRAZILIANS as a primary head (recommended earlier), with both an *sa* and "××" for "Bandeiras."[3]

Notes (Item 17)

1. Quoted by Basil Davidson in his *Black Mother* (London: V. Gollancz, 1961), p. 22.
2. *Ibid.,* p. 19, 21.
3. As precedents for "Afro-Brazilian" usage, cf. van den Berghe, *op. cit.,* especially p. 63 and 66–7.

18. *Item:* BAPTISM (p. 112)

This, too, exudes the by-now-familiar priority assigned to Christianity throughout the scheme. More than one faith, as the list itself admits in a later head, BAPTISM (HINDUISM), practices this ritual or sacrament. But Christianity again enjoys an absolute precedence.

Remedy: Add the gloss (CHRISTIANITY).

19. *Items:* BANKS AND BANKING—JEWS (p. 111); CAPITALISTS AND FINANCIERS—JEWS (p. 185)

> All Jews love money. All Jews are sensualists with a penchant for gentile virgins. All Jews are involved in a conspiracy to take over the financial and cultural life of whatever country they happen to be living in.[1]

Were *other* kinds of bankers, capitalists, and financiers accorded subheads, this might not be worth mentioning. But "Jews" appears as the *sole* subdivision, no doubt a source of warmth and comfort to anti–Semites and neo–Nazis, yet outrageous to anyone else. Such a form tempts the finder to believe that Joseph Goebbels composed it. Surely, it would have delighted him.[2]

Remedy: Either add subheads for the entire gamut of bankers, as well as "capitalists and financiers"—e.g., Lebanese, Christian, Anglo-Saxon, Teutonic, etc.—or dispense with the singled-out "Jews" altogether.[3]

Notes

1. So Gore Vidal summates "the lurid anti–Semitic propaganda of the thirties." Cf. "Number one," *New York Review of Books,* v. 14, no. 11 (June 4, 1970), p. 12.

2. In fact, venomous references to "Jewish plutocrats," "Jewish gold," "Jewish usury," and "international Jewish financiers" littered Nazi speeches and publications. Cf. "Denouncing the Jews," in Bramsted, *op. cit.,* especially p. 392; and Peter Viereck, *Meta-Politics; The Roots of the Nazi Mind* (New York: Capricorn Books, 1965), particularly p. 157–58. Viereck pointedly mentions the "popular Nazi and Wagnerian myth" that "all democracy is a secret dictatorship of Jewish capitalists" and quotes a 1921 Munich poster which declared: "Like a giant spider, the Jewish international world stock-exchange capital creeps over the peoples of this earth, sucking their blood and marrow...." *Ibid.,* p. 306. On Hitler's exhortations to the German bourgeoisie to "fight against Jewish capital and Jewish communism," cf. Mosse, *op. cit.,* p. 309.

3. A related subhead, demanding the same reform, is COMMUNISM—JEWS (p. 281). It should be common knowledge that members of many groups have been associated with Communism, but LC specifies only "Jews," again—even though unwittingly—parroting the Goebbels propaganda line, which sought to firmly identify Jews with Bolshevism. Who, asked Dr. Goebbels, "were the men 'behind the scenes of this virulent world movement ... the inventors of all this madness?' The answer was, of course, the Jews. It was they who had discovered Marxism and who were now at the head of Marxist movements everywhere. He insisted that 'only in the brain of a nomad could this satanism have been hatched.' By amassing names and alleged atrocities of countless Jews, Goebbels hoped to unmask Communism and impress on the world that it was the Fuehrer who had rendered it a signal service by setting up 'a barrier to halt world Bolshevism against which the waves of this vile Asiatic-Jewish flood break in vain.'" Cf. Bramsted, *op. cit.,* p. 380.

20. *Item:* CATHOLICS AS SCIENTISTS (p. 198)

The presumption, as with all such "as" forms, is that Catholics aren't likely to *become* scientists due to some quasihereditary or doctrinal defect. The solitary fact that Gregor Mendel was a *monk* amply discloses the spuriousness of that contention.[1]

Remedy: Assign to all relevant material the related head SCIENTISTS, CATHOLIC (p. 1147).

Note (Item 20)

1. The "as" form applied to Blacks, Jews, and Indians has earlier been commented upon. Consider, however, the magnificent assininity embodied in JEWS AS SCIENTISTS (p. 688). It fundamentally implies that men like Einstein, Salk, Oppenheimer, Freud, and Rabi are *deviants*. Similarly, "Jews as educators," though unused as a prime head (1966 ACS, p. 82), should not even be printed as a cross-reference.

21. *Item:* CHILDREN'S SERMONS (p. 222)

Since CHILDREN'S SERMONS, JEWISH immediately succeeds this unqualified head, and given the likelihood that more *Christian* sermons for children have been published than those originating from any other faith, it is practically certain that the noninverted head handles solely the Christian species. Which again ruptures what should be the universality of the scheme.

Remedy: (a) Employ the unqualified head for multireligious collections or studies.

(b) Institute an inverted form, CHILDREN'S SERMONS, CHRISTIAN, for material dealing wholly with that faith.[1]

Note (Item 21)

1. Similar "remedies" may be applied to the prime head, SERMONS

(p. 1162). No rubric appears for SERMONS, CHRISTIAN, but specific forms are given, e.g., for BUDDHIST SERMONS; SERMONS, JEWISH; etc. A like complaint may be lodged against PRAYER (p. 1019–20).

22. *Item:* INTELLIGENCE LEVELS
—Chinese
—Javanese
—Jews
—Negroes
—Shilluks (p. 660)

The particularized subheads imply that these five peoples must either be hyper- or sub-intelligent, no other comparable groups having (apparently) been the subjects of special intelligence research. Moreover, they suggest that race or ethnicity are exclusive causal factors in intelligence.

None of these imputations successfully withstands scientific examination. Many races and peoples, not merely the five shown, have been subjected to intelligence tests. And it is well established that a grand variety of factors, environmental and otherwise (not excluding the testers' presuppositions and biases), may influence "intelligence levels."[1]

Remedy: Closer, more exact cataloging, undertaken in a universalist spirit, would no doubt result in a much expanded and non-discriminatory roster of subheads: e.g., —CAUCASIAN, —AMERICAN, —AFRO-AMERICAN, —MEXICAN-AMERICAN, —BRITISH, —ANGLO-INDIAN, etc. To argue that direct subdivision to place (e.g., —UNITED STATES) would suitably encompass material on "American" intelligence begs the question. In fact, "Americans" are widely-distributed across the globe, just as Jews and Chinese are. *If* there is something peculiar about *American* intelligence, it is not necessarily a reflex of being born or living *in* the United States, but rather a result of factors like American *culture,* the nature of the American *gene-pool,* etc.

Note (Item 22)

1. Moyra Williams devotes considerable attention to "conditions and factors affecting intelligence," mentioning not only "organic factors," but also "education," "maturation," "occupation," "cultural and family environment," and "personality and emotional stability." Cf. *Mental Testing in Clinical Practice* (Oxford: Pergamon Press, 1965), p. 3–9. For a recent, well-reasoned discussion of the pitfalls inherent in even the most sophisticated attempts to link "race" and "intelligence," cf. Philip Mason, "Race, Intelligence, and Professor Jensen," *Race Today,* v. 1, no. 3 (July 1969), p. 76–7.

23. *Item:* COMMANDMENTS OF THE CHURCH (p. 276)

So ambiguous is this heading that LC supplies a scope note to explain that "if used for any church other than the Catholic, the name of the denomination is added as a subdivision." It remains quite unclear, however, why the *Catholic* Church should enjoy unqualified precedence in this case.

Remedy: Whenever used, indicate the Church in question by means of a gloss or subdivision; e.g., COMMANDMENTS OF THE CHURCH (ROMAN CATHOLIC).

24. *Item:* CONFIRMATION (p. 300)

Such a *rite de passage* is not confined to Christian peoples and denominations. Indeed, CONFIRMATION (JEWISH RITE) appears on the same page. To ease Christocentricity from the scheme, the unemended head should solely be assigned to comparative and multifaith works.

Remedy: For treatises dealing with *Christian* confirmation, add the gloss (CHRISTIAN RITE).

25. *Item:* DEVOTIONAL LITERATURE (p. 365)

Juxtaposed with DEVOTIONAL LITERATURE, HINDU; DEVOTIONAL LITERATURE, JEWISH; and DEVOTIONAL LITERATURE, MOHAMMEDAN, the Christian favoritism emerges clearly, if somewhat monotonously.

Remedy: For works on or of *Christian* devotional literature, construct an inverted head DEVOTIONAL LITERATURE, CHRISTIAN.[1]

Note (Item 25)

1. Supplements (e.g., July 1964–Dec. 1965, p. 58) have since altered this construction. The pattern is now to refer from DEVOTIONAL LITERATURE, HINDU to HINDU DEVOTIONAL LITERATURE. Significantly, the unmodified DEVOTIONAL LITERATURE remains, with an "×" for "Christian devotional literature." The result, then, of this "reform" is to make the pro–Christian bias a bit less obvious. The remedy, if all faiths are to be treated equally, would thus be to raise the unused head, CHRISTIAN DEVOTIONAL LITERATURE, to primary status, referring from DEVOTIONAL LITERATURE, CHRISTIAN.

26. *Item:* ESCHATOLOGY (p. 442)

The theological doctrine of last or final things appears in many faiths, but LC grants pre-eminence to the Christian genus, designating other creedal versions by inverted heads like ESCHATOLOGY, EGYPTIAN and ESCHATOLOGY, JEWISH.

Remedy: Apply the uninverted head only to comparative works, formulating ESCHATOLOGY, CHRISTIAN as a new rubric to encompass *Christian* material on the subject.

27. *Item:* LYNCHING
sa Vigilance committees
×× Criminal Justice, Administration of (p. 764)[1]

Note, first, that there is no "××" from HOMICIDE (p. 596), although that head is provided with references variously from and to

ASSASSINATION, DEATH BY WRONGFUL ACT, MURDER, POISONING, SUI-
CIDE, OFFENSES AGAINST THE PERSON, and VIOLENT DEATHS. Second,
there is no "xx" from MURDER, despite the fact that this form, like
HOMICIDE, is accorded many of the above named referents, plus
STRANGLING. Third, no connection is made between LYNCHING and
TERRORISM, nor between the act itself and its historically well known
victims: Black people. And fourth, the appearance of "Criminal Justice, Administration of" as the sole "xx" lends the term, as well as
the practice it denotes, a certain dignity, if not legitimacy. Coming
to fundamentals, is *lynching* somehow less "homicidal" or "mur-
derous" than "strangling" or "poisoning"? Is it not an "offense
against the person" usually resulting in a "violent death"? Are these
qualities of lynching particularly diminished because the *lynched,*
over the past century, have been largely *Black* and the *lynchers White*?
Outlining the historic role of lynching in America, van den Berghe
states that the practice

> existed before the Civil War, but it was overwhelmingly an act
> of whites against whites in attempting to control frontier law-
> lessness, where legal machinery was either absent or ineffective.
> After the Civil War, lynching assumed a different character. It
> became a racial phenomenon: most *victims* were Negroes and
> most *criminals* were whites; it was no longer a device to control
> banditry in an anarchistic frontier, but rather a *terrorist* tech-
> nique to maintain white supremacy in settled communities with
> an established legal order.[2]

Perhaps an LC savant can elucidate on how racist murder committed by White criminal gangs qualifies as the "Administration of
criminal justice," all the more so when the "punished" victims "may,
in fact, be known to be innocent of any crime" and in any event never
enjoyed due process.[3]

Remedy: (a) Eliminate "Criminal Justice, Administration
of" as an "xx."

(b) Install as "xx's" under LYNCHING:

Homicide

Murder

Offenses against the person

Terrorism

Violent deaths

(c) Create a new subhead under AFRO-AMERICANS (formerly NEGROES): —PERSECUTIONS, making cross-references from and to "Lynching."

Notes (Item 27)

1. The Sears variant (p. 372) is:
   LYNCHING
     See also Vigilance committees
     ×× Crime and criminals
2. *Op. cit.,* p. 90. Emphasis added.
3. Cf. *ibid.* for the quoted phrase.

28. *Items:* SLAVERY IN THE U.S.
—Insurrections, etc. *sa particular insurrections, e.g.* Southampton Insurrection, 1831 (p. 1187)
SOUTHAMPTON INSURRECTION, 1831
× Nat Turner's Insurrection
Turner's Negro Insurrection, 1831 (p. 1207)

> That is why the racists and the narrow-minded chauvinists do not want black people, Chicano people, Puerto Rican, Asian, and poor white people to study and know their own true history—because their history will tell the truth about America today.
>
> —Bobby Seale[1]

These "items" only underscore further what by now should be well demonstrated: that the LC scheme, whether intentionally or not, tends to minimize and sadly neglect Afro-American history, as well as dehumanizing the Black man himself. Point-by-point:

(a) Any dictionary endows the word "Revolt" with a greater intensity and broader significance than "Insurrection." The many slave

uprisings in America, especially during the 19th century, most
assuredly qualify as "revolutionary" rather than merely "insurrec-
tionary" in scope, tactics, and objectives. Gabriel Prosser, Denmark
Vesey, and Nat Turner, leaders of the three most notable rebellions,
unquestionably warrant the appellation "revolutionists."[2]

(b) Of these three major revolts, which took place, respectively,
in or around Richmond, Charleston, and Southampton, only the
Southampton event has been accorded a distinct head. The Charleston rising appears as a subhead under the city, —SLAVE INSURREC-
TION, 1822, while the Richmond enterprise goes unnoted.

(c) Raids, rebellions, expeditions, and like undertakings engineered by *White* men ordinarily merit entries under the leader's
name.[3] *Black* men, apparently, do not qualify for such a distinction.
Their deeds, if recorded at all, remain nameless. In effect, they are
reduced to ciphers, to shadows, concretely exemplifying Julius Les-
ter's contention that "we live in a world where race has meaning,
conferring superiority to white and inferiority to black. . . ."[4]

Remedy: (a) Under SLAVERY IN THE U.S., substitute —REVOLTS
for the present subhead, —INSURRECTIONS.

(b) Establish primary heads for individual revolts under the
names of the leaders, with cross-references from place; specifically:

GABRIEL PROSSER'S SLAVE REVOLT, RICHMOND, VA., 1800
    × Prosser's Slave Revolt, Richmond, Va., 1800
      Richmond, Va.—Prosser's Slave Revolt, 1800
   ×× Slavery in the U.S.—Revolts

DENMARK VESEY'S SLAVE REVOLT, CHARLESTON, S.C., 1822
    × Vesey's Slave Revolt, Charleston, S.C., 1822
      Charleston, S.C.—Denmark
      Vesey's Slave Revolt, 1822
   ×× Slavery in the U.S.—Revolts

NAT TURNER'S SLAVE REVOLT, SOUTHAMPTON, VA., 1831
    × Turner's Slave Revolt, Southhampton, Va., 1831
      Southhampton, Va.—Nat Turner's Slave Revolt, 1831
   ×× Slavery in the U.S.—Revolts

(c) The above changes will require elimination of the current *sa* note under SLAVERY IN THE U.S. — INSURRECTIONS, ETC., and the relegation of SOUTHAMPTON INSURRECTION, 1831, to an unused form.

Notes (Item 28)

1. *Seize the Time; The Story of the Black Panther Party and Huey P. Newton* (New York: Vintage Books, 1970), p. 427.
2. Bradford Chambers, among others, has so described them, noting with particular regard to Vesey that he "had devoted years to the study of revolutions in various countries, especially the slave revolts of Haiti (which had resulted in the abolition of slavery there in 1791)." Cf. *Chronicles of Negro Protest* (New York: Parents Magazine Press, 1968), p. 77. For helpful summaries of these three uprisings, cf. E. Franklin Frazier, "Slave Revolts and the Underground Railroad," Chapter V in his *Negro in the United States* (New York: Macmillan, 1949), especially p. 87–90, as well as Herbert Aptheker, *American Slave Revolts*, new ed. (New York: International Publishers, 1969), p. 293–324 ("The Turner Cataclysm"), 219–30 (on Prosser) and 268–76 (on Vesey). More detailed information may be found in the numerous sources cited by Frazier in "The Negro Under the Slave Regime," Part I of his "Classified Bibliography," p. 707–15, and Aptheker's comprehensive bibliography of primary and published material, p. 375–407.
3. Cf., for example: SHAY'S REBELLION, 1786–1787 (p. 1169), HARPER'S FERRY, WEST VA.—JOHN BROWN RAID, 1850 (p. 578), JAMESON'S RAID, 1895–1896 (p. 670), SULLIVAN'S INDIAN CAMPAIGN, 1779 (p. 1252), WAYNE'S CAMPAIGN, 1784 (p. 1397), WASHINGTON'S EXPEDITION TO THE OHIO, IST, 1753–1754, and WASHINGTON'S EXPEDITION TO THE OHIO, 2D, 1754 (p. 1392).
4. "Black and White: An Exchange," *New York Times Book Review*, May 24, 1970, p. 36.

29. *Item:* GIPSIES
×× **Rogues and vagabonds (p. 547; Sears, p. 298)**

A highly picturesque cross-reference. And also pejorative, conferring upon these people *en masse* the status of thieves, vandals, and ne'er-do-wells.[1] Undoubtedly, Gypsies—since the first of them left India in the 10th century—have pursued a wayfaring life. But whatever their faults, they cannot truthfully be characterized across-the-board as scoundrels or robbers, no more so than any other given people. In fact, contemporary Romanies, obeying their own cultural traditions, "earn a living how they can—dealing in scrap metal, selling flowers or lace and, sometimes, by telling fortunes."[2] Their original forebears—"acrobats, singers, dancers, fortune-tellers, wood-workers and horse dealers"—plied occupations "forbidden to their high-caste countrymen."[3] One Gypsy woman not long ago related to a British interviewer that "people really did still fear them—believed that they could cast spells, stop cows giving milk or hens laying, and sold babies."[4] It seems that LC, too, still believes this. Indeed, the stereotype, as the interviewer mused, may spring "from a certain envy for the gypsies," an envy of that "freedom described by one as 'the feeling of the dew underfoot in an orchard on a summer's morning.'" And the envious, he adds, "would deny to others what they themselves can't have."[5]

This introduces a less "romantic" and positively sobering aspect of the Gypsies' treatment by their "hosts" through history: they have been systematically brutalized and repressed. "In 1596," as a single instance, "106 were condemned to death simply for being gypsies."[6] Since 1530, according to one authority, "the English have persecuted their gypsies with vigor."[7] *Today* the persecutions continue in the form of evictions, together with other kinds of both private and official hostility.[8] All this might be casually dismissed as but another manifestation of stupid prejudice and know-nothingism, albeit demanding correction, except for the central, overwhelming fact of 20th century Gypsy experience, conveniently ignored in the LC scheme: that the Nazis exterminated somewhere between 200,000 and 600,000 Romanies before the Third Reich concluded, first subjecting numberless thousands to diabolical "medical experiments."[9] Well, who cares what fate befalls a pack of vile "rogues and vagabonds," of "habitual criminals and parasites"?[10] If Gypsies be less than *human*, they make no claim on human compassion nor concern. Which side *are* we on?

Remedy: (a) Delete "Rogues and vagabonds" as an "xx."

(b) Add the subhead, —PERSECUTIONS, with an "xx" for "Genocide."[11]

Notes (Item 29)

1. These remarks by William Perkins, a 17th century Puritan preacher, speaking of the English poor, fully illustrate the pejorative quality of the phrase:

> *Rogues,* beggars, *vagabonds* ... commonly are of no civil society or corporation nor of any particular Church: and are as rotten legs and arms that drop from the body.... To wander up and down from year to year to this end, to seek and procure bodily maintenance is no calling, but the life of a beast.

Quoted by J. H. Plumb, "Slavery, Race, and the Poor," *New York Review of Books,* v. 12, no. 5 (March 13, 1969), p. 4. Emphasis added.

2. Julia Bennett, "Gypsies of Europe," *Teachers World,* no. 3146 (Feb. 27, 1970), p. 25. Brian R. Goodey, summarizing a survey published by the British Ministry of Housing and Local Government in 1967, amplifies the Gypsy employment situation: 52% of the men, he notes, "continue to 'deal,'" but now in "scrap metal, rags, and waste paper," rather than horses. "Agricultural work accounts for 15%, and hawking and other traditional forms of earning officially employ ... 4% of the males." Where there are greater "agricultural opportunities," dealing "is of less importance." A "large number of gypsies in Kent," for instance, "work in the orchard and hop harvests." Cf. "Characteristics of the English Gypsy Population," *Geographical Record,* v. 58, no. 3 (July 1968), p. 488.

3. Jeremy James, "Gypsies," *The Listener,* v. 79, no. 2033 (March 14, 1968), p. 335.

4. *Ibid.,* p. 336

5. *Ibid.*

6. *Ibid.,* p. 335.

7. Goodey, *op. cit.,* p. 487.

8. Cf. Bennett, *op. cit.,* p. 24; Goodey, *op. cit.,* p. 485–87; and James, *op. cit.,* p. 334–36.

9. Cf. James, *op. cit.,* p. 336; William L. Shirer, *The Rise and Fall of the Third Reich; A History of Nazi Germany* (London: Secker and Warburg, 1962), p. 979; and Leon Poliakov, *Harvest of Hate* (London: Elek Books, 1956), p. 265–66.

10. The Gauleiter of Austrian Styria, in demanding a "National Socialist Solution for the *Gypsy Question*" even before the war began, described them as of "notoriously foul heredity ... habitual criminals and parasites within the body of our people, causing immense damage and imperiling the purity of the borderland peasant's blood and way of life." Quoted by Poliakov, *ibid.,* p. 265. Emphasis added. Other Nazi spokesmen,

labeling them "asocial," thought this a sufficient death-warrant. Is it on such high authority that LC devised its miserable cross-reference?

11. The only alterations undergone by GIPSIES in five years were the addition of three subheads, —JUVENILE LITERATURE (1967, ACS, p. 113), —LITERARY COLLECTIONS, and —RELIGIOUS LIFE (1969 ACS, p. 93), as well as the installation of a new primary head, HYGIENE, GYPSY (1969 ACS, p. 106).

30. *Item:* INDIANS OF NORTH AMERICA, CIVILIZATION OF

*Here is entered literature dealing with efforts to civilize the Indians
... (p. 635)*

A few hundred years ago there were no white people in this country. The only inhabitants of the United States were the Indians. These Indians usually lived in small bands and wandered about from place to place. They lived mostly by hunting and fishing. They were often quarrelsome. Some of the different tribes or bands had settled homes and were partly civilized, but most of them were wandering savages who did nothing to develop this great country.[1]

... It should be the role of the library to aid in overcoming another insidious application of white supremacy—cultural imperialism. Now there is literature available which decimates the "Tonto myth"; the "our-feathered-friends-a-picturesque-species-of-wildlife" stereotype; and that separates the whitewash from the war paint.[2]

If there were a competition among LC heads for sheer wrong-headedness, stupidity, distortion, and Anglo-Saxon myopia, this form would be among the top contenders. It fully embodies the "Tonto myth," accepts the preposterous "wandering savages" thesis, and culturally emasculates a varied, remarkable people whose attainments in many fields are legion and universally valuable.[3] Yes, the 19th century witnessed "the first large-scale efforts to 'civilize' the Indians by forcing on them what was believed to be the highest cultural form possible, the White man's way of life."[4] But only Tonto-mythologists could argue that the Indians *needed* "civilizing." Serious, informed students of Amerindian life, like the late anthropologist

Paul Radin, have shown in considerable detail that *before* the White Man's advent Indians had developed mighty, complex "civilizations" and registered signal accomplishments in the arts, astronomy, engineering, agriculture, conservation, pharmacy, social organization, and numerous other spheres.[5] The "civilizing" efforts encompassed in the LC head, apart from enhancing the very eradication of Indians biologically, resulted in "mental and physical degradation" for those who somehow survived.[6] A young Amerindian testified eloquently before the Commission on Indian Affairs that "The relatives you left behind are still trying to kill each other and enslave each other because they have not learned . . . that freedom is built on my respect for my brother's vision and his respect for mine."[7] Can we not, even at this late date, begin to respect our brother's vision? As well as his dignity?

Remedy: a) Delete INDIANS OF NORTH AMERICA, CIVILIZATION OF.

b) Introduce two new subheads to cover material previously assigned the excised form:

—DECULTURATION

—RELATIONS WITH MISSIONARIES, SETTLERS, ETC.

Under both should appear "xx's" for "Indians, Treatment of" and "Indians of North America—Government relations."[8]

c) While not formally cited above as an "item," it is appropriate here to observe that under INDIANS, INDIANS OF CENTRAL AMERICA, INDIANS OF MEXICO, and INDIANS OF NORTH AMERICA appears the subhead —CULTURE, usually with an "x" for "Civilization." In other words, the scheme generously acknowledges that the Mayas, Inca, Toltecs, and others—like all "primitives"—possessed a "culture," but refuses to grant that some, at least, had created "civilizations." The remedy for this absurdity is to replace —CULTURE with a new form, —CIVILIZATION AND CULTURE, which should satisfactorily embrace buffalo hunters and pyramid builders alike.

Notes (Item 30)

1. From D. L. Hennessey, *25 Lessons in Citizenship* (1969), quoted in

Synergy, no. 25 (Jan.-Feb. 1970), p. 19. The author is identified as the "Supervisor of Citizenship Classes, Northern California."

2. *Synergy, ibid.,* p. 1.

3. Peters, too, notes that "popular knowledge of the North American Indians mostly consists of myths, 'cowboys and Indians,' the Noble Savage, the torturer of brave homesteaders, etc." *Op. cit.,* p. 719.

4. Dee Frangquist, "Life with Great White Father," *Synergy, op. cit.,* p. 29.

5. Cf. especially Radin's *The Story of the American Indian* (New York: Liveright; first published in 1927, reprinted in an "enlarged Black & Gold edition," 1944). In a preface to the revised edition, Radin briefly restates his central thesis that "aboriginal American history can only be understood in terms of the spread of the great civilizations that developed in Mexico, Central America and along the Pacific coast of South America from Ecuador to Peru." Addressing himself to the "tantalizing question of what type of culture the Indians of the United States possessed before the spread of the higher elements from Mexico," he states that "although these cultures were on a non-agricultural basis, some of them were clearly more complex than has generally been assumed. It is quite within the realm of probability that, at a very early date, a fairly unified civilization, possessing pottery and a significant ritualistic and political development, stretched across North America from the northwest coast of Canada, across the northwestern plains to the Great Lakes, then along the entire area east of the Mississippi, across the Caribbean, to northeastern South America" (p. vii–viii).

On the same theme, Peggy O'Donnell declares that "the vast range of Indian peoples that inhabited this hemisphere in the 15th century covered the whole spectrum of 'civilized' experience, from the simplest form of social life to classic civilizations that in some instances operated more effectively than their European counterparts." She then limns some of the salient features of Indian culture and attainments, not the least of which being a sound ecological relationship to the environment and nonmaterialistic concept of life. On the specific question of "quarrelsome Redskins," she notes that "peace was the way of life among many of the people of the New World. A life that is spent in cooperative sharing, and in communion with the natural world, has little room for the systematic destruction of others. . . . They were more concerned in making life liveable than in making war." Cf. "The American Heritage: Gifts of the Indian," *Synergy, op. cit.,* p. 20–23.

6. Cf. Radin, *op. cit.,* p. 376.

7. Quoted by O'Donnell, *op. cit.,* p. 22.

8. For an example of "deculturation" employed by a sociologist to describe the experience of post–Conquest "indigenous societies" in Mexico, cf. van den Berghe, *op. cit.,* p. 43.

31. *Items:* CONVERTS; CONVERTS FROM BUDDHISM [CONFUCIANISM, JUDAISM, etc.] (p. 310); PROSELYTES AND PROSELYTIZING, JEWISH (p. 1038)

The note under CONVERTS unsurprisingly declares that "*Here are entered works on converts to Christianity.... Works on converts to Judaism are entered under* Proselytes and proselytizing, Jewish.... *Works on converts to other religions are entered under* Buddhist [Mohammedan, etc.] converts...." At least this is a candid admission. The arrangement may be criticized on two bases: (1) It further entrenches a pro–Christian bias; and (2) It results, from a purely logical, information-seeking viewpoint, in absolute chaos, cumbersomely strewing material on "Converts" throughout the list, although catalogue users wanting data on the general subject and its several manifestations ought certainly to find it in one convenient spot.

Remedy: (a) Excise PROSELYTES AND PROSELYTIZING, JEWISH.

(b) Reconstruct all existing heads so that they indicate, as necessary, *to* and *from* what faiths the conversions have been made; e.g.,

    CONVERTS TO BUDDHISM

    CONVERTS TO CHRISTIANITY

    CONVERTS TO CHRISTIANITY FROM HINDUISM

    CONVERTS TO JUDAISM

    CONVERTS TO JUDAISM FROM CHRISTIANITY

    CONVERTS TO ISLAM FROM BUDDHISM

(c) Replace inverted heads like CONVERTS, ANGLICAN and CONVERTS, MORMON with appropriate new forms; e.g.,

    CONVERTS TO ANGLICANISM

    CONVERTS TO MORMONISM

(d) Under the discarded head, PROSELYTES AND PROSELYTIZING, make a *See* reference to CONVERTS ... and MISSIONS. In like vein, cross-references will be required, e.g., from BUDDHIST CONVERTS to CONVERTS TO BUDDHISM, etc.

(e) On a related tangent, the missionizing religion should preface the various MISSIONS TO ... forms (1966 ACS, p. 98–9), resulting in CHRISTIAN MISSIONS TO CONFUCIANS, CHRISTIAN MISSIONS TO LEPERS, CHRISTIAN MISSIONS TO JEWS, CHRISTIAN MISSIONS TO PYGMIES, etc.[1]

Note (Item 31)

1. The new, still deficient construction, MISSIONS TO . . ., replaces the earlier MISSIONS—LEPERS, MISSIONS—JEWS, etc. (7th ed., p. 835). Sears (p. 402) continues the older form.

32. *Items:* HEAVENLY RECOGNITION (p. 583); IMMACULATE CONCEPTION (p. 621); IMPOSITION OF HANDS (p. 622); JUDGMENT DAY (p. 692); LORD'S SUPPER (p. 758; Sears, p. 371); MYSTICAL UNION (p. 871); POWER OF THE KEYS (p. 1018); VIRGIN BIRTH (p. 1376)

All these forms appear unglossed. To the well catechized Christian or student of religions it is immediately clear that they express theological concepts or doctrines. This may not be true, however, for the "outsider," especially persons reared in a milieu outside Christendom. At the risk of facetiousness, someone not overly familiar with Christianity nor schooled in Biblical teachings could easily mistake HEAVENLY RECOGNITION as referring to an aspect of astronomy, or POWER OF THE KEYS as relating to hardware, if not locksmithing. In short, these heads are not only prejudiced *toward* Christianity, but also ambiguous.

Remedy: Add glosses for clarification; e.g.,

HEAVENLY RECOGNITION (CHRISTIAN ESCHATOLOGY)
IMPOSITION OF HANDS (CHRISTIAN SACRAMENT)
JUDGMENT DAY (CHRISTIAN THEOLOGY)[1]
LORD'S SUPPER (CHRISTIAN SACRAMENT)
MYSTICAL UNION (CHRISTIAN DOCTRINE)
POWER OF THE KEYS (CHRISTIAN DOCTRINE)
VIRGIN BIRTH (CHRISTIAN DOCTRINE)

Note (Item 32)

1. As precedents, cf. the glossed form, JUDGMENT DAY (ISLAM), 1966 ACS, p. 82, and REBIRTH IN WESTERN PARADISE (BUDDHISM), 1969 ACS, p. 185.

33. *Items:* HYMNS (p. 613–14); PREACHING (p. 1020); RELIGIOUS EDUCATION (p. 1094– 95); RESURRECTION (p. 1103); REVELATION (p. 1104); SAINTS (p. 1128); SALVATION (p. 1132; 1966 ACS, p. 136)

To avoid tiresome repetition, the more detailed comments already made regarding kindred forms like ANGELS, CHILDREN'S SER- MONS, DEVOTIONAL LITERATURE, ESCHATOLOGY, GOD, and HERESY may also, with some modifications, be applied to these heads. In each case, the activity, doctrine, or category is not limited to Christianity, yet Christianity enjoys an unqualified priority.

Remedy: As appropriate, add glosses or adjectival inversions; e.g., HYMNS, CHRISTIAN[1]; RESURRECTION (CHRISTIAN DOCTRINE). Multifaith or comparative studies may be assigned the gloss (COM- PARATIVE RELIGION).

Note (Item 33)

1. The HYMNS construction, like that for DEVOTIONAL LITERATURE, has been changed so that all *non*–Christian entries are now prefaced by the name of the faith; e.g., BUDDHIST HYMNS (July 1964–Dec. 1965 ACS, p. 98). True universality, however, necessitates similar handling for *all* religions. The remedy, therefore, is to precede the unqualified rubric HYMNS with "Chris- tian," referring from "Hymns, Christian."

34. *Item:* MAMMIES
     × **Colored mammies**
     Mammies, Colored

Mammies, Negro
Negro mammies (1967 ACS, p. 159)

Annica [a Black house slave in Mississippi] got a letter from
her mammy which detected her in a lie. O! that negroes were
more truthful.
>   —Entry, dated January 25, 1855, in
>   Eliza L. Magruder's personal diary[1]

mammy . . . 2a: a Negro woman serving as a nurse to white
children esp. formerly in the Southern states. .´. . b: A Negro
woman—*often taken to be offensive*[2]

An Afro-American woman, when asked what she thought of the
word, responded unhesitatingly, "I wouldn't want to be called one."
It might be sound policy for LC catalogers to first query Black LC
staffers before elevating antebellum plantation slang to primary head
status.

Remedy: Substitute CHILD-NURSES, AFRO-AMERICAN, with an
"××" for NURSES AND NURSING as well as CHILDREN—CARE AND
HYGIENE, canceling *all* the "Mammy" referents.

Notes (Item 34)

1. Quoted from the ms. diary in Louisiana State University Library,
Baton Rouge, by Eugene D. Genovese, "American Slaves and Their His-
tory," *New York Review of Books,* v. 15, no. 10 (Dec. 3, 1970), p. 40. Miss
Magruder, White, maintained a diary for the years 1846 and 1847, as well
as 1854–57, while living with her aunt, who managed a plantation in the
Natchez area.

2. Webster, p. 1369. Emphasis added.

35. *Items:* PROVIDENCE AND GOVERNMENT
OF GOD (p. 1040); PROVIDENCE AND
GOVERNMENT OF GOD (JUDAISM)
(1966 ACS, p. 125)

The introduction of the glossed form for Judaism makes necessary the revision of the unglossed Christian centered rubric.
Remedy: Add the gloss (CHRISTIANITY).

36. *Items:* ALCOHOL AND JEWS; ALCOHOL AND NEGROES; ALCOHOL AND WOMEN (1967 ACS, p. 8)

Does no one else *drink?* Only Jews, Blacks, and women? That's surely the implication, imputing to these three groups a peculiar affection for liquor.
Remedy: (a) Scan the LC collection for similar material on the Irish, Scotch, French, Germans, etc., creating suitable prime heads like ALCOHOL AND THE IRISH.
(b) If the survey fails to disclose such material, commission the LC poet-in-residence to fill the void. It should be an engrossing addition to the bibulous literature.

37. *Item:* AUSCHWITZ TRIAL, FRANKFURT AM MAIN, 1963–1965 (1967 ACS, p. 21)

Apparently the LC cataloger was not much attuned to the ramifications of the Frankfurt trial. Otherwise, a number of cross-references would automatically have been indicated.
Remedy: Add an "xx" and *sa* for AUSCHWITZ (CONCENTRATION CAMP), together with "xx's" for GENOCIDE; HOLOCAUST, JEWISH (1939–1945); JEWS—PERSECUTIONS; and NATIONAL SOCIALISM.

38. *Item:* MUSLIMS AS SCIENTISTS (July 1964–Dec. 1965 ACS, p. 150)

The "great conversion" to "Islam" and "Muslim," footnoted under Item 6, at least reduces the objection to one plane, rather than two (as would have been the case with "Mohammedans as scientists"). B. Ben Yahia, while acknowledging that "Muslim science has been the subject of many severe and even extreme criticisms," nonetheless maintains that during the 19th century "some Arab-writers . . . produced works of great originality."[1] Moreover, in a brief retrospective passage, he notes that "the period between the 8th and 13th centuries may fairly be called the Arabs' age in the history of science" when "princes, ministers and rich patrons rivalled with one another in commissioning the translation of ancient, and the writing of new, scientific masterpieces. . . ."[2] In view of the impressive contributions in medicine, botany, geography, and the exact sciences attributed by Yahia to Muslim scientists and bulwarked by the many monographs cited in his "Bibliography," the "as" in LC's heading seems a wholly unwarranted slight.

Remedy: Cancel the head, recataloging all relevant material under SCIENTISTS, MUSLIM (1968 ACS, p. 395).

Notes (Item 38)

1. "Science in the Muslim World," in Rene Taton, ed., *Science in the Nineteenth Century* (London: Thames and Hudson, 1967), p. 573.
2. *Ibid.,* p. 572.

39. *Item:* BABIY YAR MASSACRE, 1941
  ×× **Russia—History—German occupation, 1941–1944**
  World War, 1939–1945—Atrocities
  World War, 1939–1945—Jews (1968 ACS, p. 38)

The "××'s" uncannily make it appear not that an explicit genocidal policy accounted for such atrocities, but rather that they were simply a reflex or result of the war itself. Unquestionably, the wartime German occupation of the Ukraine made the Babi Yar massacre *possible,* but does not alone explain *why* it happened. Moreover, the referents totally ignore *Ukrainian* complicity in the event.[1]

Remedy: Add "××'s" for ANTISEMITISM—UKRAINE; GENOCIDE; HOLOCAUST, JEWISH (1939–1945); and JEWS—PERSECUTIONS.

Notes (Item 39)

1. Poliakov documents the Nazi policy of inciting "pogroms and 'spontaneous' massacres" against the Jews in newly-occupied regions, like Lithuania and the Ukraine, that were "anti–Semitic by tradition." *Op. cit.*, p. 118–39. For a verbatim account of the "liquidation of the cemetery at Kiev" by the Nazi officer in charge, cf. p. 139. For explicit references to the complicity of the Ukrainian militia in these exterminations, cf. p. 125, 128, 130, and 136.

Alec Nove, in effect buttressing Poliakov's claims, writes that "unfortunately, the war also greatly stimulated antisemitism, *especially in the Ukraine*. This was apparently due partly to German propaganda, and partly to the general consequences of hardships on popular temper in *traditionally antisemitic areas*." Millions of Jews, he declares, "ended their lives in mass graves on the outskirts of Kiev, Minsk, Vilna, and hundreds of smaller places." Cf. "Jews in the Soviet Union," *Jewish Journal of Sociology*, v. 3, no. 1 (June 1961), p. 109. Emphasis added.

In describing how, as of 1961, Soviet sources rarely mentioned the wartime atrocities visited upon Russian Jewry, Nove says: "To take another example, in such places as Babi Yar, the ravine outside Kiev which was the scene of one of the biggest massacres, there is no monument or any mark of commemoration of the victims." *Ibid.*, p. 115. It may be further noted, on the basis of personal knowledge, that even when a monument *did* later appear at the massacre site, in about 1967, local Intourist guides would only conduct visitors to the grisly spot *by request*—and with visible reluctance. David W. Weiss, a Jewish-American cancer expert who attended a scientific conference in the Soviet Union late in 1965, reported a similar experience. Shortly after arriving in Kiev, he asked to be escorted to Babi Yar, only to be told that "*there was no such place as Babi Yar.*" Later, following a discussion with her Intourist superior, the guide affirmed that the site existed, but that it was hardly worth seeing. Weiss opined that "surely . . . there must be some sort of memorial to mark such a place of martyrdom; there were, after all, a variety of memorials to the Ukrainian war dead throughout Kiev!" A lengthy altercation resulted in the "compromise" that he might visit the spot if he were willing to privately hire an auto. For a full recitation of this incident, together with much evidence of continuing anti–Semitism in the Ukraine and elsewhere, cf. "The Plight of the Jews in the Soviet Union," *Dissent*, v. 13, no. 4 (July-Aug. 1966), p. 447–64. Emphasis in original.

Jacob Robinson accents the indivisibility of "Hitler's extermination order" and individual events like the Babi Yar massacre. "Despite the wide distribution of the Jewish communities involved and their relative isolation during the war years," he maintains, "the history of these communities during the Hitler era cannot be written outside the context of the total European

Jewish scene." Cf. "Research on the Jewish catastrophe," *Jewish Journal of Sociology*, v. 8, no. 2 (Dec. 1966), p. 193. His entire essay, incidentally, well indicates the continuing need to document and synthesize the experience of the "Catastrophe" or "Holocaust," as well as the immense difficulties involved in that task.

40. *Item:* SLAUGHTERING AND SLAUGHTER-HOUSES—JEWS (p. 1187)

No other people is so specified in a subdivision. To accuse LC of viciousness in this construction may be too severe, but surely it may be judged *inept*. Of course, the head refers to orthodox Jewish dietary laws, which make imperative the special, rabbinically-supervised preparation of meats. But the formulation, in view of the still vivid "slaughter" that characterized the Holocaust, requires modification.

Remedy: Create a substitute form, SLAUGHTERING AND SLAUGHTER-HOUSES, KOSHER, with an "×" for "Kosher slaughtering and slaughter-houses." Or, better yet, employ MEAT INDUSTRY AND TRADE, KOSHER as an alternative.

Chauvinism, the "Bwana Syndrome," and the Third World

Bwana, n ... used (1) in reference, 'master, owner, possessor' of slaves, house, plantation or other property, and generally 'great man, dignitary, worthy personage'; (2) in address, 'master ...'[1]

Should my Kaffirs receive communion? God forbid that I should ever allow them.[2]

Two hundred years of postcolonial history has split the world into black and white, rich and poor, powerful and powerless. We are so divided that 20 per cent of us, the White Tribe, possess 80 per cent of the world's resources and nearly 100 per cent of the world's research. It is this disproportion of resources and the inaction of the Christian and post–Christian West that has and is contributing more than anything else to a world of violence and protest.

—P. J. O'Mahony[3]

Notes

1. Inter-Territorial Language Committee for the East African Dependencies. *A Standard Swahili-English Dictionary* (Oxford University Press, first published 1939, reprinted 1963), p. 43.
2. Exclamation of a Portuguese slave-owner, quoted by Plumb, *op. cit.*, p. 4.
3. From a letter, on behalf of the Catholic Bishop's Commission for

International Justice and Peace, that originally appeared in the Sept. 21, 1970, *Times* and was later reprinted in *Namibia—Today*, v. 4 (Sept.-Oct. 1970), p. 21.

1. *Item:* NATIVE RACES as both a primary head and subhead (p. 877; Sears, p. 418–19)

This is thorny on several counts, not least because of the disparity or discrepancy between the boundaries delineated in the scope note[1] and the actual employment of the head by catalogers. In practice, the subhead, particularly, becomes an *ethnological* or *sociological* catch-all, applied to works on the life, habits, and social conditions of "races" within a prescribed land or region, as well, perhaps, as to their relations with the "governing authorities."[2] Objections to the phrase itself are manifold:

(a) "Races" is unquestionably an anachronism, no longer—if ever—sound anthropologically. Coming to the nitty-gritty, it is meant to encompass the "aboriginal" (i.e., originally-resident) *people* in a given area, whether they be a "nation," or organized tribally, by clan, etc. The overridingly important consideration here is that there may be many such "peoples" in, say, Angola, and they need not be—and often are *not*—much differentiated from one another *biologically*. If "race" retains any solid contemporary meaning it is *biological* or taxonomic, not ethnic nor cultural.[3] In short, the LC term has been misapplied to what are not *racial* (i.e., necessarily biological), but rather ethnic or social groups. As an example, the Benga, Combe, Bubi, and Fang of Equatorial (formerly Spanish) Guinea—all distinct ethnically—don't differ much *racially*. Yet LC insists on terming these *culturally*-disparate people "races." They aren't.[4]

(b) "Native" is the sort of word employed by a European or American, not an African or Asian. That it connotatively expresses a White supremacist or "bwana" attitude is perhaps nowhere better revealed than in a passage from Ezekiel Mphahlele's short story "Point of Identity." Karel, a good-natured "Coloured" mechanic who willingly lives among Black South Africans, but has just been threatened with downward reclassification, exclaims:

Look man . . . de word 'native' doesn't simply mean one's got black blood or African blood. It's a p'litical word, man. You's a native because you carry a pass, you can't go to watch-imball-er-Parliament. You can't vote, you live in dis location. One can be proud of being an African but not a *native*.[5]

To cement the point, consider Mr. Fafunwa's remarks:

The word "native" is defined [by the Shorter Oxford English dictionary] as *"One born in a place; left in a natural state, untouched by art, unadorned, simple; in modern usage, especially with connotation of non–European origin."* In Western journals, magazines and textbooks for primary school children, authors out-do themselves in making the label stick. The word "native" in terms of current usage is synonymous with the African. If no harm is meant by the users of this word, then conscious effort must be made to avoid the use of it by writers and publishers. . . .[6]

(c) It is palpably ludicrous to assign —NATIVE RACES, as a cataloguer now must, to material treating with, as examples, Xhosa and Zulu people in mid–20th century South Africa who may well be identifiable as *Xhosa* and *Zulu* (i.e., the "aboriginal"/original inhabitants) but many of whom are no longer folk- or traditionally-organized—in other words, who are modern, urbanized, relatively mobile members of the society. The foolishness only compounds with the realization that these very "native races" will one day, most certainly, become the "governing authorities" themselves, that their presently inferior political station is merely transitory, temporary.

Remedy: (a) Abolish the adjectival "Native" in all its permutations; i.e., NATIVE CLERGY, NATIVE LABOR, NATIVE RACES.

(b) Denote material on "the relations between the governing authorities and the aboriginal inhabitants" by the new head, COLONIZED PEOPLES.

(c) Identify works on the various groups within a prescribed area with the subdivision —PEOPLES (e.g., AFRICA, SOUTH—PEOPLES, which would apply equally to Boers, Britons, Xhosa, Zulu, etc.).[7]

(d) Replace NATIVE CLERGY with LOCAL CLERGY or LOCALLY-RECRUITED CLERGY, and NATIVE LABOR with COLONIES—LABOR AND LABORING CLASSES or LABOR AND LABORING CLASSES, COLONIAL.[8]

(e) Add the gloss (BIOLOGY) to the primary head, RACE, and henceforward apply this form *solely* to works dealing with gross *biological* differences and categories among humankind.[9]

Notes (Item 1)

1. *"Here are entered works on the relations between the governing authorities and the aboriginal inhabitants of colonial or other areas."*

2. LC's own confusion becomes apparent in the specified cross-references:

> × Aborigines
> ×× Ethnology

3. The Meeting of Experts acknowledged that "it would be difficult ... to dispense entirely with such terms as 'race' or 'tribe,' which are part of current scientific terminology; they should, however, be used correctly." *Op. cit.,* p. 4. The conference further declared, on a more general plane, that "special attention should ... be paid to the use of terms which have passed into the everyday speech of the colonizing peoples and which, because of their colonialist origin, carry overtones of racial superiority vis-à-vis the one-time colonies. These terms could implant the seeds of racialism in the minds of former colonizing peoples; in any event, they offend the susceptibilities of peoples who were once colonized." The meeting thus recommended "that 'after-effects of colonialism' be eliminated as rapidly as possible." Amen.

4. The *SSHI* errs similarly, noting, e.g., under ABORIGINES: "*See* ... also names of aboriginal *races,* e.g. Eskimos," v. 57, no. 4 (March 1970), p. 1. Emphasis added.

On the biotypology of Guinea peoples, cf. Sanford Berman, *Spanish Guinea: An Annotated Bibliography* (Washington, D.C.: Photoduplication Service, Catholic University of America, 1961), p. 285–86, 301.

5. *In Corner B* (Nairobi: East African Publishing House, 1967), p. 69. Emphasis in original.

6. In Meeting of Experts, p. 25. Emphasis in original. "Librarians" was probably omitted from the last sentence by oversight.

The "native" cancer, unexpectedly, also appears in the *API* as NATIVE PEOPLES, *op. cit.,* p. 42, though it was apparently dropped from later issues. Not so unexpectedly, the *SSHI* uses it, too. Cf., e.g., v. 57, no. 3 (Dec. 1969), p. 81. And *Habari,* monthly newsletter of the Washington Task Force on African Affairs (P.O. Box 13033, Washington, D.C. 20009), in a regular survey-feature, "Towards a Racist Press," finds the malady rampant in the U.S. newspapers. The March 1970 issue, for instance, reports that "to read American press coverage of Africa one would think the continent is half populated with dimwits consumed with self-destructive politics. The other half is 'native,' a word usually followed by some erroneous and condescending unfact." Excerpts from the pages of *Time, Newsweek,* and the Washington *Star* conclusively prove the point. V. 2, no. 3, p. 5–6.

7. The Meeting of Experts suggested that "the word 'inhabitant' should be used in preference to the word 'native.'" *Op. cit.,* p. 4. While the recommended substitute may not be appropriate to library practice, the complaint regarding the term that we are currently using is worth heeding.

8. For a precedent, cf. LABOR LAWS AND LEGISLATION, COLONIAL (p. 711). To turn once more to South Africa, it is sufficient to employ the usual, unqualified term —LABOR AND LABORING CLASSES for material dealing with *African* labor in the postcolonial period, though the subhead in this instance might be made even more precise by adding "African" as an inverted adjective.

9. On "Race" as an essentially *biological* concept, cf. Sonia Cole, *Races of Man* (London: British Museum, 1965), especially Chapter I, "Definition of Race," p. 9–13, in which the author declares that "Nationality has not necessarily any connection with race, nor has language or culture, though they have been responsible for isolating certain groups and thus indirectly affect gene frequencies.... A race, in fact, differs from other races only in the frequency of the genes it possesses...."; Ashley Montagu, ed., *The Concept of Race* (New York: The Free Press; London: Collier-Macmillan Ltd., 1964), a provocative anthology in which the editor himself raises the question "as to whether, with reference to man, it would not be better if the term 'race' were altogether abandoned," p. 12; and van den Berghe, *op. cit.,* who on p. 9–11 critically examines four "definitions" of "race," revealing how actual usage of the term has become impossibly muddled and contradictory.

For LC precedents, cf. DEATH (BIOLOGY), p. 352; LIFE (BIOLOGY), p. 742; SEX (BIOLOGY), distinguished from SEX (PSYCHOLOGY), p. 1165; and VARIATION (BIOLOGY), distinguished from VARIATION (MUSIC), p. 1361.

The glossed head RACE (SOCIAL SCIENCE) could be usefully assigned to studies like those by Montagu and van den Berghe, cited above. To achieve even greater accuracy, both should also be catalogued under RACE (BIOLOGY) and the van den Berghe work further treated under RACE RELATIONS. Still another way out of the maze might be to create a composite form, RACE (BIOSOCIOLOGICAL CONCEPT), which would economically and fairly handle at least the major thrust of the Montagu/van den Berghe volumes.

2. *Item:* DISCOVERY AND EXPLORATION as a subdivision under names of continents and countries (p. 374; Sears, p. 58, 627)[1]

What are such concoctions as AFRICA—DISCOVERY AND EXPLORA-
TION and AMERICA—DISCOVERY AND EXPLORATION if not colossal
specimens of ethnocentrism? Cortez no more "discovered" Mexico
for the Aztecs than Livingstone did Victoria Falls for the Leya people, who much earlier had named it "Nsyungu Namutitima."[2] Unqualified, "—Discovery and exploration" represents an insult to the
many peoples and lands which, so it appears in our library catalogues, didn't really *exist* until Whites happened to notice them.[3]

Remedy: Employ the subhead *only* with a gloss indicating *who*
did the discovering and exploring, or *for* whom it was done (e.g.,
French, European, American, English, Spanish, Portuguese, Chinese).[4]

Notes (Item 2)

1. Sears apparently uses this subdivision for only "America" and "The
West," otherwise preferring "—Description and travel." Cf. note on p. 203.
2. Cf. George M. Musowe, "Requiem for Mujimaizi," *Jewel of Africa,*
v. 1, no. 4 (1968), p. 12–3.
3. In this regard, Joan Marshall adds, the list "reflects, and thereby
helps perpetuate, the Western European view that the world was created bit
by bit as it was discovered by Western Europeans." Personal communication, *op. cit.*
4. Joan Marshall, who reports hearing an East African "relate with
great humor his view of the Western European view that his country was discovered by Vasco da Gama," suggests another "remedy": first, the establishment of a primary head for EUROPE, WESTERN (to match the current EUROPE,
EASTERN); second, the introduction under "discovered" areas like AFRICA,
EAST of a subdivision, —FIRST KNOWLEDGE OF IN EUROPE, WESTERN; and
third, the automatic assignment of a duplicate entry —FIRST KNOWLEDGE OF
IN, e.g., AFRICA, EAST under EUROPE, WESTERN (since, as Marshall notes,
"while Vasco," for instance, "was discovering Africa, Africa was discovering
him"). *Ibid.*

3. *Items:* FRANCE–COLONIES (p. 511); GREAT BRITAIN–COLONIES (p. 562); U.S.–INSULAR POSSESSIONS (p. 1346); U.S.–TERRITORIES AND POSSESSIONS (p. 1348; Sears, p. 613)

Under the prime head COLONIES appears this helpful note: *"also subdivision* Colonies *under names of countries, e.g.,* France– Colonies."[1] The "disinterested" reader, however, who in all innocence turns to the subdivisions under U.S., finds

U.S.–Colonies
     See U.S.–Insular possession
     U.S.–Territories and possessions[2]

How quaint and self-righteous that the United States does not now (and never did) have "colonies" (an unpleasant word), but only "territories and possessions"! That is, Cubans, Guamians, Filipinos, Okinawans, Puerto Ricans, Midway, Marianas, Caroline, Marshall, and Virgin Islanders, Hawaiians, Haitians, Samoans, Indians, and Mexicans, unlike their less fortunate brothers and sisters in Africa, Asia, and South America, were spared a "colonial" experience. Except, of course, that they weren't.[3] Which nicely illustrates a transparent double-standard built into the scheme.[4]

Remedy: Replace the euphemistic —INSULAR POSSESSIONS and —TERRITORIES AND POSSESSIONS with the pure, straightforward —COLONIES applied so painlessly to *other* imperialist powers like France and Great Britain.

Notes (Item 3)

1. P. 272.
2. P. 1342. Sears' note under U.S.—TERRITORIES AND POSSESSIONS (p. 613) is even more candid: "Use this subdivision under U.S. only. For other countries use the subdivision COLONIES."
3. Sir Denis Brogan, limiting his remarks to strictly 19th-century events, frames it this way:

> At the end of this ignominious conflict [i.e., the Spanish-
> American War], the United States had demonstrated to Europe

not only that it had become a serious power with an important navy, but that it had become an imperial power. Cuba was formally 'freed'; Puerto Rico was annexed as a straight colony; and, across the Pacific, near the shores of China, the United States made itself the heir of Spain by annexing the Philippines. This involved them in a war with the Philippine rebels or patriots, and as the 19th century drew to a close the country of the Declaration of Independence was involved in imposing its authority by force, 'puking up its principles,' as the philosopher William James put it.

Cf. "USA: The Years of Expansion," *History of the 20th Century*, no. 2 (1968), p. 40.

In an angry apostrophe to "Anglos," Chicano student leader William Martinez exclaims: "Your schools teach that the United States respects other nations, so it skips over the Mexican War in a hurry and never explains why you invaded Mexico and *took away more than half her territory*. It's like that." Cf. "A Mexican American Talks About White Supremacy," *Interracial Books for Children*, v. 2, no. 4 (spring 1970), p. 5. Emphasis added. Cf. also Michael Meyerson's aptly-titled "Puerto Rico: Our Backyard Colony," *Ramparts*, v. 8, no. 12 (June 1970), p. 50–1+ and "Puerto Rico: Colony in Revolution," *Tricontinental Bulletin*, v. 5, no. 48 (March 1970), p. 16–21.

Following World War II some 2,141 Pacific islands, including the Marianas, Caroline, and Marshall groups, became an American-administered "Trust Territory," which enjoys only limited self-government through an elected legislative body, the Congress of Micronesia. The Micronesian Congressmen themselves harbor no illusions about their status. In a report rejecting Commonwealth affiliation with the U.S., they declared that "Under our present *quasi-colonial* system, the identity, individuality and dignity of the people of Micronesia are being suppressed." Cf. Robert Trumbull, "U.S. Ties with Micronesia Strained," *The New York Times*, Aug. 23, 1970, Section 1, p. 14. Emphasis added.

4. A similar double-standard, based on the canons of "Marxist-Leninist epistemology," appears to thrive in Soviet subject cataloging. "For a treaty," says R. L. Cope, "between the U.S.A. and Mali on economic assistance, the headings chosen [by the Fundamental Library of Social Sciences] were U.S.A.—External Affairs—Documents: and Economic Expansion, American in Mali Republic. But for works dealing with economic aid by socialist countries to under-developed areas the type of heading used is 'Economically under-developed countries—Aid from Socialist Countries.'" Cf. "Soviet Views on Subject Cataloguing: A Brief Review of Some Writings," *Australian Library Journal*, v. 19, no. 4 (May 1970), p. 130–31.

African and other beneficiaries of such "socialist" aid, which may include numberless apothecary jars and hopelessly aged chemical compounds, might well question the implicit distinction between the two types of "assistance."

4. *Items:* SOCIETY, PRIMITIVE (p. 1195; Sears, p. 551), together with its multiple variations (ART, PRIMITIVE; CLOTHING AND DRESS, PRIMITIVE; MUSIC, PRIMITIVE; RELIGION, PRIMITIVE; etc.)

"Primitive" in these inverted heads inaccurately and—according to popular conceptions of the word—slurringly describes various forms and aspects of human life.[1] No self-respecting social scientist is likely to use it. Why then, should librarians? It is heavily overlaid with notions of inferiority, childishness, barbarity, and "state of nature" simplicity, whereas the societies, arts, economic modes, music, and religions it purportedly covers may be extremely complex, ingenious, creative, humane, and—depending on taste and *Weltanschauung*—admirable.[2] The term additionally implies, erroneously, a *bygone* period, although a "primitive" artist, for example, may be a contemporary.

   Remedy: (a) Replace the inverted adjective in SOCIETY, PRIMITIVE with "Folk," "Traditional," or—on a structural basis—"Kin-organized."[3]

   (b) Most other inverted forms require special reconstruction; e.g., HUNTING, PRIMITIVE (p. 608) may become HUNTING (ETHNOLOGY), HUNTING IN FOLK SOCIETIES, or HUNTING WITH TRAPS, BOW AND ARROW, ETC., while INDUSTRIES, PRIMITIVE (p. 642) might be changed to INDUSTRIES (ETHNOLOGY); INDUSTRIES, NONMECHANIZED; or INDUSTRIES, HAND.

   (c) If the politico-anthropological distinction between "kin" and "civil" society is accepted, KINGS AND RULERS, PRIMITIVE (p. 703) needs to be dismantled, for the "primitive" element becomes a *non sequitur.* By *definition,* most folk- or kin-organized societies are essentially egalitarian and communal. Once "kings" or "rulers" emerge who govern at least partly by fiat, the society is no longer (in the original ethnological sense) "primitive." Should a heading still be required for material on "primitive" *leaders* or *nominal* "rulers," CHIEFS AND HEADMEN IN FOLK SOCIETY, CHIEFS AND HEADMEN (ETHNOLOGY), or CHIEFS AND HEADMEN IN KIN-ORGANIZED SOCIETY may be instituted.

Notes (Item 4)

1. The Meeting of Experts assailed "primitive," as well as "savage," "backward," and "uncivilized," as examples of "contemptuous, unjust or inadequate" phraseology. p. 4.

2. "The Oxford dictionary," notes Fafunwa, "defined the word as *'simple, rude or rough like that of early times: old-fashioned.'* Again, this word is often used to stereotype some African art, culture, mores, religion or stage of development. By setting ourselves up as the sole arbiter of who is 'primitive' and who is 'civilized,' and what is 'good' and what is 'bad,' it means that we are playing God and that role can only lead to greater misunderstanding and intolerance among the peoples and nations of the world." *Op. cit.,* p. 26. (Emphasis in original.)

Lest anyone protest that the LC heading-manufacturers never intended the term as ethnocentric or "intolerant," turn to the first column on p. 1137 and notice, about a quarter of the way down:

> Savages
> *See* Man, Primitive

The reader hoping to locate entries under such an outmoded, soul-warping head royally deserves to find *nothing* at all, not even a thoughtful *See* reference to a not-much-better form.

With particular reference to Africa, Basil Davidson asks two elemental questions: Is its sculpture "primitive"? Is its religion "primitive"? He then quotes William Fagg to the effect that African plastic-forms have assumed a high and influential place among "the world's great art traditions," and to his second query replies that "many African peoples ... have systems of belief about themselves and the universe that are subtle and developed." Cf. *Old Africa Rediscovered* (London: Victor Gollancz, 1965), p. 231.

3. Leonard W. Doob affirms that "anthropologists have been seeking euphemisms to replace adjectives such as 'uncivilized,' 'primitive,' and 'savage'; but the ones they prefer—preliterate, non-literate ... etc.—possess no special advantage." *Becoming More Civilized; A Psychological Exploration* (New Haven: Yale University Press, 1960), p. 3. "Non-literate" presupposes literacy as a touchstone of societal differentiation, although "non-

literate" peoples have evolved complex, super-kin sociopolitical organizations that render them unclassifiable as "primitive" or "folk." "Preliterate" posits a series of evolutionary stages, a rigid, immutable progression *toward* "literacy," that in the case of any specific people simply cannot be demonstrated or known *in advance.*

The late Ralph Linton, like many other anthropologists, made a necessary distinction between "band-" or "tribe-" organized groups and "civil" societies (i.e., states). "The tribe," he maintains, "is a social entity, while the state ... is a *political* entity," characterized chiefly by "a fairly strong central authority with power to coerce [its] members." Cf. "Tribe and State," chapter 14 in his *Study of Man* (New York: Appleton-Century-Crofts, first published 1936; copyright renewed 1964), p. 231–52.

As LC precedents for conversion to "Folk" as an alternative, cf. FOLK ART, FOLK LITERATURE, etc., p. 494–500. Indeed, the July 1964–Dec. 1965 ACS on p. 80 and 125 completely *canceled* LITERATURE, PRIMITIVE as a prime head, referring directly to FOLK LITERATURE. But this appears to be an isolated instance of de-primitivization. All the sister-forms remain untouched.

5. *Item:* AFRICA, SOUTH—HISTORY (p. 23)

Obviously inconsonant with both modern scholarship and ordinary intelligence are primary heads and subheads like NATIVE RACES; SOCIETY, PRIMITIVE; NATIVE LABOR; and NATIVE CLERGY. Surely, as indicated earlier, these can be either abandoned or humanized. Less obvious, perhaps, but equally disturbing, are certain more specific topics. Nosipho Majeke, a South African, in 1952 proclaimed that

> When non–Europeans write the full history of the past, they will have to find other names for the so-called Great Trek and 'Kaffir' Wars.... We shall need a new vocabulary, for language itself has become distorted in the service of herrenvolkism [master-racism]. The very word 'Non-European' is an absurdity, when a man must needs describe himself as the negative of another man.[1]

Now, what do we find as subdivisions under AFRICA, SOUTH—HISTORY?:

    —KAFIR WARS, 1811–1878
    —GREAT TREK, 1836–1840

The list, in short, defines these events entirely from the viewpoint of the rigidly Calvinist and thoroughly racist Boer invaders.[2] It has likewise appropriated wholesale the term "Kafir" (or "Kaffir"),[3] originally an Arabic designation for "unbeliever" or "infidel" which Europeans in South Africa applied—in a connotative sense like "nigger"—to *all* Bantu peoples in the region, or, more particularly, to the Xhosa and their Nguni-speaking neighbors.[4] Librarians can certainly muster enough imagination to devise more honest and objective forms. Rubbish left over from the days of pith helmets and Gatling guns simply doesn't belong in a modern library catalogue.[5]

Remedy: (a) As possible alternatives under AFRICA, SOUTH—HISTORY, replace the present second and third subdivisions with:

—XHOSA-BOER WARS, 1811–1878[6]

—BOER MIGRATION, 1836–1840

(b) To eliminate utterly the obnoxious "Kafir" in its remaining forms with respect to both the people it lamely attempts to identify and their language, substitute XHOSA (AFRICAN PEOPLE) and XHOSA LANGUAGE, with cross-references from the variant "Xosa."[7] Further: replace HYMNS, KAFIR with HYMNS, XHOSA (AFRICAN PEOPLE).

Notes (Item 5)

1. *The Role of the Missionaries in Conquest* (Cape Town), p. ii.
2. Should this delineation seem excessively harsh, consider that carefully conducted attitude studies in South Africa revealed Afrikaners, compared with other elements of the population, to be "both more anti–African and more authoritarian." Cf. Tajfel, *op. cit.,* p. 91. The author additionally cites the "religious elements in the hierarchy of human groups built by the Bible-carrying early Boers" as an example of the sort of self-justifying ideology fabricated by social groups "imbued with a fairly definite code of values and morals" who find themselves enjoying advantages over other groups that need to "be explained away in terms which would not conflict with the code." Hence the Boers' Bible-based notions of "inherent superiority and inferiority" (p. 95).

On the heated question of "Who got there first?," cf. Robert Weisbord's so-titled article in the Feb. 1966 *Africa Today* (v. 13, no. 2), p. 10–12. Weisbord's examination of evidence "from three sources: archaeology, oral tradition, and the accounts of shipwrecked Portuguese seamen" leads him to conclude "that the Bantu and not the Europeans were the first to come to South Africa. If there is an interloper in South Africa it is the white man."

3. Cf. KAFIR LANGUAGE (BANTU), p. 696; KAFIRS (AFRICAN PEOPLE), p. 697; and HYMNS, KAFIR (BANTU) p. 614.

4. "kaf-fir *or* kaf-ir . . . 1 *also* caf-fer or caf-fre . . . a *usu cap*: a member of a group of southern African Bantu-speaking peoples of Ngoni stock b *sometimes cap* a South African or Negroid ancestry—*usu used disparagingly*. . . ." *Webster's Third*, p. 1230. Emphasis added.

W. J. Plumbe, University of Malawi Librarian, in a paper delivered at the mid–1969 Conference of Commonwealth Africa University Librarians in Lusaka, forthrightly stated: " 'Kafir' is an offensive word that, to say the least of it, cannot be used in the light of present-day—or even 1948—knowledge." Quoted from an unprocessed copy of his "Classification and Cataloguing of Africana."

The Meeting of Experts also condemned the term as equivalent to "Nigger," p. 4, while the April 1970 *Race Relations News* classified it with defamatory labels like "native" and "munt" (v. 32, no. 4), p. 9.

An anonymous contributor to *Sechaba* succinctly highlights the sociopolitical role and all too frequent outcome of such tabs. "It is not," he writes, "as men that the victims of genocide are attacked. They must first be depersonalized. Men do not enslave other men. They enslave those who they have first deprived of their humanity by labeling them 'Kaffirs,' 'Wogs'— subhumans, fitted by their nature to be slaves. It is not just chance that racism as a social theory came into being with the rise of colonialist, imperial expansion with the clear function of justifying slavery and other forms of exploitation." Cf. "Brutality and Race," v. 4, no. 3 (March 1970), p. 7. A later *Sechaba* issue reports a concrete case of the epithet being used by Johannesburg policemen who allegedly attacked a young Soweto woman, calling her both a "kaffir" and "communist pig." Cf. "Banned Woman Assaulted," v. 4, no. 7 (July 1970), p. 24.

5. Indeed, SCAUL (the Standing Committee on African University Libraries) is now undertaking just such a project for Africana; i.e., codifying the names of African peoples and languages into a generally acceptable list which will indicate recommended forms plus variants.

6. To firmly establish that the so-called "Kaffir Wars" were, in fact, a century-long conflict between trekking Boers and militant, cattle-herding Xhosa, cf. chapter 9, "Boer, Bantu, and Briton," in Donald L. Wiedner's *A History of Africa South of the Sahara* (New York: Vintage Books, 1962), especially p. 126.

7. With appalling typicality, the LC list at present does exactly the reverse; i.e., refers from XOSA, which it thereby implicitly recognizes as the correct *African* terminology, to the Boer-derived KAFIR. Cf. p. 1425. To be fair, there also appears on p. 1425 a primary head for the unglossed XOSA

with an "×
×" from KAFIRS (AFRICAN PEOPLE), the unmistakable inference being that the Xhosa, among others, are "Kafirs" (i.e., "niggers").

6. *Item:* AFRICA, SOUTH—RACE QUESTION
× Apartheid (p. 23)

The subhead —RACE RELATIONS, discussed above, more appropriately handles material dealing with the interaction between
"racial" groups in South Africa and elsewhere. What needs to be
stressed at this juncture is that "Apartheid"—the practice, as well as
policy or philosophy, of racial separation—is no longer restricted,
lamentably, to the South African milieu. It is a theory in its own
right, argued and exposited—if not implemented—in many other
places (most notably, though not exclusively, Rhodesia).[1]

Remedy: "Elevate" APARTHEID to a primary head, with both
"sa" and "×
×" references for AFRICA, SOUTH—RACE RELATIONS; RHO-
DESIA—RACE RELATIONS; RACISM; and SEGREGATION.[2]

Notes (Item 6)

1. For monthly reportage on apartheid in its various guises, cf. *Anti-
Apartheid News* (89 Charlotte Street, London, W. 1). For two valuable ex-
positions of the concept and system as they have arisen in South Africa, cf.
Jean-Paul Sartre, "The Cancer of Apartheid," *London Bulletin*, no. 6
(autumn 1968), p. 47–9, and A. Sachs, *The Violence of Apartheid* (London:
an International Defence and Aid Fund pamphlet issued by Christian Action Publications Ltd., 1969). Justin V. J. Nyoka, a Black journalist, examines the legislative "cornerstone" of Rhodesian *Apartheid*, presaging the
establishment of South Africa–like "Bantustans," in "Rhodesia's New Land
Tenure Act—More Forced Migration of Southern Africans," *Migration Today*, no. 14 (spring 1970), p. 25–32. Also: the many UN documents, most
available gratis, that are conveniently listed on p. 7 of the April 1970 *African
Studies Newsletter* (v. 3, no. 2).
  The UN General Assembly had identified "*apartheid*, racial discrimination and colonialism" as "interlocking evils." Cf. *Objective: Justice*,
published by the United Nations Office of Public Information, v. 1, no. 1
(1969), p. i.

An apologist minces few words in announcing the general relevance of apartheid to Africa. "The policy," says L. E. Neame, "that is variously described as Differentiation or Segregation or Apartheid simply recognizes that there are different races in the continent; that they are likely to remain different; and that they cannot be merged into a homogeneous people any more than the races in Europe or Asia or America." He later elucidates that "if White Man's Africa is to survive there must be further consolidation and entrenchment. The process must have its centre in the Union [now Republic], which is obviously the stronghold of the White race in the sub-continent. What may be called the White settler areas may wish to be included in the orbit of the Union." *White Man's Africa* (Cape Town: Stewart, 1952), p. 93, 99.

2. As a precedent for employing APARTHEID as a primary head, cf. the Oct.–Dec. 1969 *BHI* (no. 4), p. 5.

7. *Item:* UNDERDEVELOPED AREAS (p. 1338; Sears, p. 598)

The list editors opted for "Underdeveloped" instead of "Backward." Which merits some applause. But not much. For the chosen term nonetheless qualifies as a species of chauvinistic negativism, emphasizing a distinction between the superior "We" and inferior "They." "It would be permissible," said the UNESCO experts, "to speak of rich, industrialized countries and of poor, still essentially agricultural countries."[1] The LC head is not so lucid.

Remedy: Substitute either DEVELOPING AREAS or THIRD WORLD.[2]

Notes (Item 7)

1. Meeting of Experts, p. 4.
2. A number of academic organs have sagely taken this tack; e.g., *The Journal of Developing Areas* (Macomb, Ill.), *International Development Review* (Washington, D.C.), *Economic Development and Cultural Change* (Chicago), *Tiers-monde* (i.e., "Third World"; Paris), *Journal of Development Studies* (London), *Overseas Development* (London), and *The Developing Economies* (Tokyo). There doesn't appear to be a single scholarly vehicle titled, e.g., *The Journal of Underdeveloped Areas*. According to a report

in the May 15, 1970, *Library Journal* (v. 95, no. 10), Central Michigan University has lately established an interdisciplinary undergraduate program on "Developing Nations" and concurrently issued a guide to its Dag Hammarskjold Collection on Developing Nations. P. 1819. Also, Denmark, one of the most enlightened and highly-respected of Western nations, maintains a Secretariat for Technical Cooperation with Developing Countries within its Ministry of Foreign Affairs.

Perhaps predictably, the *API* selected "Third World" over both "Developing" and "Underdeveloped," though *RG* unhappily continues in the LC rut.

Since "Backward areas," even as a *See* reference (p. 103), constitutes an unjustifiable, superiority-laden judgment, it should be permanently removed.

On p. 278 of the 1967 ACS, LC belatedly recognized that the term "developing" *can* be applied, but steadfastly refused to *do* it. What appears is:

> UNDERDEVELOPED AREAS
>   × Developing countries

On page 454 of the 1968 ACS it similarly acknowledged the relevance of "Third World," but merely introduced it, too, as a *See* reference to UNDERDEVELOPED AREAS.

8. *Item:* **BARBARIAN INVASIONS OF ROME (p. 113)**

The impropriety of "Barbarian" is much like that described for "Primitive." The *sa* roster mentions "Goths," "Huns," "Lombards," and "Vandals," as well as "Migrations of nations." To subsume these peoples or "nations" under "Barbarian" is to *judge* and *damn* them, which is hardly the function of a "disinterested" subject-heading scheme.[1]

Remedy: Excise "Barbarian" from the head and add, following a comma, the inclusive dates representing the period during which Goths, Lombards, and other peoples invaded Rome. Or, as an alternative, eliminate the head entirely, relying on an appropriate subdivision under ROME—HISTORY, in tandem with MIGRATIONS OF NATIONS, to perform the same task.[2]

Notes (Item 8)

1. The appellation "Barbarian" would probably seem strange and in-defensible to any *child* who had read Kate Seredy's *White Stag* (New York: Viking, 1937). A pity that *adults* forget so quickly.
2. For an LC precedent, cf.

CHINA
  —History
    —Invasions
      × Invasions of China

in the July 1964–Dec. 1965 ACS, p. 36.

9. *Item:* TRIBE as a descriptive gloss under names of particular groups (e.g., BUBE [AFRICAN TRIBE], p. 163) or an element in primary heads (e.g., IBO TRIBE, p. 616)

A tribe, in popular 'American,' suggests a group of primitives, savages, the pre-civilized-who-swing-from-the-trees-in-the-jungle. It is an offensive term....[1]

Mr. Fafunwa states, with understandable rage, that

The word "tribe" is defined [by the *Shorter Oxford dictionary*] as *"A group of persons forming a community and claiming descent from a common ancestor"*; it is also defined as *"A race of people; now applied especially to a primary aggregate of people in a primitive or barbarious condition under a headman or chief."* It is interesting to note that the word tribe is principally used now-adays to describe African ethnic groups. It used to cover groups in Asia and other non–European communities but since most of the Asian countries became independent between 1947 and 1954, the word gradually disappeared from the textbooks and journals.... How an ethnic group with two or ten million peo-ple in East or West Africa, with a parliamentary government, can be described as a tribe and not the Irish, the Scot, the Welsh, the French or the English, still baffles the non–Euro-pean.[2]

He is wrong, however, in thinking that this willy-nilly application of
"tribe" baffles only "non–Europeans." It equally baffles Europeans
and North Americans even slightly conversant with anthropological
literature who appreciate the enormous complexity—defying easy
categorization—of "non–European" societies.[3] To be sure, it is easy
and convenient to term the Bube or Ibo a "tribe" without troubling
over such niceties as the specifics of their sociopolitical organization,
etc. In fact, the Bube had evolved a proto-state on the West African
island of Fernando Poo whose further development was stymied
only by the advent of English and Spanish colonialists.[4] The Ibo, as
every literate person knows, are a numerous people who first pio-
neered in the creation of federal Nigeria and then formed their own
nation/state, Biafra.[5] They are no more "tribes" than the Bavarians
or Danes.

Remedy: (a) Since harried catalogers cannot be expected to
determine the *precise* anthropological or political definition for
groups like the Bube or Ibo, they may satisfactorily substitute for
"tribe" the sufficiently broad and inoffensive term "People"; e.g.,
BUBE (AFRICAN PEOPLE) and IBO PEOPLE.[6]

(b) As a corollary: Eliminate DETRIBALIZATION as a primary
head (p. 364; July 1964–Dec. 1965 ACS, p. 57) since it is highly
questionable that the process-term has—or will be—applied exclusively to people who may safely be characterized as "tribal." Two existing heads, CULTURE CONFLICT (p. 341) and URBANIZATION (p. 1356),
should do the job for much of this material, while a new form, CUL-
TURE CHANGE (in preference to ACCULTURATION, p. 7, which inaccurately implies a one-way process that is seldom the case), should
suitably handle the rest.[7]

Notes (Item 9)

1. Margaret Snyder, "Paternalism and the African Sculpture Exhibit
at the National Gallery," *Habari*, v. 2, no. 3 (March 1970), p. 19–20.
2. *Op. cit.*, p. 25. Emphasis in the original.
3. Van den Berghe, on p. 3 of the "Introduction" to *Africa; Social
Problems of Change and Conflict*, a collection of readings he edited in 1965
(San Francisco: Chandler Publishing Co.), writes of the word "tribe" that,

"apart from the invidious connotations of the term . . . (and of its derivatives such as *tribal, tribalism, detribalization*)," it "has been used in many different senses, and is therefore hopelessly confusing." Emphasis in original. After noting that "tribe" has become obsolete in French anthropology, he cites "at least six different meanings" ascribed to the word by "English-speaking scholars." In a later contribution to the same volume, Paul Mercier discourses brilliantly and at length "On the meaning of 'tribalism' in Black Africa," p. 483–501. And elsewhere van den Berghe has reiterated, "I have been especially careful in all my writings to avoid the word 'tribalism' altogether because of its highly ethnocentric connotations." Cf. "Pluralism and Conflict Situations in Africa: A Reply to B. Magubane," *African Social Research*, no. 9 (June 1970), p. 686.

4. Cf. the annotations under NATIVE POPULATION—BUBIS in Berman, *Spanish Guinea, op. cit.,* p. 288–93. The author, incidentally, admits the use of "*Native* population" as an error of youth, although the introduction to that 1961 opus describes "native" as "a term largely in disrepute for its ethnocentric and patronizing connotations," stating that its employment in heads like NATIVE POLICY and NATIVE POPULATION was intended "denotatively to refer to indigenous peoples." p. 16.

5. Cf., e.g., Stanley Diamond, "Who Killed Biafra?," *New York Review of Books*, v. 14, no. 4 (Feb. 26, 1970), especially p. 18–21. Also: Conor Cruise O'Brien, "Biafra Revisited," *New York Review of Books*, v. 12, no. 10 (May 22, 1969), especially p. 26, where the Irish author declares, after assaulting "the habit of referring to the Ibo-speaking peoples—more numerous than many European nations, including my own—as a 'tribe,'" that "we all tend to think in analogies and stereotypes about situations of which we have no direct experience. The white grid of analogies and stereotypes about Africa has served to promote racial arrogance among whites inside and outside Africa."

6. This *has* been done, either as an afterthought or merely in helter-skelter fashion, for some groups—e.g., FAN (AFRICAN PEOPLE), p. 468—which only underscores the wisdom and necessity for applying the principle evenly throughout the scheme. For another bibliographic precedent, cf. the headings BUBIS (AFRICAN PEOPLE), BUICO (AFRICAN PEOPLE), BUJEBA (AFRICAN PEOPLE), etc., in Berman, *Spanish Guinea, op. cit.,* p. 71ff.

7. On "acculturation" as an "inadequate theory" and "static approach," cf. van den Berghe, *Africa, op. cit.,* p. 2.

10. *Item:* ACQUISITION OF TERRITORY (p. 8)

A pleasant, if somewhat awkward, euphemism for what in most cases was territorial theft. If the prime head is allowed to stand, the

"sa's" and "xx's" need to be expanded, in the interest of truth and
clarity alike, to better reveal the scope. At present two *sa*'s appear:
"Annexation (International law)" and "Occupancy (International
law)." The lone "xx" is for "Territory, National."

   Remedy: Add to both the "*sa*" and "xx" rosters: "Colonies"
and "Imperialism."

11. *Item:* ANGOLA (p. 53)

> Let us follow the path that today is ours.
> With guns, we shall march to build the world we want.
>
> The boundaries of our free land are widening.
> Our fields
> Our schools
> Our hospitals are growing
> With each passing day the darkness of oppression
> Recedes before the light of our hopes.
>
> The image of our victory rises clear
> From our collective labour
> It has already the beauty of revolution.
>
> All the land will be ours,
> The world will be ours
> We are freedom, comrade.
>   —Marcelino dos Santos[1]

   In that this is the first of the still-colonial areas to appear in the
list, it may serve as the basis for a general observation. Briefly put:
the list makes colonialism in such areas as Angola, Mozambique,
Guinea-Bissau, Namibia, and Zimbabwe appear to be immutable.
As now constructed, it locks these lands into a permanent colonial
status, even though movements like FRELIMO (Mozambique Liberation Front), COREMO (Mozambique Revolutionary Committee),
MPLA (People's Movement for the Liberation of Angola), and PAIGC
(African Independence Party of Guiné and the Cape Verdes) are
struggling mightily toward independence, and in the specific instance

of Guinea-Bissau have actually liberated much of the country from alien rule.[2]

Remedy: (a) Introduce a subhead, —NATIONAL LIBERATION MOVEMENT, or, under —HISTORY, indicate —WAR FOR NATIONAL LIBERATION, with the appropriate open date[3] and—in view of the typical mode of warfare—an "××" for "Guerrillas."[4]

(b) Establish NATIONAL LIBERATION MOVEMENTS as a new primary form to embrace multi-area studies (e.g., comparative material on the NLF, ZAPU, ANC, etc.), with "××'s" for both "Colonies" and "Guerrillas," as well as an *also* note referring to the subhead "National liberation movement" or "War for national liberation" under names of specific colonies and countries.[5]

(c) For once- or still-colonial areas, establish under —HISTORY a further subhead, —COLONIAL PERIOD, with an appropriate commencement date representing the first year of hegemony over the land by the foreign, metropolitan power.[6] If, as in the case of South West Africa and the Philippines, more than one colonial power has dominated the area, specify the powers in separate glosses; e.g.,

> AFRICA, SOUTHWEST
> —HISTORY
> —COLONIAL PERIOD (GERMAN), 1884–1915
> —COLONIAL PERIOD (SOUTH AFRICAN), 1915–   [7]

The date should remain open for not-yet-independent countries.

(d) For originally-independent Third World states subsequently occupied or colonized by an alien power, construct an "Occupation" subhead under —HISTORY; e.g.,

> ETHIOPIA
> —HISTORY
> —ITALIAN OCCUPATION, 1936–1941[8]

Notes (Item 11)

1. "We Are Freedom," in *Poems from Mozambique,* an undated, mimeographed collection of ten verses by FRELIMO guerrillas, p. 3. For an

explanation by FRELIMO's Central Committee of the "Role of Poetry in the Mozambican Revolution," cf. *Africa Today*, v. 16, no. 2 (April-May 1969), p. 19–22.

2. Paul M. Whitaker maintains that PAIGC now controls two-thirds of the territory, including half the total population. Cf. "The Revolutions of 'Portuguese' Africa," *Journal of Modern African Studies*, v. 8, no. 1 (April 1970), p. 26.

3. In the Angolan case, it should probably be: 1961– ; LC currently specifies a subhead, —MASSACRE, 1961, for what most observers instead regard as the first year of a yet-continuing revolt against Portuguese over-lordship. Cf., for instance, Rene Pelissier, "Nationalismes en Angola," *Revue Française de Science Politique*, v. 19, no. 6 (Dec. 1969), p. 1197–1201; Clifford Parsons, "The Makings of a Revolt," Patricia McGowan Pinheiro, "Politics of a Revolt," and Basil Davidson, "The Oldest Alliance Faces a Crisis," all in *Angola: A Symposium; Views of a Revolt* (London: Oxford University Press, 1962); K. Madhu Panikkar, *Angola in Flames* (Bombay: Asia Publishing House, 1962), p. 71–82; and Anders Ehnmark, "Angola," in *Angola and Mozambique; The Case Against Portugal*, coauthored by Ehnmark and Per Waestberg (London: Pall Mall Press, 1963), p. 15+.

Respective beginning dates for the national liberation wars—i.e., full-fledged military activity—in Mozambique and Guinea-Bissau are 1964 and 1962. Cf. Whitaker, *op. cit.*, p. 16–7.

4. As a partial LC precedent for the suggested subhead, cf. CATALONIA —HISTORY—AUTONOMY AND INDEPENDENCE MOVEMENTS (1969 ACS, p. 33).

5. It should be obvious that older rubrics like REVOLUTIONS (p. 1105) and PEASANT UPRISINGS (p. 955) just don't fill the bill.

For details on the liberation struggles in Portuguese-speaking Africa, cf. Whitaker, *op. cit.*, p. 15–35; the press releases and occasional pamphlets issued by the Committee for Freedom in Mozambique, Angola & Guiné (531 Caledonian Road, London, N. 7); K. Shingler's *Portuguese and Colonial Bulletin* (10 Fentiman Road, London, S.W. 8); Basil Davidson, "The Liberation Struggle in Angola and 'Portuguese' Guinea," *Africa Quarterly*, v. 10, no. 1 (April-June 1970), p. 25–31; "Talk with a Guinean Revolutionary," a frank, incisive interview with Mr. Gil Fernandez, Cairo representative of PAIGC, on both the guerrilla war and radical social transformation engineered in Guinea-Bissau by Amilcar Cabral, described by Basil Davidson (*ibid.*, p. 29) as "one of the most remarkable men that Africa has yet produced," in the inaugural, spring 1970 issue of *Ufahamu; Journal of the African Activist Association* (UCLA), p. 6–21; and the war communiqués, together with other periodicals and pamphlets, published by the movements themselves: FRELIMO (Information Dept., P.O. Box 15274, Dar es Salaam, Tanzania; quarterly letterpress organ: *Mozambique Revolution*), PAIGC (B. P.

298, Conakry, Guinea; monthly, French-language bulletin: *Actualités*), MPLA (P.O. Box 20793, Dar es Salaam; irregular magazine: *Angola in Arms*), and COREMO (P.O. Box 1493, Lusaka, Zambia; mimeoed, English-language newsletter: *O Combatente*). Also: Basil Davidson, *The Liberation of Guiné* (Harmondsworth: Penguin Books, 1969); Eduardo Mondlane, *The Struggle for Mozambique* (Baltimore: Penguin Books, 1969); Amilcar Cabral, *The Struggle in Guinea* (Cambridge, Mass.: African Research Group, P.O. Box 213, O2138, 1969); and G. Chaliand, *Armed Struggle in Africa; With the Guerillas in Portuguese Guinea* (New York: Monthly Review Press, 1969).

Periodicals issued by ZAPU (Zimbabwe African Peoples Union), ANC (African National Congress of South Africa), and SWAPO (Southwest African Peoples' Organisation) are fully described in Berman's "African Magazines for American libraries," *op. cit.*, p. 1292–93 (SWAPO, however, also issues a bimonthly bulletin, *Namibia—Today*, from its Dar es Salaam office at P.O. Box 2603). The Zimbabwe African National Union (ZANU), another group seeking to free Rhodesia from minority rule, issues a monthly journal, *Zimbabwe News*, from its Lusaka headquarters (P.O. Box 2331). Material on the long-standing but relatively little-known guerrilla war waged by Anyanya against Arab suzerainty in the Southern Sudan or "Nile State" appears most extensively in *The Grass Curtain* (Southern Sudan Association, Ltd., Room 19, 29 Ludgate Hill, London, E.C. 4), which began publication in May 1970.

For a compact overview of the whole liberation-scene in southern and Portuguese-occupied Africa, cf. the entire April-June 1970 issue of *Africa Quarterly*, *op. cit.*, which includes contributions by Colin Legum, Kenneth W. Grundy, P. T. Makonese, and S. P. Singh, as well as "A Bibliographical Survey" prepared by Anrudha Gupta (p. 53–60). As more general sources covering developments not only in Africa, but also Latin America and Asia, cf. *Liberation; Colonial Freedom News*, bimonthly organ of the Movement for Colonial Freedom (313/5 Caledonian Road, London, N. 1), and *Tricontinental Magazine*, issued bimonthly by the Organization of Solidarity of the Peoples of Africa, Asia, and Latin America (Havana, Cuba: OSPAAAL, Apartado 4224). Also: the monthly bulletin *Afro-Asian Peoples*, together with a monograph series, "Afro-Asian Publications," both issued by the Permanent Secretariat of the Afro-Asian Peoples' Solidarity Organization (89, Abdel Aziz Al Saud Street, Cairo, U.A.R.), the latter including: *National Liberation Wars in the Portuguese Colonies* (no. 31, Jan. 1970, 150 p.), *International Conference in Support of the Peoples of the Portuguese Colonies and Southern Africa; Khartoum, 18–20 January 1969* (no. 32, Jan. 1970, 76 p.), and *Zimbabwe: History of a Struggle* (no. 34, June 1970, 68 p.).

6. For an LC precedent, cf. U.S.—HISTORY—COLONIAL PERIOD, p. 1344.

7. Cf. *Statesmen's Year-Book*, 1969–1970. 106th ed. (London: Mac-millan/St. Martin's Press, 1969), p. 1305. Also, for more detailed historical background: Ruth First, *South West Africa* (Harmondsworth: Penguin Books, 1963), especially Parts Two through Five; and Chapter 2, "Genesis: From Conquest to Mandate," in *South West Africa: Travesty of Trust*, a collection of "expert papers and findings" edited by First and Ronald Segal (London: Andre Deutsch, 1967).

In that SWAPO and its sister liberation movements term the land "Namibia" and are pledged to so designate the country once it attains independence, and since the United Nations General Assembly on 12 June 1968 "proclaimed that South West Africa should henceforth be known as Namibia," a *See* reference should be made from "Namibia" to AFRICA, SOUTHWEST. Cf. *Yearbook of the United Nations*, 1967 (New York: United Nations Office of Public Information, 1968), p. 689. By the same token, "Zimbabwe (territory)" should appear as a temporary "×" under "Rhodesia," the gloss being necessary to distinguish the contemporary polity from both the ancient city which bore the same name and its actual archeological site, located some 17 miles southeast of Victoria in Mashonaland. For an authoritative SWAPO statement on the proper nomenclature for Southwest Africa, cf. "Why Namibia" in the Oct.–Dec. *Namibia News*. More information concerning Bantu-built Zimbabwe, whose monumental stonework dates from the 15th century Monomotapa Empire, may be found in Wiedner, *op. cit.*, p. 97–8; Gertrude Caton-Thompson, *The Zimbabwe Culture: Ruins and Reactions* (London: Oxford University Press, 1931); and Basil Davidson, *Old Africa Rediscovered, op. cit.*, p. 199–230.

8. Cf. *Statesmen's Year-Book, op. cit.*, p. 884.

For precedents, cf. entries for the various *European* states occupied by Nazi Germany during World War II; e.g., DENMARK—HISTORY—GERMAN OCCUPATION, 1940–1945, p. 360.

12. *Item:* CANNIBALISM
   ×× **Ethnology**
   Society, Primitive (p. 181; Sears, p. 125)

If Ronald M. Berndt is correct in claiming that "authentically substantiated cases of cannibalism are less common in anthropological literature than one might expect,"[1] the referents to "Ethnology" and "Society, Primitive" qualify as gratuitous and misleading.

Remedy: Eliminate both "××'s," simultaneously adding an "×" for "Anthropophagy" to placate the tidy-minded.

Note (Item 12)

1. "Cannibalism," in Julius Gould and William L. Kolb, eds., *A Dictionary of the Social Sciences* (London: Tavistock, 1964), p. 65. Indeed, Berman's examination of frequent "cannibal" allegations regarding the Fang, the most numerous people of Equatorial Guinea, as well as members of the syncretistic Mbueti Sect, disclosed that no regular nor widespread anthropophagic practice could be established for the Fang in either antiquity or modern times (only occasional "consumption of slain enemies" for purposes of "sympathetic magic"), and that the Mbueti sacrificed animals, rather than humans, at their rites. Cf. the annotations under ANTHROPOPHAGY in Berman, *Spanish Guinea, op. cit.*, together with p. 299–301 and 304–05. Moreover, Stanley M. Garn and Walter D. Block, both of the Center for Human Growth and Development at the University of Michigan, have calculated, on the basis of normal protein requirements, that "less than one man [eaten] per week for a group of 60 would not appear to be nutritionally worthwhile, even as a protein supplement to a cereal or tuber diet with limiting amino acids." Their conclusion: "While human flesh may serve as an emergency source of both protein and calories, it is doubtful that regular people-eating ever had much nutritional meaning." Cf. "The Limited Nutritional Value of Cannibalism," *American Anthropologist*, v. 72, no. 1 (Feb. 1970), p. 106. In short, while "cannibalism" has mainly occurred among folk peoples, it is in no wise a common nor frequent ingredient of folk or traditional culture. To refer thrill-seekers to the immense ethnological literature for data on anthropophagy is to send them on an essentially wild-goose chase, as well as further propagating the exceedingly tenuous "primitive-cannibal" nexus.

Suhl also pinpoints in the *Doctor Dolittle* series of children's books a cannibal/primitive/African syndrome literarily at least as old as Shakespeare's *Othello*. In *The Voyages*, "Bumpo Kahbooboo," Oxford-educated "Crown Prince" of the West African kingdom of "Jolliginki," when confronted by Polynesia, a garrulous parrot, with the problem of a stowaway sailor "who has been eating up the ship's store of salt beef," suggests: "Would it not be good political economy . . . if we salted the able seaman and ate him instead?" The parrot reminds the *African* prince that he is no longer at home, adding "those things are not done on white men's ships." A smarter parrot than Polynesia would have known that "those things" aren't done in West African kingdoms either. *Op. cit.*, p. 7.

13. *Items:* CIVILIZATION, ANGLO-SAXON; CIVILIZATION, ARAB; CIVILIZATION, ARYAN; etc. (p. 253–54; Sears, p. 158–59)

> In the olden days there was no peace among the black people. There were many wars. People attacked one another without provocation, they killed one another and captured each other's cattle.... Such freedom from fear and want as we enjoy today did not exist; instead, fighting was a daily occurrence.... Truly, we who live today ought to thank God that we did not live in those days, but rather live in these days of peace, and of plenty, and of happiness.[1]

The reader seeking CIVILIZATION, AFRICAN will look in vain. By the glaring omission of this head it appears that the whole continent has been history*less*, a vast cultural desert, whereas in fact "scholars ... unencumbered by colonial ties" have in recent years discovered that "Africa was not a *tabula rasa*, but that it had a past, a history which could be reconstructed; that it was a continent which knew empire builders at a time when large areas of Europe stagnated in the Dark Ages; that it knew art and commerce."[2] The LC vacuum reflects a common tendency "in the North Atlantic world," as anthropologist Stanley Diamond puts it, "to stereotype the peoples and cultures of the continent, to regard them as a ... featureless, backward, and largely passive mass."[3]

Remedy: Establish at once the primary head, CIVILIZATION, AFRICAN.[4]

Notes (Item 13)

1. Translated by Kunene, *op. cit.*, from *Sesotho Readers for Standards 2 and 3*, p. 641.

2. Edith R. Sanders, "Rape of African History: The Hamitic Hypothesis," *Liberator*, v. 10, no. 4 (April 1970), p. 13. Given the lately-published flood of material on African history and culture, the case for African "civilization" hardly needs much elaboration. The novice, however, may well begin with Basil Davidson's *African Past; Chronicles from Antiquity to Modern Times* (London: Longmans, 1964), in which the author notes that the study

of Africa's past "is not only possible, but is also useful and even indispensable, to a closer understanding of the general condition of mankind," p. 4–5. Perhaps the most succinct, yet many-faceted, brief for African "civilization" appears as Chapters 10 and 11 of Davidson's *Old Africa Rediscovered, op. cit.* "But *civilization?*," he begins, "isn't that, after all, saying too much?" And then argues conclusively that the appellation fits, on many counts.

3. "Introduction: Africa in the Perspective of Political Anthropology," in Stanley Diamond and Fred G. Burke, eds., *The Transformation of East Africa* (New York/London: Basic Books, 1966), p. 5. This entire chapter should be consulted for information on the dynamics and forms of state building in much of sub–Saharan, precolonial Africa. Probably the most reliable, objective index of "civilization," as Diamond regularly contends, is the emergence of social stratification and civil authority, represented in Africa, as examples, by the several empires of antiquity like Songhay, Benin, Mali, and Monomotapa, and more recent kingdoms or "proto-states" such as Ankole and Dahomey. LC, in fact, admitted this sociopolitical "leap" from *folk* to *civil* society (or civilization) when it introduced the subhead, —KINGS AND RULERS under AFRICA (July 1964–Dec. 1965 ACS, p. 5).

The sterotyping persists in portions of Africa itself, as Ezekiel Mphahlele relates from his own experience: "In history, social studies and civics, the black pupil had to be taught to accept as facts the hypotheses that the white man came to South Africa to civilize savage indigenes; that the black man was underdeveloped . . . immature . . . and could not exercise the vote nor represent his people in Parliament." Cf. "Censorship in South Africa," *Censorship Today*, v. 2, no. 4 (Aug.-Sept. 1969), p. 14. Cf. also the epigraph above, excerpted from school texts fashioned for Black South African children. "The tragedy of Africa," adds Kunene, "the basic problem that confronts us, is that of the contemptuous rejection of the African by the European. So Europe came to Africa and to varying degrees Europeanized Africa, but totally refused to be Africanized by Africa." *Op. cit.,* p. 646.

It should occasion little wonder that a Project Africa study conducted among American secondary school students found that "students see Africa south of the Sahara as a land of 'no history' when the survey of basic knowledge shows that they have virtually no knowledge of the region before the coming of the Europeans. Students simply have never heard of Zimbabwe, Benin, and Ashanti, or of Sonni Ali, Osei Tutu, or Mansa Musa." E. Perry Hicks and Barry K. Beyer, "Images of Africa," *Journal of Negro Education,* v. 39, no. 2 (spring 1970), p. 164. The authors add that "the mis-information that students have about Africa may come primarily from the popular media. Students may never have heard of Africa's Sudanic kingdoms, but they probably have heard of Tarzan, Jungle Jim and King Solomon's mines. If Tarzan lives in the jungle along with his lion and elephant friends and this is all that a student knows about Africa, the student's image of Africa will certainly not be accurate." *Ibid.* Further, the surveyors discovered that even in world history courses the continent is usually studied 'from the point of view of European exploration, colonialism, and imperialism. The students see the region and its peoples through the eyes of explorers, missionaries, entrepreneurs, and adventurers. They study it only as an appendage of European history, as an arena in which the destinies of western civilization were enacted. This culture-bound view distorts Africa's past and gives little insight into the present." *Ibid.,* p. 166. For additional, commonplace faults of imbalance and out-datedness in Africa-related teaching, cf. the full article, p. 158–66. References to the library responsibility for this widespread distortion and misinformation concerning Africa are all the more alarming for their complete *absence.*

4. The only "new" civilizations acknowledged in LC supplements since the 7th ed. are CIVILIZATION, MYCENAEAN (1968 ACS, p. 87), CIVILIZATION, AEGEAN; CIVILIZATION, BAROQUE; and CIVILIZATION, MINOAN (1969 ACS, p. 42).

14. *Items:* ETHNIC TYPES   ETHNOLOGY
      ***sa* Caucasian race   *sa* Native races**
           Race   Race problems
      ×× **Race (p. 445)   *also names of races...***
                                        × **Races of man**
                                       ×× **Native races**
                                              (p. 445–46;
                                              Sears, p. 242)

Through much of the nineteenth century the concepts of biological race, language, and culture were confused; one was inferred from the other, and reconstruction of human development combined all three aspects. Ethnology was historically oriented from the start and attempted to account for extant races, languages, and cultures in terms of migration, diffusion, and other historical processes.

In the twentieth century, "ethnology" has come to mean the comparative study of documented and contemporary cultures and has largely excluded their bioanthropology, archeology, and linguistics....[1]

The LC continues to suffer from and mirror the 19th century confusion. Now that we are 70 years into another century, no one could sensibly charge LC with unseemly haste were it to finally recognize the scientifically-established dichotomy between "race" and "ethnicity."[2]

Remedy: (a) Eliminate ETHNIC TYPES as a primary head, since its intended meaning is biological, rather than ethnological.

(b) Remove the above-listed "sa," "×" and "××" referents under ETHNOLOGY.

(c) As corollaries, excise "Art and race," "Music and race," and "Race awareness" as *sa*'s under ETHNOPSYCHOLOGY (p. 447). Indeed, the first two forms are highly-suspect *primary* heads, which could be well abandoned or recast as ART AND ETHNICITY and MUSIC AND ETHNICITY.[3]

Notes (Item 14)

1. Harold E. Driver, "Ethnology," in Sills, *op. cit.,* v. 5, p. 178.

2. On this point, cf. also van den Berghe, *Race and Racism, op. cit.,* p. 10, where he admits that "the distinction between a racial and an ethnic group is sometimes blurred by several facts," but maintains that "the distinction between race and ethnicity remains analytically useful."

3. Sears would also contribute to clarity in this area by canceling the *See* reference from "Ethnic psychology" to "Race psychology," p. 241.

15. *Item:* PHILIPPINE ISLANDS
 —HISTORY
 —TO 1521
 —1521–1898
 —INSURRECTION, 1896–1898
 —JAPANESE OCCUPATION, 1942–1945
  (p. 970; 1968 ACS, p. 330)

The determining considerations for Western policy were never what the Asians considered to be good for themselves but what

the West judges to be good for Asia. Often this meant, in actual practice, that what is good for the West is good for Asia.
—Salvador P. Lopez[1]

The Yankee imperialism already noted under U.S.—TERRITORIES AND POSSESSIONS becomes even more evident in LC's treatment of the Philippines. Except for the cited Japanese incursion during World War II, the supplied headings abysmally fail to indicate that the islands had endured colonialism under two successive foreign powers for no less than 351 years, that American dominion was imposed for a number of less admirable reasons than mere "tutelage," and that nationalist discontent had arisen during the 19th century, flaring into open revolution at the time of the Spanish-American War.[2] The LC schema reduces the experience of "our little brown brothers" to an inconsequential charade, with only the war-mongering Japanese cast as culprits.

Remedy: Reconstruct the —HISTORY subdivisions as follows:

—TO 1521
—COLONIAL PERIOD (SPANISH), 1521–1898
—REVOLT, 1896–1901
—COLONIAL PERIOD (AMERICAN), 1898–1946
—1946–

Notes (Item 15)

1. From an address delivered at the opening session of the International Press Institute's 19th Assembly in Hong Kong on May 18, 1970, quoted in *IPI Report*, v. 19, no. 2/3 (June/July 1970), p. 19. Mr. Lopez is Chancellor of the University of the Philippines and a former Philippines Foreign Secretary.
2. For a recapitulation of U.S.-Philippine relations from annexation to independence by two "apologists" who hold that America regarded her administration of the islands as a "trust," cf. Garel A. Grunder and William E. Livezey, *The Philippines and the United States* (Norman: University of Oklahoma Press, 1951). An "Introduction" sketches pre–American Philippine history, noting the "spirit of unrest" and outright "dissatisfaction" that emerged among Filipinos in the 19th century, culminating in the Aguinaldo-led

"revolution" which erupted in 1896 and only ended with the leader's capture in 1901. In passing, the authors note regarding Aguinaldo that "there is no indication at any time that he expected less than full autonomy," p. 24. They further admit, on p. 28, the commercial and missionary impulses toward "acceptance of American responsibility for control of the Islands," themes which Julius W. Pratt explores extensively in his *Expansionists of 1898; The Acquisition of Hawaii and the Spanish Islands* (Gloucester, Mass.: Peter Smith, 1959; originally published by Johns Hopkins Press in 1936). Cf. especially Chapters 7 and 8, "The Business Point of View" and "'The Imperialism of Righteousness,'" p. 230–316. Anyone still unsure that American motives (and rationales) vis-à-vis the Philippines significantly differed from those of other colonial powers elsewhere need only digest President McKinley's account of the answer to his prayers, quoted by Pratt on p. 334–35. The President states, in part, "that we could not leave them to themselves — they were unfit for self-government — and they would soon have anarchy and misrule over there worse than Spain's was; and . . . that there was nothing left for us to do but to take them all, and to educate the Filipinos, and uplift and civilize and Christianize them, and by God's grace do the very best we could by them, as our fellow-men for whom Christ also died." Less eminent figures, clerics and businessmen alike, echoed the President's sentiments with talk of the American duty to uplift the "barbarious" and Anglo-Saxonize mankind.

16. *Items:* GREAT AWAKENING (p. 562); NORTHWEST, OLD (p. 899); RECONSTRUCTION (p. 1084; Sears, p. 503); REFUGEES, SOUTHERN (p. 1089); STATE RIGHTS (p. 1224; Sears, p. 563); THE WEST (p. 1401; Sears, p. 627)

> *USA all the way.*
>
> —Slogan attached to American flags by construction workers at New York office building site.[1]

All these forms appear unglossed. All express a facet of distinctly *American* history or politics which lay foreigners — and perhaps some Americans themselves — cannot reasonably be expected to appreciate.

They therefore represent an all too common ailment, "Americocentrism," as well as being unclear.[2]

> *Remedy:* Add glosses for clarification; e.g.,
>
> GREAT AWAKENING (U.S. RELIGIOUS HISTORY)
> NORTHWEST, OLD (U.S.)
> RECONSTRUCTION (U.S. HISTORY)
> REFUGEES, SOUTHERN (U.S. HISTORY)
> STATE RIGHTS (U.S. CONSTITUTIONAL HISTORY)
> THE WEST (U.S.)

Notes (Item 16)

1. As reported by Alfred Kazin, "Our Flag," *New York Review of Books,* v. 15, no. 1 (July 2, 1970), p. 3.
2. Conor Cruise O'Brien expands knowledgeably and incisively on the question of "Americocentrism" in "America First," *New York Review of Books,* v. 14, nos. 1/2 (Jan. 29, 1970), p. 8+.

17. *Items:* LEGENDS; LEGENDS, BUDDHIST; LEGENDS, CELTIC [GREEK, etc.]; LEGENDS, GERMANIC; LEGENDS, JEWISH; LEGENDS, ORIENTAL (p. 731)

What's awry here is that, if one halves the world into Occident and Orient (which is done commonly—though brainlessly—enough), the Occident, like Christianity in so many other forms, is assumed to be dominant. As *sa*'s ranging from "Chansons de geste" to "Saints" unequivocally demonstrate, the unqualified head is meant to embrace Western—or, more particularly, European—material. The *other* half of the world's legendary heritage (again, *given* such a bifurcation) thus occupies a place much-removed from the initial head and distinguished merely by an inverted adjective just as legends derived from Celts and Greeks are. Such handling perpetuates the

Kiplingesque notion that the "Orient" exists only as a kind of exotic, inscrutable adjunct to the Occident, a pagoda-shaped, dragon-decorated, curry-and-soy-sauce-smelling doll house operated for the amusement of wonder-craving Westerners.

Remedy: Admitting the usefulness of inverted forms, the travesty presently made of Oriental civilization can be overcome by instituting a complementary head, LEGENDS, OCCIDENTAL, and reserving the simple form, LEGENDS, for material of genuinely global nature.[1]

Note (Item 17)

1. The same rectification should then be made under ARCHITECTURE (p. 67–8), ART (p. 74–6), etc. LC itself affords precedents for such polaric forms. Cf., for example, CIVILIZATION, OCCIDENTAL (p. 253) and OCCIDENTAL STUDIES (1967 ACS, p. 185).

18. *Item:* Biafran Conflict, 1967–1970
See Nigeria—History—Civil War, 1967–1970
(1969 ACS, p. 22)

Regardless of pro– or anti–Biafra feelings, the fact remains that such a state *did* secede from federal Nigeria and managed to endure as an independent entity for some three years. The Confederate States of America did not last much longer, yet they enjoy two full columns of primary and subordinate headings (p. 299). Why, then, is "Biafra" totally buried under "Nigeria" with no primary head representing its actual, if short-lived, existence? Because *Black* Africans engineered its birth in open defiance of Big Power (not to mention Big Money) wishes? Because its very *being* wrecked paternalistic Western illusions about how Africans are *supposed* to behave and indirectly reflected badly on the former imperialists' border-erecting abilities?

Remedy: Establish BIAFRA (1967–1970) as a primary form, with an *sa* and "××" for "Nigeria—History—Civil War, 1967–1970."[1]

Note (Item 18)

1. For an extra–LC precedent, cf. the May 10, 1970, *RG* (v. 70, no. 6), p. 43.

Section III

Politics, Peace, Labor, Law Enforcement, etc.

1. *Items:* ANARCHISM AND ANARCHISTS (p. 49); COMMUNISM (p. 281); COMMUNISTS (p. 282); CONSERVATISM (p. 303); DISSENTERS (p. 377); LIBERALISM (p. 737); REVOLUTIONISTS (p. 1105); SOCIALISM (p. 1194); SOCIALISTS (p. 1195)

At first glance, these heads appear satisfactorily to cover the full political spectrum, past and present, Left to Right. But which rubric would the cataloger assign to material on the New Left, to composite studies on groups like the German and American SDS, Peace and Freedom Party, Ausserparliamentarische Opposition (APO), and International Socialists; to leaders and theoreticians like Herbert Marcuse, Staughton Lynd, Paul Buhle, Jerry Rubin, Rudi Dutschke, Tariq Ali, Bobby Seale, and Dave Dellinger? "Dissenters" misses the mark, for it seems to sidestep the activist, militant, Movement quality that characterizes these persons and organizations. Additionally, it implies a "reformism" which they hardly endorse or personify.[1] Likewise, "Revolutionists" may apply, in part, to some, but fails to capture the ideological dimension and many-faceted activities that typify the subjects. Similarly, "Communism" and "Socialism" are only *approximate* labels, failing to convey the distinctive "new" Left-oriented moods, lifestyles, strategies, and tactics.[2]

111

Remedy: Initiate a new head, RADICALISM AND RADICALS, with both "××'s" and *sa*'s for ANARCHISM AND ANARCHISTS, DISSENTERS, REVOLUTIONISTS, and SOCIALISM, as well as *See* references from "Extraparliamentary Opposition" and "New Left."[3]

Notes (Item 1)

1. The same argument disqualifies SOCIAL REFORMERS, a new head appearing on p. 208 of the July 1964–Dec. 1965 ACS.

2. An absolutely vital, current guide to "radical" organizations and publishing is the monthly *Red Notes*, issued by Agitprop Information (160 North Gower Street, London, N.W. 1). "Movement" reportage accents British and continental European events, but coverage of new magazines, books and pamphlets is international.

For additional data on these groups and publications, cf. *Guide to the American Left; Directory and Bibliography* (Kansas City, Missouri: Box 1832, 64141); *Directory of America's Most Controversial Periodicals* (Berkeley, Calif.: Guidelines Publications, 2813 Telegraph Avenue, 94705); and the 2d, hugely-expanded edition of Robert F. Muller's *From Radical Left to Extreme Right; Current Periodicals of Protest, Controversy or Dissent—U.S.A.* (Ann Arbor, Mich.: Campus Publishers, 711 North University Avenue, 48108, 1970), coedited by Theodore J. and Janet M. Spahn, which includes whole chapters on the "Marxist-Socialist Left" and "Radical Left," together with listings for "Anarchist" and "Libertarian" titles. Also: the section on "Left-of-center" magazines in Katz, *Magazines for Libraries, op. cit.,* p. 107–111; Paul Jacobs and Saul Landau, eds., *The New Radicals: A Report with Documents* (New York: Random House, 1966), featuring a representative selection of "radical" writings together with an introductory survey of the "Movement"; and T. B. Bottomore, *Critics of Society; Radical Thought in North America* (London: George Allen and Unwin Ltd., 1967), which traces "radical" ideas and undertakings in both the U.S. and Canada from before the Progressive Era to the present.

3. The 1968 ACS on p. 366 finally introduced RADICALISM as a primary head, but skimped on cross-references, indicating only an "××" for "Political Science." The innovation still bears improvement.

Sears on p. 495 makes a *See* reference from "Radicals and radicalism" to "Anarchism and Anarchists; Reformers; Revolutions," which represents a broader *approach* than LC's, but results in an unsatisfactory hodge-podge, still failing to account for New Left–style radicals.

2. *Items:* ANARCHISM AND ANARCHISTS
sa Terrorism (p. 49)
TERRORISM
sa Anarchism and Anarchists (p. 1288)

Popular mythology merrily associates "terrorism" with "anarchism."[1] But what intelligent person would concur that a document like the LC list should be based on popular mythology? Admittedly, *some* anarchists have espoused or practiced "terrorism." Others, like the towering Prince Kropotkin, Judith Malina and Julian Beck of the "Living Theater," the prolific and pacific Paul Goodman, Errico Malatesta, and most contemporary "communards" have *not.*[2] In any event, "terrorism" is hardly a theory or tactic peculiar to anarchists. Ultra-conservative groups like the Minutemen and KKK have embraced it; so, it might be argued, have the "Liberals" who developed "saturation bombing" during World War II, dropped the atomic bomb on Japan, authorized "search and destroy" missions, together with massive defoliation, in Vietnam, etc.[3] Yet under neither CONSERVATISM nor LIBERALISM does an *sa* to "Terrorism" appear.[4]

Remedy: Drop both references and exercise some constraint when applying TERRORISM as a primary head to Kropotkinites and others who may be *anarchists,* but not *ipso facto* of the violent variety.

Notes (Item 2)

1. Sears, in which "Terrorism" doesn't figure as a prime head, settles for "Assassination" as an "×" referent.

2. On the latter-day "communards," cf., as examples: "Community News," *Modern Utopian,* v. 3, no. 2 (Nov.-Dec. 1968/Jan.-Feb. 1969), p. 45–7; Paul Encimer, "Resistance Communes," *ibid.,* p. 41; "Notes from New Mexico," *ibid.,* p. 4–7; and Joyce Gardiner, "From Cold Mountain to Warm Vermont," *ibid.,* p. 2. For additional data on *The Modern Utopian,* easily the most authentic and important source of information on current libertarian and communal movements, cf. Katz, *op. cit.,* 109–10, and Sanford Berman's review in the March 15, 1969, *Library Journal* (v. 94, no. 6), p. 1119.

On the "positive side," Daniel Guerin in the final chapter of *Anarchism* (New York: Monthly Review Press, 1970), opines that "workers' self-management" may be attributed to the Anarchist Movement as its "most original creation." Quoted in the MRP spring 1970 checklist, p. 6. Noam Chomsky confirms this judgment in a lucid, thoughtful exposition of "libertarian socialism" or "council communism" as both doctrine and practice, noting, for instance, that "the workers' control movement has become a significant force in England in the past few years" and that "on the continent, there are similar developments." Cf. "Notes on Anarchism," *New York Review of Books*, v. 14, no. 10 (May 21, 1970), p. 31–5. From the Chomsky-Guerin discussions emerges what may be a useful illumination in this area: the addition of "Libertarian socialism" and "Council Communism" as "×" referents under ANARCHISM AND ANARCHISTS, as well as SOCIALISM.

Says Ashley Montagu in a foreword to the Porter Sargent edition of Kropotkin's major opus, *Mutual Aid:*

> For Kropotkin anarchism was a part of philosophy to be treated by the same methods as the natural sciences. He saw anarchism as the means by which justice (that is equality and reciprocity) in all human relations could be established throughout the world of humanity. This could best be achieved by the complete elimination of the state and all governmental processes, and their replacement by a free and spontaneous co-operation among individuals, groups, regions, and nations. *Kropotkin abhorred violence of any kind. . . .*

(Boston), p. [5] of foreword. Emphasis added.

Remarks Roderick Kedward of Malatesta, "[He] was the nearest of the major anarchists to the ideal of the labouring, sociable individualist, and his ideas had the basic force of Kropotkin's. . . . 'By definition,' he wrote in 1913, 'an anarchist is he who does not wish *to be oppressed nor wishes to be himself an oppressor;* who wants the greatest well-being, freedom, and development for *all* human beings.' From this, from his repeated denunciation of 'supermen rebels,' and *his restriction of violence to self defence,* it is clear that he believed anarchism to be a constructive proposition for all societies." Cf. "The Anarchists," *History of the 20th Century*, no. 10 (1969), p. 257. Initial emphases in original; last emphasis added.

As current, reliable sources for anarchist thought and activity, cf. the weekly *Freedom* and monthly *Anarchy,* both issued by Freedom Press (84b Whitechapel High Street, London, E. 1).

3. On the extensive "military" use and "macabre" effects of herbicides in Vietnam, cf. Navroz Mody, "Chemical Warfare in Vietnam," *Economic and Political Weekly* (Bombay), v. 5, no. 24 (June 13, 1970), p. 948–49. Also: George Wald, "Corporate Responsibility for War Crimes," *New York Review of Books*, v. 15, no. 1 (July 2, 1970), p. 4–6.

4. "Terrorist," of course, has long proven a convenient epithet for threatened rulers or classes to hurl at those who would upset the status quo and challenge their authority. "In all history," declares a front-page *Sechaba* editorial, "whenever men have fought for freedom they have been called names: In Algeria they were called terrorists; in Vietnam they were called bandits; in Kenya they were called criminal gangs; and in Southern Africa itself those who refuse to say 'Ja baas' are also called names: terrorists— saboteurs—agitators.... They try to destroy us by swear-words because they fear what we really are—Freedom Fighters!" V. 4, no. 1 (Jan. 1970).

Rene Pelissier, writing of the Angolan revolt, himself speaks of "resistants," but notes that the Portuguese insist on using the term "terroristes." *Op. cit.*, p. 1202.

Van den Berghe, discussing the "development of new terrorist tactics to supplement the other mechanisms of racial subordination" in the post– Reconstruction South, writes that "secret organizations such as the Ku Klux Klan resorted to intimidation, brutality, and murder as their major means for keeping Negroes and 'nigger-lovers' in their place, but so did spontaneous groups of unorganized private citizens as well as the police, which, in the South, has traditionally played the role of uniformed vigilantes in the service of the dominant whites. The most notorious and extreme form of terrorism was lynching, but other tactics were also used such as beatings, cross-burnings, masked night rides through Negro districts, verbal threats, hate rallies, public humiliations, and random discharging of shotguns in windows." *Race and Racism, op. cit.*, p. 90. This grisly recitation argues convincingly for a bona fide "Terrorism" *sa* under both KU KLUX KLAN (p. 707) and RECONSTRUCTION (p. 1084). It additionally prompts the already-suggested form, AFRO-AMERICANS — PERSECUTIONS, as a cross-reference from and to both RECONSTRUCTION and KU KLUX KLAN.

3. *Item:* PEACE—SOCIETIES (p. 954)

This subdivision may suitably handle material on the nearly 2,000 individual peace groups like MOBE, the War Resisters League, Kampagne für Abrustung, and CND, but miserably under-represents the worldwide Peace Movement, an aggregate of organizations and persons—in fact, a spirit and style made manifest in yearly "Easter Marches," the "V" sign (freely exchanged and readily understood everywhere), and the starkly simple "peace symbol," much seen on posters, stickers, flags, walls, jewelry, clothing, etc., as well as in internationally circulated publications like *Peace News,* the *Journal of Peace Research, Peace Press,* and *WIN.*[1]

Remedy: Establish a new form, PEACE MOVEMENT.[2]

Notes (Item 3)

1. For bibliographic data and descriptive notes on *Peace News* and *WIN,* cf. Katz, *op. cit.,* p. 106–8. Each number of *Peace Press,* distributed by the International Confederation for Disarmament and Peace (6 Endsleigh Street, London, W.C. 1), focuses on a specific problem area; e.g., Laos in the June-July 1969 issue (v. 5, nos. 6/7). Universitetsforlaget in Oslo, Norway (P.O. Box 307, Blindern) publishes the quarterly *Journal of Peace Research,* "An interdisciplinary and international journal of scientific reports in the field of peace research." As basic guides to the burgeoning peace literature, cf. Charles H. Gray, and others, comps., *A Bibliography of Peace Research* (Eugene, Ore.: General Research Analysis Methods, 1059 Hilyard Street, 97401, 1968), and Blanche Wiesen Cook, ed., *Bibliography on Peace Research in History* (Santa Barbara, Calif.: ABC-Clio Press, 1969), which covers "all phases of antiwar (peaceful) activities in the West" and features lists of relevent organizations and journals. Also: Universitetsforlaget in early 1970 commenced publication of a useful abstract quarterly, *The Bulletin of Peace Proposals,* whose intent is "to motivate research . . . inspire future oriented thinking . . . [and] promote activities for peace." Marek Thee of the International Peace Research Institute in Oslo edits. Initial categories include "Science and Development," "Socio-Political Issues," "World Peace and Disarmament," and "The Vietnam Conflict." Cf. further the listings under "Peace" in Muller, 2d ed., *op. cit.*

2. Even so, while eschewing a "numbers-game," the literally scores of primary heads and subheads relating to Armies and Armed Forces, together with specific weapons, in toto far out-bulk the relatively meagre subject attention to Peace and Disarmament. Note, as a single, depressing example, that the prime head ART AND WAR (p. 77) has thus far not been balanced with an ART AND PEACE, although it seems likely that *some* work has dealt with this topic, employing Picasso's "Guernica" and many dove-motifs (one of which adorns a bright, giant tapestry at the Brecht-Theater in East Berlin), Goya's "Disasters of War," and similar material as illustrations. Indeed, a study or collection of such graphics and plastics—particularly the horrendous statements on human brutality and military madness like Käthe Kollwitz's "Seven Woodcuts on War" or Georg Grosz's "Ecce Homo"—better warrant ART AND PEACE as a head than ART AND WAR, the former more faithfully reflecting the artists' intent and inspiration. Says H. W. Janson of "Guernica": "With

a series of powerful images, it evokes the agony of total war. The destruction of Guernica was the first demonstration of the technique of saturation bombing which was later employed on a huge scale during the Second World War; the mural was thus a prophetic vision of doom—the doom that threatens us even more in this age of nuclear warfare." *History of Art* (Englewood Cliffs, N. J.: Prentice-Hall; New York: Harry N. Abrams, 1966), p. 524. A new head PEACE IN ART *does* appear in the 1966 ACS, p. 115, but is not semantically equivalent to ART AND PEACE.

The initial *API* number includes five closely printed entry-columns under PEACE MOVEMENT, *op. cit.,* p. 44–6.

Libraries with extensive holdings in this area, especially if they include much retrospective material, may wish to sophisticate the head by creating *two* chronologically distinct forms:

> PEACE MOVEMENT, 1843–1945
> PEACE MOVEMENT, 1946–

1843 represents the year in which the first international peace congress took place in London, while the open entry 1946–   would embrace the postwar movement, essentially dissimilar in tone, program, and tactics from the previous period. For a short overview of "Peace movements," centering upon various approaches and historical development, cf. Johan Galtung, "Peace," in Sills, *op. cit.,* v. 11, p. 494–96. On the particular aims and attitudes of the current Peace Movement in America, cf. Bottomore, *op. cit.,* p. 92–5.

4. *Items:* EMPLOYEE OWNERSHIP (p. 425); EMPLOYEES REPRESENTATION IN MANAGEMENT (p. 426; Sears, p. 230)

The first head covers material on profit-sharing and stock-ownership plans, while the second deals with *Mitbestimmungsrecht* (the original German term), i.e., schemes for worker-participation in industrial management. Both are valid forms, though the rejected variant, CO-DETERMINATION (INDUSTRIAL RELATIONS), might be preferred to the used head in that it posits a degree of labor-management equity in control, EMPLOYEES REPRESENTATION IN MANAGEMENT suggesting a largely paternalistic concession *by* management *to* labor, perhaps a variety of cooptation.

At any rate, events within the labor movement, notably in England, Algeria, and Yugoslavia, have rendered both heads inapplicable to the theory and system now widely called "Workers' Control," which extends well beyond profit-sharing and "codetermination" to *total* ownership and administration *by* workers.[1] No existing LC term satisfactorily comprehends this relatively new phenomenon.

Remedy: Institute a new head, WORKERS' CONTROL, with cross-references from and to the two "Employee" forms.[2]

Notes (Item 4)

1. As examples of the growing literature on this theme, cf. the quarterly *Bulletin* issued by the Institute for Workers' Control (91 Goldsmith Street, Nottingham NG1 5LT, U.K.); Ken Coates, "Workers' Control: The Next Phase," *The Spokesman,* no. 1 (March 1970), p. 9–10; the symposium on "Workers Participation in Management: An International Comparison" that composes nearly the entire Feb. 1970 issue of *Industrial Relations* (v. 9, no. 2), p. 117–214; Emerik Blum, "Workers' Management of an Enterprise and its Director," *Socialist Thought and Practice: A Yugoslav Quarterly,* no. 38 (Jan.–Mar. 1970), p. 27–44; Tony Topham, "Workers' Control: Two Case Studies," *Spokesman,* no. 4 (June 1970), p. 9–15; Ken Coates and Wyn Williams, eds., *How and Why Industry Must Be Democratised* (Nottingham: Institute for Workers' Control, 1970); David Pickett, "Workers' Control Conference," *Freedom,* v. 31 no. 3 (Jan. 24, 1970), p. 4; Charles Levinson, "Workers' Control: The Answer to the Giant Company," *Voice of the Unions; For Socialism with Democracy,* May 1970, p. 3–6; the 1970 "literature kit" on "Workers' Control" assembled by the Canadian quarterly, *Our Generation* (3934 rue St.-Urbain, Montreal 131, Quebec); Predrag Aleksic, "Lenin and Self-Management," *Review of International Affairs* (Belgrade), v. 21, no. 481 (April 20, 1970), p. 31–3; Borivoj Romic, "Twenty Years of Self-Management; Preparations for the Second Congress of Self-Management," *ibid.,* v. 21, no. 479 (March 20, 1970), p. 25–8; M. J. Broekmeyer, "Holland Self-Management," *ibid.,* v. 21, no. 480 (April 5, 1970), p. 24–5; Ken Coates and Anthony Topham, *Industrial Democracy in Great Britain: A Book of Reading and Witnesses for Workers' Control* (London: Macgibbon & Kee, 1968); Robert Kilroy-Silk, "Contemporary Theories of Industrial Democracy," *Political Quarterly,* v. 41, no. 2 (April–June, 1970), p. 169–81; Desimir Tochitch, "Some Aspects of Workers' Management," *Review* (Study Centre for Jugoslav Affairs, London), no. 4 (1964), p. 235–

52; and the 41 books and pamphlets listed under "Labour" in *Critical Politics; International Research Publications,* 2nd ed. (London: Agitprop Information, 1970), p. 2–3. Also: Denis Butt, "Workers' Control," *New Left Review,* no. 10 (July-Aug. 1961), p. 24–33, emphasizing the necessity to both *transfer* and *transform* industrial "power"; and "Retreat from Industrial Democracy," *ibid.,* no. 4 (July-Aug. 1960), p. 32–8, by Royden Harrison, who concludes that "only social ownership can—within the limits that are inherent in any co-operative organisation—allow men to run their lives in their own way." Cf. further: "Industrial Democracy—Yugoslavia, Czechoslovakia, Sweden, 1968," *Agenor* (Brussels), no. 13 (Nov. 1969), p. 38–40, and the several in-depth studies on "Workers' Participation in Management" that have appeared in the International Institute for Labour Studies *Bulletin* (Geneva); e.g., the background and progress reports in no. 2 (Feb. 1967), p. 64–125, no. 3 (Nov. 1967), p. 141–43, no. 4 (Feb. 1968), p. 162–63, and no. 5 (Nov. 1968), p. 136–220, as well as specific country-analyses on India, no. 5 (Nov. 1968), p. 153–87, Poland, *ibid.,* p. 188–220, France no. 6 (June 1969), p. 54–93, West Germany, *ibid.,* p. 94–148, the U.S., *ibid.,* p. 149–86, Israel, no. 7 (June 1970), p. 153–99, Japan, *ibid.,* p. 200–51, and Spain, *ibid.,* p. 252–85.

Further: A. Globerson, "Spheres and Levels of Employee Participation in Organizations; Elements of a Conceptual Model," *British Journal of Industrial Relations,* v. 8, no. 2 (July 1970), p. 252–62; Adolf F. Sturmthal, *Workers Councils—A Study of Workplace Organization on Both Sides of the Iron Curtain* (Cambridge, Mass.: Harvard University Press, 1964); and J. Y. Tabb and Amira Goldberg, *Workers' Participation in Management—Expectation and Experience* (Haifa: Technion Research and Development Foundation, 1968).

2. It will be readily apparent that EMPLOYEE CONTROL or EMPLOYEE MANAGEMENT as possible alternatives violate the very essence of "*Workers' control.*" The essential point is that "employees" would no longer exist under such a system, for every worker would be part-owner, part-manager. As early as the late 1920s and early 30s in Spain "workers' participation in management" was understood by the workers' movement, whose "ideology was based on anarchist trade union doctrines," to mean "control and autonomy," not *co*-determination. Cf. "Workers' Participation in the Management of Undertakings in Spain," IILS country-study no. 8, *op. cit.,* p. 284.

The *API* affords a precedent for this new form, *op. cit.,* p. 68.

In view of the connection established by Guerin, Chomsky, and others between anarchism and workers' control, *sa* references seem advisable from and to ANARCHISM AND ANARCHISTS, while "×" referents would be appropriate for "Council Communism," "Liberatarian Socialism," and "Industrial Democracy."

5. *Item:* BOYCOTT
×× **Competition, Unfair (p. 155)**

What is necessarily "unfair," as the "××" implies, about a labor-generated boycott—like that of the California farm workers—conceived as a form of pressure upon recalcitrant employers to negotiate worker demands? Is it not equally "unfair" that such bosses refuse either to recognize a bona fide union or to grant their employees a living wage plus certain minimal amenities taken for granted by most of the population?[1] The "boycott" is merely one among relatively few weapons in the labor arsenal. When compared with the many employer options, like dismissal, blacklisting, and scab-hiring, it hardly merits the appellation "unfair."

Remedy: Remove "Competition, Unfair" as an "××."

Note (Item 5)

1. On the strike and international boycott mounted by the United Farm Workers Organizing Committee (UFWOC, AFL-CIO), cf. the union's biweekly organ, *El Malcriado,* published in both English- and Spanish-language editions (P.O. Box 130, Delano, California 90063); George Ballis, and others, *Basta* (Delano: Farm Workers Press, 1966); John Gregory Dunne, *Delano* (New York: Farrar, 1967); Eugene Nelson, *Huelga: The First Hundred Days of the Great Delano Grape Strike* (Delano: Farm Workers Press, 1966); Andy Zormeno, *Don Sotaco,* a cartoon-collection (Delano: Farm Workers Press, 1966); and the "special issue" of *Peace News* on the "California Grape Strike," no. 1751 (Jan. 16, 1970), p. 2–3, 8–9. Also: the periodic analyses contributed by Anne Draper to the *Los Angeles Free Press* and other "underground" publications.

The New York Civil Liberties Union, positing the "right of unions to bargain collectively through representatives of their own choosing as a fundamental civil liberty," characterized the California grape boycott as "the only means available to UFWOC to implement that fundamental civil liberty." Cf. "NYCLU Backs Grape Boycott," *Civil Liberties,* no. 265 (Dec. 1969), p. 5. Also: "Suits Assist Grape Pickers, Condemn Pesticide Poisoning, Violence, Threats," *ibid.,* no. 261 (Apr. 1969), p. 6; and Martin Garbus, "Migrant Labor Fights for Freedom," *ibid.,* no. 254 (March-April 1968), p. 12.

6. *Item:* COLLECTIVE SETTLEMENTS (p. 270)

"Classic" communal ventures like the Oneida Community and Brook Farm are well enough covered by this form. But it doesn't suffice as a rubric for the experiments in cooperative living that have recently blossomed in both metropolis and wilderness, from ultra-urban Berkeley and Berlin to teepee-dotted northern New Mexico. These newer incarnations differ in important respects from the older varieties, often serving—for instance—as loci for political action, and frequently interacting with one another in a fashion that their progenitors never did. Such postwar politico-ecological undertakings are described by most practitioners as "intentional communities."

Remedy: Create two new forms, INTENTIONAL COMMUNITIES, RURAL, 1946– , and INTENTIONAL COMMUNITIES, URBAN, 1946– , WITH "××'s" for COLLECTIVE SETTLEMENTS, COOPERATION, etc.[1]

Note (Item 6)

1. Since many such communitarians also regard themselves as "libertarians" or "anarchists," it would be well to add cross-references from and to ANARCHISM AND ANARCHISTS.

The *API* prefers COMMUNES, RURAL and COMMUNES, URBAN, *op. cit.*, p. 15. These seem altogether acceptable forms. If selected instead of INTENTIONAL COMMUNITIES, there should be a *See* reference *from* "Intentional communities." Likewise, *See* references *from* "Communes, Rural" and "Communes, Urban" are advisable if INTENTIONAL COMMUNITIES becomes the prime head.

ONEIDA COMMUNITY, incidentally (p. 919), deserves an "××" for Collective settlements," as does BROOK FARM (p. 162).

7. *Item:* MOLLY MAGUIRES
×× Crime and criminals (p. 842)

The provocation under which the miners lived day by day in the 1870's was immense; one need only mention the starvation

wages, the company-owned homes, the blacklisting and the
terror and violence used against the Mollies and miners in
general. During the sharp economic crisis of 1873 the burden
was shifted to the workers in the form of unemployment,
wage cuts and longer working hours. In the 1870's the largest
number of strikes—304—were in Pennsylvania. In the absence
of a powerful labor movement to fight for their rights, the
miners fought injustice with violence and terrorism until the
mining union was reorganized. After this such tactics were
almost entirely abandoned. If the movement is viewed against
the background of class and ethnic struggles, then the coal
miners of eastern Pennsylvania had added a tactic which, if
not particularly pretty, is not surprising.

—Ann J. Lane[1]

The Mollies, says the *Encylopaedia Britannica,* were "certain
men in the anthracite coal–producing counties of Schuylkill,
Luzerne, Carbon and adjacent counties in Pennsylvania, who violated property rights of coal-mine operators and even committed
murder during the years 1862 to 1876...." Reluctantly, the *EB* expert admits that "there is some justification for considering the Molly
Maguire episode as an aspect of labour struggles in the coal
mines...."[2]

Through its single "××," LC chooses to emphasize the Mollies'
alleged criminality, entirely ignoring the labor-struggle dimension of
the "episode." That terror erupted in the Pennsylvania coalfields
during the 1870s nobody denies. But that the "Mollies" deserve
responsibility for that terror remains an unresolved question. Indeed, studies by Anthony Bimba and others conclude that far from
being hooligans and murderers, the Mollies were "pioneers and mar-
tyrs in a determined struggle of the miners to improve their miserable
working conditions."[3] Bimba, in particular, holds that the railroad
company owning the mines itself organized the "terror" and managed
"the frame-up trial that sent the Mollies to the gallows."[4] A court
well attuned to the wishes of the "robber baron" Establishment and
patently unsympathetic to working-class organization *convicted* the
Mollies on capital charges. But history has yet to *prove* them guilty.
If, however, their "guilt" inheres in having "violated" the coal
operators' "property rights," then the owners themselves must be

adjudged no less "guilty" for having violated the miners' *human* rights. But no "××" for "Crime and criminals," naturally, appears under COAL MINES AND MINING, the standard head for the industry (p. 262). Until the matter of the Mollies' asserted "gangsterism" is finally settled, it is incumbent on subject-schemes to tread warily — in terms of our own legal precepts, to presume them innocent.[5]

Remedy: (a) Delete the "××" for "Crime and criminals."

(b) Introduce two nondebatable "××'s": COAL-MINERS — PENNSYLVANIA and LABOR AND LABORING CLASSES — PENNSYLVANIA.

Notes (Item 7)

1. "Recent Literature on the Molly Maguires," *Science and Society,* v. 30 (summer 1966), p. 319.

2. (Chicago: Encyclopaedia Britannica, Inc., 1967), v. 15, p. 673–74.

3. Bimba's 1932 work, *The Molly Maguires,* has been reissued by International Publishers in New York. The quote derives from IP's *Book News Letter,* v. 6, no. 2 (May-July 1970), p. 1.

4. *Ibid.*

5. Indeed, Lane — at the outset of her judicious review of "Molly" studies — straightforwardly announces that "little … can be said of the Molly Maguires upon which all knowledgeable persons can agree and for which there is some convincing evidence." *Op. cit.,* p. 310.

8. *Item:* COMMUNIST STRATEGY (p. 282)

Since the head posits a single, monolithic Communist movement which in reality has not for some time — if ever — existed, it is foolish and careless. Beyond that, however, it reflects a distinctly Western, "Free World," Cold War bias in that no correlative form has been devised for what Soviet or Cuban ideologues and analysts might well term "Capitalist strategy." Both terms, admittedly, represent over simplifications. Still, if the one can claim any merit, so can the other. The very isolation of COMMUNIST STRATEGY attributes to Communist "bloc" activities a singular, sinister quality. "Sinister" and nefarious they well may be, but not — in view, e.g., of widely-known CIA machinations in both the West and Third World — singular.[1]

Remedy: Either institute CAPITALIST STRATEGY as a complementary form or dispense completely with COMMUNIST STRATEGY,
employing in its place such fully-adequate and far less-slanted rubrics as COMMUNISM, WORLD POLITICS—1945–   , RUSSIA—FOREIGN
RELATIONS, etc.

Note (Item 8)

1. To refresh faulty memories on CIA "strategy" and operations, cf.,
for example, Andrew Kopkind, "CIA: The Great Corrupter," *New States-
man*, v. 73, no. 1876 (Feb. 24, 1967), p. 249–50; George Morris, *CIA and
American Labor; The Subversion of the AFL-CIO's Foreign Policy* (New York:
International Publishers, 1967); Warren Hinckle, Robert Scheer, and Sol
Stern, "The University on the Make; or How MSU Helped Arm Madame
NHU," in *A Muckraker's Guide to 1968 and Other Horrors from the Pages of
Ramparts* (San Francisco: Ramparts, 1969), p. 52–60; Sol Stern, "A Short
Account of International Student Politics & the Cold War, with Particular
Reference to the NSA, CIA, etc.," *ibid.*, p. 87–97; Michele Ray, "In Cold
Blood: How the CIA Executed Che," *ibid.*, p. 142–49; Robert E. Light and
Carl Marzani, *Cuba Versus CIA* (New York: Marzani & Munsell, 1961);
David Wise and Thomas B. Ross, *The Invisible Government* (New York:
Random House, 1964); and Paul W. Blackstock, *The Strategy of Subversion;
Manipulating the Politics of Other Nations* (Chicago: Quadrangle Books,
1964). Also: Murray Hausknecht, "CIA and the Universities," *Dissent*, v. 13,
no. 4 (July-Aug. 1966), p. 348–50, and Lewis Coser, "The CIA—Enemy
or Promise?," plus comments by Michael Walzer and Stanley Plastrik, *ibid.*,
v. 14, no. 3 (May-June 1967), p. 274–83.

9. *Items:* CONSCIENTIOUS OBJECTORS (p. 303); MILITARY SERVICE, COMPULSORY (p. 825)

Events have overtaken these heads, for resistance to the draft,
largely a reflex of the continuing Vietnam War and accompanying
radicalization of youth, has increasingly been based on nonreligious
and frankly political considerations. CONSCIENTIOUS OBJECTORS,
mainly and traditionally limited to religion-inspired pacifists who
make formal application for military exemption, fails to describe

satisfactorily the now much-enlarged area of draft resistance, typi-fied by conscription-eligible young men who may refuse even to register with government authorities, exile themselves to Canada and elsewhere, etc., frequently on ethical or ideological grounds.[1]

Remedy: (a) Add the subhead —RESISTANCE TO MILITARY SER-VICE, COMPULSORY, with an "××" and *sa* for "Conscientious objec-tors."

(b) Under this new form introduce "Draft resistance" as an "×."

Note (Item 9)

1. For a selection of material on this phenomenon, cf. the *API* entries under "Draft Exiles" and "Draft Resistance"; Ken Cloke, *A Pocket Manual on Draft Resistance* (New York: The Guardian, 197 E. 4th Street, 10009); Arlo Tatum and Joseph S. Tuchinsky, *Guide to the Draft* (Boston: Beacon, 1969); Leslie Rothenberg, *The Draft and You* (Garden City, N.Y.: Anchor Books, 1968); periodicals like *Counterdraft Magazine* (Box 74881, Los Angeles, California 90004) and *AMEX* (American Exiles in Canada), Box 187, Station D, Toronto 165, Ontario); and the weekly *Los Angeles Free Press* question-and-answer column, "Shaft the Draft."

10. *Item:* COMPANY UNIONS
×× **Independent unions (p. 283)**

>...a labor union consisting of the employees of a single firm, having no affiliation with a larger outside union, and *often felt to be dominated by the employer.*[1]

"Independent" of larger, "international" unions, yes. But not usually *independent* of management, as any student of labor history appreciates. The "××," however, does not make this absolutely essential distinction, mistakenly implying that "company unions" are in fact, truly and fully "independent."

Remedy: Remove "Independent unions" as an "××."

Note (Item 10)

1. *Webster's Third,* p. 461. Emphasis added.

11. *Item:* CUBA—HISTORY—1959—   (p. 340)

This subhead immediately follows —REVOLUTION, 1935. Regardless of personal views toward the transformation undergone by Cuba since 1958-59, the events of those two years, culminating in the overthrow of Batista's regime and marking the outset of a thoroughgoing reconstruction of society, no less qualify as a "Revolution" than the upsurge 25 years earlier.[1]

Remedy: Precede CUBA—HISTORY—1959— with CUBA—HISTORY—REVOLUTION, 1958–1959.

Note (Item 11)

1. For a brief, readable account of Cuban history through 1968, cf. Byron Williams, *Cuba: The Continuing Revolution* (New York: Parents Magazine Press, 1969). The last three chapters chronicle and analyze Castro's "New Society."

12. *Items:* EMPLOYEE MORALE (p. 425); PSYCHOLOGY, INDUSTRIAL (p. 1044); WORK (p. 1417)

The "××" referents for these forms include "Incentives in industry" and "Job satisfaction." Remarkably, however, there is no reference to a primary head on *alienation* as an ingredient or aspect of worker psychology, though Marx introduced the concept more than a century ago and numerous commentators have elaborated it since. The present referents, in true Babbitt fashion, tend to "accentuate the positive," whereas objective studies tend to substantiate the grimmer, estrangement-producing side of the workplace.[1]

Remedy: Establish ALIENATION (SOCIAL PSYCHOLOGY) as a primary head, with cross-references from and to EMPLOYEE MORALE; PSYCHOLOGY, INDUSTRIAL; and WORK.[2]

Notes (Item 12)

1. As examples of "alienation theory" and its applications, cf. Melvin Seeman, "On the Personal Consequences of Alienation in Work," *American Sociological Review*, v. 32, no. 2 (April 1967), p. 273–85; Herbert Aptheker, ed., *Marxism and Alienation; A Symposium* (New York: Humanities Press, 1965); Giuseppe Bonazzi, *Alienazione e Anomia nella Grande Industria; Una Ricerca sui Lavoratori dell'Automobile* (Milan: Edizioni Avanti, 1964); John L. Horton, "Dehumanizaton of Anomie and Alienation; A Problem in the Ideology of Sociology," *British Journal of Sociology*, v. 14, no. 4 (Dec. 1964), p. 283–300; A. G. Neal and S. Rettig, "Dimensions of Alienation Among Manual and Non-Manual Workers," *American Sociological Review*, v. 28, no. 4 (Aug. 1963), p. 599–608; B. B. Seligman, "On Work, Alienation, and Leisure," *American Journal of Economics*, v. 24 (Oct. 1965), p. 337–60; Louis A. Zurcher, Jr., and others, "Value Orientation, Role Conflict, and Alienation from Work: A Cross-Cultural Study," *American Sociological Review*, v. 30, no. 4 (Aug. 1965), p. 539–48; Gerald Sykes, ed., *Alienation* (New York: Braziller, 1964); Erich Fromm, *Marx's Concept of Man* (New York: Ungar, 1961), including the verbatim texts of Marx's *Economic and Philosophical Manuscripts*, in which he early expounded the *Entfremdung* (i.e., alienation) theory; Fritz Pappenheim, *Alienation of Modern Man* (New York: Monthly Review Press, 1959); Ronald Fraser, comp., *Work; 20 Personal Accounts* [originally published in the *New Left Review*] (Harmondsworth: Penguin Books, 1968); R. Blauner, *Alienation and Freedom* (Chicago: University of Chicago Press, 1954); and David Armstrong, "Meaning in Work," *New Left Review*, no. 10 (July-Aug. 1961), p. 16–23, which commences with an excerpt from Marx's "Estranged Labour." The Horton piece, in particular, should be consulted as a solid historical treatment of the concept, tracing its origins to both Marx and Durkheim. S. R. Parker and J. Child furnish useful, albeit brief, definitions, together with additional bibliographical references (particularly to studies by Fromm, Veblen, and Weber) in their *Sociology of Industry* (London: George Allen and Unwin, 1967), p. 154–55 and 168–69. For a short discussion of "alienation" and its broader ramifications beyond the workplace itself, cf. Bottomore, *op. cit.*, p. 74–5.

2. Precedents: *API* employs "Alienation and Anomie"; *SSHI* uses precisely the suggested form, "Alienation (Social psychology)." Cf. v. 57, no. 3 (Dec. 1969), p. 4.

It is a pleasure to report that the July 1964–Dec. 1965 ACS on p. 9 did install ALIENATION (SOCIAL PSYCHOLOGY) as a prime head. However, its two "××'s" are solely for "Social isolation" and "Social psychology," while a later "×" (1967 ACS, p. 9) refers merely from "Estrangement (Social Psychology)." In short, it still fails to relate the concept to "Employee morale," etc. Further, its utility may be enhanced by the addition of an "×" for "Entfremdung" and an "××" for "Anomy" (p. 56).

13. *Items:* LIBRARIES AND FOREIGN POPULATION; LIBRARIES AND LABOR; LIBRARIES AND SCHOOLS; etc. (p. 740)

No one can fair-mindedly expect that LC compilers would be blessed with the gift of prophecy to a greater degree than anyone else. Hence, noting the list's failure to indicate the lately-expanded social concerns of the profession can hardly be interpreted as a criticism. This is a useful opportunity, however, to suggest that the next edition reflect what may properly be termed a near-revolution in library services and professional philosophy, already incarnated, print-wise, in many studies and such periodicals as *Response*, "the newsletter of the N.Y.C. Librarians Roundtable on Social Responsibilities," and the ALA Social Responsibilities Round Table *Newsletter*,[1] as well as *The Liberated Librarian, Sipapu,* and the Bay Area Reference Center's vibrant, "with it" *Synergy*.

   Remedy: Establish, as the literature warrants, such new forms as

    LIBRARIES AND THE COMMUNITY
    LIBRARIES AND SOCIETY
    LIBRARIES AND SOCIAL CHANGE
      × Social change and libraries
    LIBRARIES AND THE POOR
      × Libraries and ghettos
        Libraries and slums
        Libraries and the disadvantaged
        Libraries and the inner city
    LIBRARIES AND PEACE
      × Peace and libraries

Note (Item 13)

1. Both available from the SRRT Clearinghouse, c/o George Hathaway, Secretary, Brooklyn College Library, Bedford Avenue and Avenue H, Brooklyn, NY 11210.

14. *Items:* LONDON—BOMBARDMENT, 1940 (p. 757); ROTTERDAM—BOMBARDMENT, 1940 (p. 1118)

It is irresistibly tempting to ascribe the inclusion of these forms to the close political and cultural affinities felt toward wartime allies and, similarly, to explain the *ex*clusion of certain other heads in terms of political and cultural antagonism toward erstwhile enemies. Whatever the real reasons, the agonies undergone by our "friends" are duly noted in the list, while the no-less-horrendous suffering inflicted *by* us upon our adversaries passes unremarked. From February 13th through 15th, 1945, the RAF in tandem with the USAF completely destroyed the refugee-swollen city of Dresden with phosphorus and high-explosive bombs, producing an estimated 300,000 deaths and casualties. No other German city during World War II experienced a bombardment of such magnitude in death and destruction.[1] No inkling of this event appears on p. 386, merely two entries for safely-distant episodes: DRESDEN, BATTLE OF, 1813, and DRESDEN, PEACE OF, 1745. On August 6, 1945, the USAF dropped an atomic bomb on Hiroshima. The result: 260,000 dead; 163,263 missing or wounded; 60 percent of the city devastated.[2] And three days later another atomic device fell on Nagasaki, almost totally wrecking the city, wounding 40,000 and killing 36,000.[3] There are no entries for even the *names* of these two cities. Nor is there any indication—*21 years later*—under either ATOMIC BOMB or ATOMIC WARFARE that the weapon had in fact *ever been used*. It would seem from this LC treatment—or lack of it—that nuclear weapons had never *hurt* anybody, that the dead, mangled, and deformed of Hiroshima and Nagasaki inhabit only some hyperactive imaginations. It is a stupendous achievement in make-believe.[4] But for fairy tales most persons prefer Grimm or Andersen, not the LC subject-list. The charred corpses in Dresden's streets were real enough. So is the Hiroshima-demonstrated threat of nuclear annihilation. This *is* the Atomic Age. Let us face it. And let us further face the perhaps unsavory fact that evildoing on a terrible scale has not always been the exclusive province of our foes. As the Dean of St. Albans explained when banning the use of St. Albans Abbey for a thanksgiving service on August 15, 1945: "I cannot give thanks to God for an event brought about by a wrong use of force, by an indiscriminate massacre."[5]

Remedy: (a) Institute three new forms:

DRESDEN—BOMBARDMENT, 1945[6]

HIROSHIMA—ATOMIC BOMBARDMENT, 1945

NAGASAKI—ATOMIC BOMBARDMENT, 1945

(b) Under each of the above, as well as under the London and Rotterdam entries, place an "××": "World War, 1939–1945—Atrocities."

(c) Under both ATOMIC BOMB and ATOMIC WARFARE make an *sa* reference to Hiroshima and Nagasaki.

(d) To correct any missuppositions that "Massacres" only happen on the ground, effected with bows-and-arrows, rifles, knives, or cannon, establish another new form, MASSACRES, AERIAL, with a note: *sa the subdivisions* BOMBARDMENT *and* ATOMIC BOMBARDMENT *under names of places, e.g.* HIROSHIMA—ATOMIC BOMBARDMENT, 1945, *and* ROTTERDAM—BOMBARDMENT, 1940.

Notes (Item 14)

1. Cf. *Der neue Brockhaus.* 3e, völlig neubearb., Aufl. (Wiesbaden: F. A. Brockhaus, 1965), Bd. 1, p. 615, and David J. C. Irving, *The Destruction of Dresden* (New York: Holt, Rinehart, & Winston, 1964).

2. *Der neue Brockhaus, op. cit.*, Bd. 2, p. 551. According to Godfrey Featherstone, these are Japanese estimates. The Allies claimed a death toll of "up to 135,000 people." Cf. "Across the bomb-site...," *Peace News*, no. 1780 (Aug. 7, 1970), p. 3.

3. *Ibid.*, Bd. 3, p. 592. Featherstone places the "Allied estimate" at

"74,000 dead and 75,000 wounded," adding that "Japanese figures confirm this estimate." *Op. cit.*

4. Only slightly lessened by the institution of — PERSONAL NARRATIVES as a subhead under ATOMIC BOMB — PHYSIOLOGICAL EFFECT (1969 ACS, p. 16).

5. Quoted by Nigel Young, "1945 — How Britain Reacted," *Peace News*, no. 1780 (Aug. 7, 1970), p. 2.

6. LC assigned to Irving's volume, *op. cit.*, the heads WORLD WAR, 1939–1945 — DESTRUCTION AND PILLAGE — GERMANY — DRESDEN and DRESDEN — HISTORY, the first unassailable but the second a classic example of slipshod, milktoast cataloging that succeeds in rendering an altogether ghastly, dishonorable event wholly *invisible.* Cf. *National Union Catalog, 1963–1967* (Ann Arbor, Mich.: J. W. Edwards, 1969), v. 20, p. 399.

15. *Item:* FASCISM
— ARGENTINE REPUBLIC
— BRAZIL
— GERMANY
— ITALY (p. 470)

Fair enough. But not *complete* enough, for fascist movements have thrived — and continue to flourish — elsewhere, not merely in the Axis countries and *cacique*-prone Latin America. The virus has also infected Great Britain, Finland, America, Spain, France, Portugal, and South Africa.[1]

Remedy: Add subheads for the above-named states, together with any others indicated by the literature.

Note (Item 15)

1. The outstanding U.S. examples in recent years are the American Nazi and National Renaissance parties, whose chief publications are annotated in Robert H. Muller, ed., *From Radical Left to Extreme Right* (Ann Arbor, Mich.: Campus Publishers, 1967), especially p. 96–8. F. L. Carsten, in his *Rise of Fascism* (London: Batsford, 1967), traces "the history of the principal Fascist movements as they developed in the course of the 1920s and 1930s." A final chapter (p. 230–37) delineates their common traits. E. J.

Woolf's 1968 anthology, *European Fascism* (London: Weidenfeld and Nicolson), includes an analysis by H. R. Trevor-Roper of "The Phenomenon of Fascism," as well as individual sections on Italy, Germany, Austria, Hungary, Rumania, Poland, Finland, Norway, Great Britain, France, Spain, and Portugal. It concludes with Christopher Seton-Watson's survey of "Fascism in Contemporary Europe," plus a partially annotated reading list. On fascism in South Africa, cf. especially Brian Bunting, *Rise of the South African Reich*, rev. ed. (Harmondsworth: Penguin Books, 1969).

16. *Item:* MANAGEMENT RIGHTS

> *Here are entered works dealing with the rights and powers essential to the operation of a business, such as hiring, production methods, and the like, which management may claim to be outside the scope of collective bargaining and over which management commonly maintains authority and responsibility* [p. 775].

An initial reaction to this form, in light of the growing segment of labor that aims at *total* control of industrial and business enterprises, is that there are. *no longer* such unquestioned "management rights." In fact, many of the scope-note prerogatives have long been contested—and eroded—even by relatively "moderate" unions. "Union shop" and "closed shop" arrangements surely inhibit management's hiring "rights," while disputes, as an example, over speed-ups on an assembly-line certainly encroach on the manager's alleged rights concerning "production methods."[1] A secondary response, however, centers on the ethical geometry of the head. In a word, it is disturbingly *asymmetrical*. The cataloger who turns to p. 711 and p. 712 expecting to find a correlative entry, LABOR RIGHTS, sandwiched between LABOR REST HOMES and LABOR SERVICE, will be disappointed. No such head exists. Which leads to the interesting, inescapable conclusion, worthy of Ford, Carnegie, or Rockefeller, that Management enjoys certain God-given, indestructible rights, while Labor, by contrast, is entitled to *none*.

Remedy: Either delete MANAGEMENT RIGHTS as a superfluous, moribund form or install LABOR RIGHTS as a symmetry-making rubric with an equivalent scopenote; e.g.,

> *Here are entered works dealing with the rights and powers essential*
> *to the well-being of workers, such as hiring, production methods,*
> *union organization, shop conditions, and the like, which labor may*
> *claim to be within the scope of collective bargaining but over some of*
> *which management, until recent times, has commonly maintained*
> *full authority and responsibility.*

Note (Item 16)

1. A Working Party established by the Department of Christian Education and Training of the National Christian Council of Kenya found, in the course of examining "some attempts [in Yugoslavia, West Germany, and elsewhere] to associate industrial workers with the management of their enterprise," that "sometimes the distinction is made between the *external* responsibilities of management: sales, purchasing, etc., about which most employees have little contribution to make, and their *internal* responsibilities: *production, methods, personnel,* etc., with which the man on the shop floor is very much concerned." Cf. *Who Controls Industry in Kenya?* (Nairobi: East African Publishing House, 1968), p. 242–43. First two emphases in original, last added.

The "erosion" of traditional managerial "rights" appears as a virtual *Leitmotif* throughout the 16 papers assembled by Philip D. Bradley in his 1959 anthology, *The Public Stake in Union Power* (Charlottesville: University Press of Virginia). Cf., e.g., David McCord Wright's remarks on labor demands for "tight, centralized planning," seniority based promotion, closed-shop contracts, and "participation," the latter, in his opinion, being likely to "hamstring management and efficiency," p. 119. Albert Rees, in "Some Non-wage Aspects of Collective Bargaining," expands on the seniority question, p. 124–42, while H. Gregg Lewis, in "Competitive and Monopoly Unionism," particularly discusses the closed shop and dues check-off, as well as "make-work," "share-work," and "featherbedding" practices, all aspects of labor encroachment on the once-sacred administrator's domain, p. 181–208.

G. Warren Miller further cavils against "exploitative" union behavior, manifest in "work rules of various kinds, employment guarantees, output royalties for union benefit, penalty rates of various types (e.g., overtime pay) and so on." In Miller's view, "as far as industrial unions are concerned, all exploitation tends toward the ultimate 'optimum': syndicalism." p. 299–300.

17. *Item:* ANTI-COMMUNIST MOVEMENTS (p. 584; Sears, p. 69)

The head suggests a polarity that the list itself fails to express. For if there are "anti–Communist movements," then certainly there are also "anti–Capitalist movements."

Remedy: Establish a *See* form:

Anti-Capitalist movements
　See Anarchism and anarchists
　　Communism
　　Radicalism and radicals
　　Socialism

18. *Item:* POOR (p. 1009)

The 20 *sa* and 13 "××" referents, ranging from "Almshouses" and "Begging" to "Benevolence" and "Tramps," effectively dehumanize the poverty-stricken. The twin emphases are upon *external* amelioration of their condition (e.g., "Benevolence" and "Charities") and the pitiably low state to which they have fallen (e.g., "Tramps" and "Unemployed"). No hint appears of the actions and campaigns mounted by the poor themselves to improve their lot,[1] nor of the socioeconomic systems to which large scale poverty—or, more accurately, a marked disparity in income distribution—seems invariably wedded.[2]

Remedy: (a) Create three new forms, RENT STRIKES, TENANTS' UNIONS, and WELFARE RIGHTS MOVEMENT (U.S.), providing each with an "××" for POOR.[3] Each of the first two heads should also become both an *sa* and "××" under the other, as well as under LANDLORD AND TENANT (p. 716), while WELFARE RIGHTS MOVEMENT (U.S.) will require an "××" for PUBLIC WELFARE—U.S. (p. 1050).

(b) Add "Capitalism," "Feudalism," and "Laissez-faire" to the "××" rosters for both POOR and POVERTY (p. 1018).

(c) Add "Migrant labor" as an *sa* entry under POOR.

Notes (Item 18)

1. Cf., for instance, issues of *Now*, bulletin of the National Welfare Rights Organization, and Roger H. Davidson's "War on Poverty: Experiment in Federalism," in American Academy of Political and Social Science, *Annals*, v. 385 (Sept. 1969), p. 1–13. Davidson underscores "political activity on the part of disadvantaged citizens" as an integral element of the five-year-old "anti-poverty program." Other contributors to the same volume expand on this facet of the program. Also: "Poor Protest Court Fees in Eviction, Divorce Suits," *Civil Liberties*, no. 261 (April 1969), p. 6, and Paul Bullock, "On Organizing the Poor," *Dissent*, v. 15, no. 1 (Jan.-Feb. 1968), p. 65–70+.

2. Without once mentioning "capitalism" or "laissez-faire" economics, Pamela Roy's discussion, "Inequality: A Trend Analysis," by emphasizing "the interpretation of poverty in terms of inequality in high-income industrial nations," in effect joins poverty with essentially capitalist, free-enterprise systems. Cf. in *Annals, op. cit.,* p. 110–17. Michael Harrington makes such a linkage more explicit. Cf., for example, "The Politics of Poverty," *Dissent*, v. 12, no. 4 (autumn 1965), p. 412–30. So, likewise, does Bottomore in the course of examining Galbraith's views on "redistribution of income." *Op. cit.*, p. 70–2.

3. For precedents, cf. the initial *API*, which uses RENT STRIKES (p. 54) and WELFARE MOVEMENT (p. 67). For reportage on a typical rent strike and the dynamics of organizing a tenants' union, cf. Peter H. Denton and Nancy Holstrom, "Ann Arbor Rent Strike," *IS*, no. 13 (Oct. 1969), p. 20. Also: *Not a Penny on the Rents*, plus other recent pamphlets and studies on housing and tenant resistance available from Agitprop Information, *op. cit.*; and "Court Holds Retaliatory Eviction Illegal, Hits Landlords Who Punish Complainers," *Civil Liberties*, no. 261 (April 1969), p. 6.

19. *Item:* NAPALM
×× **Metallic soaps (1968 ACS, p. 296)**

Napalm is a purely American invention. It was compounded by Professor Louis Fieser at Harvard University in World War II and has since experienced considerable refinement. The *early formulations were metallic soaps gelled with gasoline*. . . . In recent years the Air Force has adopted a new type of napalm, designated "Napalm B," which consists of 50% polystyrene mixed with 25% each of gasoline and benzene. This blend, which was developed by the Dow Chemical Company, is said to impart superior qualities of "adhesion" to the product. . . .

Napalm was used extensively in the Pacific theatre in World War II, and a total of 32,215 tons was dropped in the three years of the Korean war. Figures released by the Defense Department in early 1968 revealed the napalm escalation in Vietnam: 2181 tons dropped in 1963; 1777 tons in 1964; 17,659 tons in 1965, and 54,670 tons in 1966. For the first six months of 1967, napalm spending came to $2,949,929 per month. By March of 1968 it was estimated that the Air Force alone had dropped in excess of 100,000 tons in Vietnam; the Navy also uses napalm bombs and the Army employs substantial quantities in flame-throwers.[1]

> Napalm sticks to kids, napalm sticks to kids,
> When'll those damn gooks ever learn?
> We shoot the sick, the young, the lame,
> We do our best to kill and maim,
> Because the 'kills" all count the same,
> Napalm sticks to kids.[2]

Since the 1969 ACS made no further emendation to the new head, it appears that the role of this chemical mixture remains both harmless and even helpful. Were its uses confined to purely peaceful soap production, it would warrant no comment here. But the Air Force has not dropped 100,000 tons of *soap* on Vietnam, though one might fervently wish that it had. Napalm, as everyone who has merely scanned the daily newspaper or fitfully watched TV news reports over the past few years well knows, is a flesh-scorching chemical *weapon*, whose employment in Vietnam has often been wholly indiscriminate.[3] Not only does it inflict severe burns, but may also kill by asphyxiation—i.e., carbon monoxide poisoning—persons who have "sheltered" themselves out of the open air.[4] It cannot be claimed that LC just doesn't know about napalm's extra-soap aspects. It has already cataloged a 1967 title that dealt specifically with this substance as a chemical warfare agent.[5] Why, then, the obfuscation, the same "Let's pretend" posture earlier noted with respect to the atomic bomb?

Remedy: Add to the "××" for "Metallic soaps" further references for "Chemical warfare," "Offenses against the person,"

"Vietnamese Conflict, 1961–   —Atrocities," "Vietnamese Conflict, 1961–   —Chemistry," and "World War, 1939–1945—Chemistry."

Notes (Item 19)

1. J. B. Neilands, "Vietnam: Progress of the Chemical War," *Asian Survey*, v. 10, no. 3 (March 1970), p. 213. Emphasis added.

2. First verse of a little ditty composed by 1st Cavalry Divison (Airmobile) "skytroopers" at Phuoc Vinh, Vietnam, as reported by John E. Woodruff from Saigon in the June 15, 1970, Baltimore *Sun* and quoted by I. F. Stone in his *Bi-Weekly* for June 29, 1970 (v. 18, no. 13), p. 2. Woodruff notes that "agreement was by no means complete on whether the [songwriters] were protesting the war or mocking a 'bad image' that many helicopter pilots and gunners feel they have acquired unfairly in the course of the war." Still, the ballad seems to verify, however crudely, Neilands' point regarding the product's "adhesive" quality, as well as evincing the essentially racist ("gook") attitude toward Asians mentioned earlier with respect to YELLOW PERIL.

3. Cf. *ibid.,* p. 214. Its use as a military agent, however, has by no means been limited to World War II, Korea, and Vietnam. Whitaker reports that the Portuguese reacted to the eruption of military resistance in Angola in the early 1960s "with indiscriminate air attacks using bombs and napalm." *Op. cit.,* p. 17. Jet aircraft regularly drop napalm, as well, on the liberated zones of Guinea-Bissau, hoping to "disrupt . . . rebel control." *Ibid.,* p. 25.

4. Cf. Gilbert Dreyfus, "Napalm: "What It Is; What It Does," *London Bulletin,* no. 4 (winter 1967-68), p. 152–55. Dr. Dreyfus, professor of biochemistry at the University of Paris Medical School, made a detailed report on the various forms and effects of napalm to the second session of the Bertrand Russell War Crimes Tribunal. He concluded that "whether it is used strategically on the battlefield or in the bombardment of urban areas or village collectives, [napalm] is a means of extensive, nondiscriminatory destruction. It affects primarily human beings, livestock, crops and light flammable structures such as habitations. Its employment in heavily populated areas will produce immense loss of life from burning and asphyxiation. In survivors, corporal injuries of the greatest gravity with functional sequels which prevent the resumption of normal life are the rule" (p. 158).

5. John Takman's *Napalm; Ett Internationallt Symposium om Kemisk och Biologisk Krigföring i Var Tid* (Stockholm: Raben & Sj³/₈gren). Cf. *Library of Congress Catalog. Books: Subjects, Jan.–March 1969* (Washington, D.C.: Library of Congress, 1969), p. 712.

20. *Item:* PUBLIC RELATIONS—POLICE
× Police-community relations (1968 ACS, p. 361)

Some of the published literature may, indeed, require this head. But some also requires a heading akin to that reduced to an "×" referent. For "Public relations"—PR—is ad-world jargon. In this context, it signifies "image-building" undertaken by the police, *not* their de facto relationship with the communities they ostensibly "serve and protect." Just as TEACHERS AND COMMUNITY is not equivalent to PUBLIC RELATIONS—TEACHERS, neither is POLICE AND COMMUNITY or POLICE-COMMUNITY RELATIONS the same as PUBLIC RELATIONS—POLICE.[1] An additional form is needed, particularly since police activities have become the subject of much controversy and concern within the past few years.[2]

Remedy: Introduce POLICE AND COMMUNITY as a new head, with an "×" for "Police-community relations," deleting this latter referent under PUBLIC RELATIONS—POLICE. The literature may also demand further heads like POLICE AND AFRO-AMERICANS, POLICE AND YOUTH, and POLICE MALPRACTICE.

Notes (Item 20)

1. TEACHERS AND COMMUNITY appears on p. 446 of the 1968 ACS.
2. Cf., for example, Chapter V, "The Police," in Bullock, *Watts, op. cit.,* and "Police and the Panthers," *Black Politician,* v. 1, no. 3 (Jan. 1970), p. 17–9, which voices "the great concern that [police-implemented] repression is being aimed [at] and will extend to all blacks." Also: Kathy Boudin, and others *The Bust Book: What to Do Till the Lawyer Comes* (New York: Grove Press, 1970); Donald H. Bouma, *Kids and Cops: A Study in Mutual Hostility* (Grand Rapids, Mich.: Eerdmans, 1969); and the frequent items on alleged police malpractice appearing in the ACLU's monthly *Civil Liberties;* e.g., "LA Police Escape Crime Prosecutions," "No Crime or Charge— Just Jail for Negro," and "Albuquerque Police Hit with Rights Suit for Crippling Negro," all on p. 8 of the March 1970 issue (no. 267); "N.J. Police Suit Asks Receiver" and "CLU Raps St. Louis Police Practices," no. 269 (May 1970), p. 5; "Chi Police Raid School," *ibid.,* p. 8; "Grand Jury Slams Paterson Police, Confirms NJACLU's Abuse Charge," no. 259 (Dec. 1968),

p. 5; "Police Beat, Jail Student," no. 253 (Feb. 1968), p. 2; and "Epileptic Asks Damages for Police Beating During Seizure," no. 254 (March-April 1968), p. 3. Further: the abundant material cited under POLICE, POLICE BRUTALITY, and POLICE RIOT in the initial *API* number, *op. cit.*, p. 47–8. Further: the detailed account of "Police violence" on the UCLA campus prepared by the Chancellor's Commission on the Events of May 5, 1970, reprinted in the *UCLA Daily Bruin*, Jan. 19, 1971, p. 9–12, which alleges police attacks upon "many innocent persons," arrests "for no sensible reason," and invasion of two university buildings "for no useful purpose whatever." The report concludes that "the pattern of attack and arrest was discriminatory: the longhairs, the Blacks, the Mexican-Americans, the Asian-Americans and American Indians were prime targets; there was one illustration of anti–Semitism."

21. *Item:* SOCIAL PROBLEMS
sa Crime and criminals
Discrimination
Race discrimination
Race problems
Suicide [etc.] (p. 1192–93; Sears, p. 548)

Some 44 *sa* referents appear under this head. In the light of previous discussions and recommendations, more are needed to suitably contemporize the coverage.

Remedy: Add to the *sa* roster, after canceling "Race discrimination" and "Race problems":

> POLICE AND COMMUNITY
> POVERTY
> RACE RELATIONS
> RACISM

22. *Item:* PREVENTIVE DETENTION

> *Here are entered works on long-term detention as a correctional measure against habitual criminals. Works on the detention of suspects before trial are entered under the heading Arrest.*

x **Detention, Preventive**

xx **Arrest**
   Criminal Justice, Administration of
   Detention of persons
   Imprisonment
   Prisons
   Punishment
   Recidivists (p. 1025)

Whether "habitual criminals" can, in fact, be readily and unerringly identified, and how efficacious "preventive detention" is likely to prove in combating recidivisim are matters for jurists, lawyers, and penologists to determine. The theory and practice undoubtedly exist. And, as of mid–1970, some four bills on the subject were pending before the U.S. Congress. The LC treatment adequately conveys the *penological/administrative* dimension of the topic, but entirely fails to show its *legal* and *civil* libertarian aspects. Who could possibly imagine from the scope note and seven "xx" referents that "preventive detention" is equally the subject of profound ethical and juridical dispute, that the very *idea* has been denounced as "alien to the American concept of law-enforcement and our tradition"?[1] In short, there's more to the matter than meets LC's eye.

Remedy: (a) Introduce additional "xx's" for CIVIL RIGHTS, CONSTITUTIONAL LAW, and DUE PROCESS OF LAW.

(b) Since material on *pretrial* detention is ignominiously buried by LC under ARREST, although such imprisonment is often imposed for punitive or "preventive" reasons,[2] a new primary form is indicated:

PRETRIAL DETENTION
   x Detention, Pretrial

   xx Arrest
      Civil rights
      Constitutional law
      Detention of persons
      Due process of law

Imprisonment
Preventive detention
Prisons
Punishment

Notes (Item 22)

1. This is Arthur J. Goldberg's opinion, quoted in "Union Forms Group to Block Preventive Jail," *Civil Liberties,* no. 269 (May 1970), p. 5. The national ACLU, together with its National Capital Area affiliate, in a letter sent to all Congressmen, called one of the four pending bills "indistinguishable from a 60-day jail sentence imposed without a crime having been committed." *Ibid.*

2. Cf., for example, "Detention Without Trial," in Sachs, *op. cit.,* p. 23–7, which describes the practice in contemporary South Africa. For a recent American example of quasipunitive imprisonment inflicted on 21 Black defendants *awaiting trial,* but not "already judged guilty" in court, cf. Murray Kempton, "The Panthers on Trial," *New York Review of Books,* v. 14, no. 9 (May 7, 1970), p. 38–42. A form of pretrial-cum-preventive-detention especially common in the Soviet Union is to place "protesters," like General Grigorenko, in mental hospitals. The authorities, by declaring an undesirable "insane," thus seem to "observe 'the norms of Socialist legality.'" Cf. Victor Zorza, "1984 Arrives for Amalrik," *Guardian Weekly,* May 30, 1970, p. 5. Also: "Lenin centenary," a summary of the report by the British Section of Amnesty International which maintains that many dissident intellectuals are confined in "special psychiatric hospitals in the Soviet Union ... with or without trial...." *AIR; Amnesty International Review,* no. 31 (May 1970), p. 1–2.

23. *Item:* WIRETAPPING

sa Eavesdropping

×× Criminal investigation
Eavesdropping
Evidence (Law)
Evidence, Criminal
Telephone—Laws and regulations
(p. 1409)

Wire tapping is admitted to be a form of "eavesdropping." Eavesdropping on p. 397 is associated by an "××" with "Privacy, Right of." Why, then, is no connection made between *wiretapping* and the right of privacy? Because most *anyone* can eavesdrop, while wiretapping, which requires more sophisticated technology, is largely the preserve of governmental agencies? Or simply because no LC catalogers, fortuitously, have *been* wiretapped (just as none, thankfully, has been napalmed)?[1] Beyond that, the larger *issue* of wiretapping as a publicly-employed instrument to protect "national security" or secure criminal indictments goes unnoted, much as with "preventive detention." In brief, "wiretapping" is *not* merely one among many investigative techniques, nor solely a mode for securing evidence to be placed before judge-and-jury; it is also a means of coercion or repression, a Constitutionally questionable way for official bodies like the Department of Justice to gather information on "dissident" or "controversial" persons and groups. Indeed, there has been vigorous debate on both wiretapping as a *means* and the *ends* for which it is used.[2]

Remedy: Install "××'s" for CIVIL RIGHTS; CONSTITUTIONAL LAW; DUE PROCESS OF LAW; POLITICAL CRIMES AND OFFENSES; and PRIVACY, RIGHT OF.

Notes (Item 23)

1. It would be lamentable, however, if sensitivity to political and social questions were wholly contingent upon firsthand experience. It should not, for instance, be necessary to witness or undergo tear-gassing during a demonstration in order to appreciate both the physiological and *political* effects of such "control" methods. Still, it must be confessed that personal exposure of that nature—as the author learned from a gas-dispersed protest at the British High Commission in Lusaka in late July 1970—tends to heighten and crystallize one's perceptions. Which is not to suggest that a tear-gas canister should be exploded at LC for instructional purposes, but rather that catalogers might at least benefit from *other* people's experience in this sphere.

2. Cf., for example, "Dissenters Sue to Stop U.S. Wiretapping, Eavesdropping," *Civil Liberties,* no. 263 (Aug. 1969), p. 1+. The plaintiffs in this case, who asked a federal district court "to declare Justice Department and

Federal Bureau of Investigation wiretapping policies and practices unconstitutional" and "to prohibit all electronic surveillance of members of controversial organizations," included "nine anti-war, civil rights and black power" groups, among them the Congress for Racial Equality, American Servicemen's Union, and Catholic Peace Fellowship.

Section IV

Man/Woman/Sex

1. *Item:* WOMEN AS ACCOUNTANTS [ARCHITECTS, ARTISTS, ASTRONAUTS, SOLDIERS, etc.] (p. 1412–13; Sears, p. 631)

> It is quite true there are no limits to masculine egotism in ordinary life.
>
> —Lev Trotskii[1]

The same objection applies to these forms as to NEGROES AS BUSINESSMEN, etc. The "as" strongly suggests that women are not ordinarily competent or otherwise equipped to work at accountancy, bear arms, or fly to the moon. Implicit is the wholly indefensible stereotype that relegates women to "hearth and home."[2] Skeptics not convinced that the "as" is a reflex of male chauvinism are invited to cite comparable terms assigned to the other sex; e.g., MEN AS ACCOUNTANTS. But they needn't bother, of course. They aren't there.[3]

Remedy: As with the "Negroes" forms, remove the "as"; e.g., WOMEN ACCOUNTANTS [ARCHITECTS, ARTISTS, ASTRONAUTS, SOLDIERS, ETC.][4]

Notes (Item 1)

1. From *Problems of Life* (London: Methuen & Co., 1924), quoted by Sheila Rowbothams, "Alexandra Kollontai: Woman's Liberation and Revolutionary Love," *Spokesman,* no. 4 (June 1970), p. 30.

145

2. Fay Ainscow states that "Society has developed certain sex stereotypes that need realistic reexamination. One cliché assumption is that the
well-adjusted male should try to get ahead or be aggressive. If a female
seems aggressive, then it's often assumed that she's frustrated, is compen-
sating for some lack or she'll be labeled 'pushy.'" Cf. "Targets of Prejudice,"
Freethinker, v. 90, no. 13 (March 28, 1970), p. 103.

3. Anita R. Schiller, research assistant professor at the University of Illinois, forcefully underscores this critique:

> An interesting sidelight, which illustrates how out-of-touch with
> the times we are, is provided by the subject headings librarians
> have devised to categorize the attainments of women in the
> various professions: The Library of Congress ... for example,
> uses the term "Women *as* authors," not "Women authors";
> "Women *as* physicians," not "Women physicians"; "Women *as*
> librarians," not "Women librarians," etc.... While it is delight-
> ful to note the cross reference "Women, see also Charm," and
> disturbing to find the heading "Women as colonists," it is clear
> that this terminology, which arose in a bygone age, is not in
> keeping with present conditions.

Op. cit., p. 346. Emphasis in original. The author later includes among
a number of proposals for achieving female equality within the library profession a suggestion that "subject headings which reflect customary prejudice toward women should be reconsidered and revised," observing in particular that *"Library literature* used the term 'Women as librarians' until
1952, when the wording was changed to read 'Women librarians.'" *Ibid.,*
p. 349. Joan Marshall adds that the general "as" form "does not merely imply, it *states* that all segments of society other than white Christian males
who achieve (anything) are merely role-playing. Women *are* doctors; they
do not simply act *as* doctors." And she asks: "Why is WOMEN AS LIBRARIANS
included? Logically, given our profession and the construction of the list,
MEN AS LIBRARIANS should be a subject heading. In this field, at least, women
are the majority."

As another, later eruption of what may be called the masculinocentric
reflex note that the 1967 ACS on p. 166 innovated MEN NURSES as a primary
head without making even a cross-reference from "Men *as* nurses," though
they are statistically less common than women in that profession.

4. Where this produces a conflict with or duplication of certain inverted heads (e.g., AUTHORS, WOMEN), which heretofore have encompassed
mainly biographical material, prefer the already-established form, broaden-
ing its scope to now include "attainments of women as authors," etc. The
BHI furnishes numerous precedents; e.g., WOMEN ATHLETES, WOMEN

CLERGY, WOMEN DIRECTORS, WOMEN PEERS, WOMEN PILOTS. Cf., e.g., the 1968 cumulation, p. 514–15.

The 1967 ACS on p. 291 exacerbates the mischief by installing two new heads: WOMEN AS CONSUMERS and WOMEN AS PHOTOGRAPHERS, while the 1968 ACS on p. 492 still further worsens the situation with WOMEN AS AUTOMOBILE DRIVERS, WOMEN AS PUBLISHERS, and WOMEN AS SPIES.

2. *Item:* ABORTION
×× **Birth control**
Conception—Prevention
Criminal law
Fetus, Death of
Infanticide
Obstetrics
Offenses against the person
Sex and law (p. 3)

It is not the prime head itself, but rather the "××'s" that need repair, particularly "Infanticide" and "Offenses against the person." These two "related" heads, when cited under ABORTION, imply a judgment concerning a matter that has long been—and remains—in contention. In effect, they equate "Abortion," advocated by an impressive array of medical, civil libertarian, and women's groups, with "crime."[1]

Remedy: Excise both terms from the "××" roster and apply them as primary heads with great caution.

Note (Item 2)

1. For a highly objective, heavily documented overview, maintaining that "abortion guilt is, in large measure, culturally determined," cf. Edwin M. Schur, "Abortion," in American Academy of Political and Social Science, *Annals,* v. 376 (March 1968), p. 136–47. On the controversy itself, the *RG* for March 1968–Feb. 1969 (v. 28) on p. 2–3 offers no fewer than 18 citations. Cf. also: Donald Gould, "Abortion in Perspective," *New Statesman,* v. 78 (July 11, 1969), p. 42–3; Sheila Golden, "Abortion Now!,"

Madison Kaleidoscope, v. 2, no. 3 (Feb. 4, 1970), p. 1+; Jefferson Poland, "Death Issue," *Modern Utopian*, v. 3, no. 2 (Nov.-Dec. 1968), p. 34; Carol Driscoll, "The Abortion Problem," *Women; A Journal of Liberation*, v. 1, no. 2 (winter 1970), p. 7–9; Evelyn Frankford, "Social Workers & Abortion," *ibid.*, p. 18–9; "Union Hits Cal. Abortion Laws, Backs Rights of Women, MDs," *Civil Liberties*, no. 262 (June 1969), p. 4; John L. Broom, "Can Abortion Be Rationally Justified?," *Freethinker*, v. 90, no. 7 (Feb. 14, 1970), p. 53; Daniel Callahan, *Abortion: Law, Choice and Morality* (New York: Macmillan, 1970); American Friends Service Committee, *Who Shall Live? Man's Control Over Birth and Death* (New York: Hill & Wang, 1970); and "Is Abortion a Right?," three probes by Charles H. Bayer, K. Danner Clouser, John Moore and John Pamperin, *Christian Century*, v. 87, no. 20 (May 20, 1970), p. 624–31. Further: Lawrence Lader, *Abortion* (Boston: Beacon Press, 1967), which includes a lengthy "Bibliography and Sources," plus citations for relevant legal cases; and Group for the Advancement of Psychiatry, Committee on Psychiatry and Law, *The Right to Abortion; A Psychiatric View* (New York: Scribner's, 1970).

3. *Item:* WOMAN—RIGHTS OF WOMEN (p. 1412; Sears, p. 631)

> Woman is made the slave of a slave and is reckoned fit only for companionship in lust.
>
> —Eugene V. Debs[1]

> Eve's biological role was to bear children . . . her romantic role was to love her husband . . . her vocational role was to be second in command. . . . Wife, mother, homemaker, this is the appointed destiny of real womanhood.
>
> —Billy Graham[2]

It might not easily have been foreseen in 1966, but there has since arisen a vocal and powerful movement among women that transcends in its spirit and approach the conventional "feminist" demands or agitation for "rights." This new surge accents radical change within the whole society, with particular emphasis on restructuring the institutions of "family" and "marriage."[3] "Women," in short, "are asking for nothing less than the total transformation of the world."[4] The old head may well enough cover the earlier, "feminist" period, but it does not adequately handle the new era.

Remedy: Add a subhead, —LIBERATION, or introduce another entry, WOMEN'S LIBERATION MOVEMENT, with both an "xx" and *sa* for WOMEN—RIGHTS OF WOMEN, as well as RADICALISM AND RADICALS.[5]

Notes (Item 3)

1. Quoted by Eric Bentley, "The Red, White, and Black; A Patriotic Demonstration," *Liberation*, v. 15, no. 3 (1970), p. 39.

2. Quoted from a *Ladies' Home Journal* article in *The Ethiopian Herald*, v. 8, no. 270 (Nov. 24, 1970), p. 3.

3. It has already spawned a host of magazines, articles, and studies; as examples, cf. Maxine Williams, "Black Women and the Struggle for Liberation," *Militant*, v. 34, no. 26 (July 3, 1970), p. 12–3; the *Milwaukee Kaleidoscope's* "Woman Liberation Special," v. 2, no. 23 (7 Nov. 1969); Marlene Dixon, "Why Women's Liberation?," *Ramparts*, v. 8, no. 6 (Dec. 1969), p. 57–63; Susan Brownmiller, "Sisterhood Is Powerful," *New York Times Magazine*, March 15, 1970, p. 26+; Ellen Gay Detlefsen and Patricia Schuman, "The Women's Liberation Movement—I," *WLB*, v. 44, no. 9 (May 1970), p. 962+; Sheila Rowbotham, *op. cit.*, Bonnie Eisenberg, "Women's Liberation and Self-Defense," *IS* (i.e., *International Socialist*), no. 16 (Feb. 1970), p. 20; "Berkeley Campus Women's Liberation Program," *ibid.*, Carol Rosenbaum, "Sex Segregation: On the Job and in the Schools," *ibid.*, p. 9; Alice S. Rossi, "Sex Equality: The Beginnings of Ideology," *Humanist* (Buffalo, N.Y.), v. 29, no. 5 (Sept.-Oct. 1969), p. 3–6+; the "literature kit" on "Women's Liberation" prepared in early 1970 by *Our Generation, op. cit.*; and "Women's Liberation," a radical précis of the new movement by a pseudonymous "Eve," *Sechaba*, v. 4, no. 6 (June 1970), p. 15–7. Also: the 30 inexpensive items from various offbeat publishers cited under "Women's Liberation and Sexual Oppression" in *Critical Politics, op. cit.*, p. 6; the listings under "Women's Liberation" in Muller, 2nd ed., *op. cit.*; and issues of the 5-times-yearly *Women: A Journal of Liberation* (3011 Guilford Avenue, Baltimore, Md. 21218), of which the first three numbers (v. 1, nos. 1–3) were titled, respectively, "Inherent Nature or Cultural Conditioning?," "What Is Liberation?," and "Women in History: A Recreation of Our Past." Further: Evelyn Reed, *Problems of Women's Liberation*, 5th ed. (New York: Pathfinder Press, 1970); Robin Morgan, ed., *Sisterhood Is Powerful; An Anthology of Writings from the Women's Liberation Movement*

(New York: Vintage Books, 1970); Branka Magas, "Women's Liberation," *New Left Review*, no. 61 (May/June 1970), p. 31–4, which holds that "what separates the feminist from the revolutionary at present is the lack of a theory of the specificity of women's oppression, and its relationship to other forms of exploitation"; Jenny Sims and Valerie Hart, "Birmingham Women's Liberation Group," *Peace News*, no. 1775 (July 3, 1970), p. 3; Jan Williams, "Emerging from Passive Female Shells," *ibid.*, p. 6; the roster of 26 active "Women's Lib. Groups in Britain," *ibid.;* Carol Brown and Celeste West, "News from the Front," *Synergy*, no. 27 (May-June 1970), p. 35, a supplement to their initial, annotated bibliography in the Dec. 1969 issue; and Sonya Okoth, "Liberation Must Also Include the Women of Africa," *Africa and the World*, v. 6, no. 60 (June 1970), p. 17–9.

    4. "Editorial," *ibid.*, v. 1, no. 2 (winter 1970), inside front cover.

    5. The *RG* early in 1970 recognized this necessity, instituting WOMEN'S LIBERATION MOVEMENT as an independent head. Cf., e.g., v. 69, no. 22 (Feb. 10, 1970), p. 340. *API* uses the shorter form, WOMEN'S LIBERATION, *op. cit.*, p. 67.

4. *Item:* DELINQUENT WOMEN (p. 358)

Since unused terms like "Female offenders," "Woman—Crime," "Women as criminals," and "Woman offenders" all refer to DELINQUENT WOMEN, the implication, an apparent reflex of male gallantry with an admixture of condescension, is that members of the "fairer sex" can't possibly commit bona fide delicts or pursue a genuinely criminal life in the fashion that *men* can. "Delinquent," as any dictionary reveals, occupies a much lower rung on the sociopathological ladder than "criminal." LC practice assigns female felons to the same category as wayward children and youths.[1] If candor is to take precedence over Camelot-like chivalry, our subject lists must discard such forms of "favorable" discrimination and acknowledge—as in this case—that *some* women are just as capable of serious misbehavior as *some* men.[2]

    Remedy: (a) Excise DELINQUENT WOMEN.

    (b) Introduce two new heads: MALE CRIMINALS and FEMALE CRIMINALS.[3]

    (c) Abandon "Women as criminals" and "Woman—Crime" as

See referents, replacing them with "Women criminals" and "Women —Crime."

Notes (Item 4)

1. Cf. DELINQUENT GIRLS and DELINQUENTS, p. 358.
2. Joan Marshall comments further that the construction "implies that women are not full and equal members of society and cannot therefore commit a crime against society; women, instead, have certain duties in society which they may be *delinquent* in performing. This implication is patently untrue." Personal communication, *op. cit.*
3. CATHOLIC CRIMINALS, JEWISH CRIMINALS, and NEGRO CRIMINALS—all discussed earlier—constitute precedents for such an adjectival form, as does the 1968 *BHI*'s WOMEN CRIMINALS, p. 514.

5. *Items:* HOMOSEXUALITY
xx **Sexual perversion (p. 598)**
LESBIANISM
xx **Sexual perversion (p. 734)**

With the advent of the Wolfenden Report, the liberalization in many lands of laws regarding homosexual relations, and recent birth of an outspoken, self-confident "Gay Liberation Movement," the stigma traditionally attached to homosexuality has markedly lessened, and—among the more enlightened—vanished.[1] Increasingly, homosexuality has come to be regarded as only one among many varieties of sexual or social liaison, not intrinsically better or worse than the others. "Perversion," however, unmistakably brands it "worse," a form of "corruption" or "maladjustment." The referent thus smears and blemishes a large and already much-harrassed body of men and women, whose habits may be different, but not therefore more dangerous, disagreeable, or censurable, than those of the heterosexual majority.

Remedy: Delete "Sexual perversion" as an "xx" under both heads, and similary eliminate "Homosexuality" and "Lesbianism" as *sa*'s under the prime head SEXUAL PERVERSION (p. 1167).

Note (Item 5)

1. Carl Wittman's "Gay Manifesto," in *Liberation,* v. 14, no. 10 (Feb. 1970), pointedly declares that "Homosexuality is *not* a lot of things. It is not a makeshift in the absence of the opposite sex; it is not hatred or rejection of the opposite sex; it is not genetic; it is not the result of broken homes except inasmuch as we could see the sham of American marriage. *Homosexuality is the capacity to love someone of the same sex*" (p. 18–24). Emphasis in original. Cf. also: the "Gay Liberation Supplement" to the 13–26 Feb. 1970 *Milwaukee Kaleidoscope* (v. 2, no. 26); Great Britain. Committee on Homosexual Offences and Prostitution. *Report* (London: H.M.S.O., 1957; Command paper 247); issues of *Red Butterfly,* a "radical gay newsletter," which began publication in March 1970 (Box 3445, Grand Central Station, New York, N.Y. 10017); the "Homosexual" section in Muller, 2nd ed., *op. cit.:* and Bill Katz's annotations for *The Ladder; A Lesbian Review* and *Tangents, op. cit.,* p. 105. Don Slater, *Tangents* editor, estimates the homosexual population in the U.S. at 17,000,000. The magazine's editorial viewpoint, says Katz, is "clear: the homosexual is a human being who should not be treated as a criminal or far-out sexual deviate." *Ibid.* Gore Vidal further underpins this view in the course of exploding the myriad myths surrounding bi-, homo-, and heterosexual activity. *Op. cit.,* p. 8–14.

Editor David Reynolds, in the April 18, 1970, *Freethinker* (v. 90, no. 16), maintains that "Psychologists are fast agreeing that sexual deviation is not the manifestation of a diseased mind. By what authority," he asks, "does the [Church of England Evangelical] Council class homosexuals as perverts and presumably heterosexuals as sexually perfect? Are they not both equally perfect within their own definitions of the term?" (p. 122).

Great Britain, through the Sexual Offences Act of 1967, legalized "homosexual relations in private between consenting adult men." Cf. Denis Cabell, "Thou shalt not...," *Freethinker,* v. 90, no. 20 (May 16, 1970), p. 156.

6. *Items:* MONASTIC AND RELIGIOUS LIFE; MONASTIC AND RELIGIOUS LIFE OF WOMEN (p. 842)

One need not be a Catholic to appreciate that there are—and have been for centuries—monastic orders for men *and* women, "brothers" *and* "sisters." Yet by specifying a head for "Women," it appears that *male* orders are the norm, the usual, the unexceptional, while female varieties are *ab*normal, *un*usual, etc., which is hardly the case in fact.[1] "Sisters" ought rightly to take umbrage at the suggestion that "brothers" are somehow more *natural* and *proper*.

Remedy: Either delete MONASTIC AND RELIGIOUS LIFE OF WOMEN or complement it with MONASTIC AND RELIGIOUS LIFE OF MEN, allowing the unqualified MONASTIC AND RELIGIOUS LIFE to apply strictly to works dealing on a general plane with life in monasteries and convents.

Note (Item 6)

1. Indeed, some authorities hold that such women's groups probably *antedated* similar organizations among men. Says the *Encyclopaedia Britannica:*

> In all ages, women, hardly less than men, have played their part in monasticism. In the earliest Christian times the veiled virgins formed a grade or order apart, more formally separated from the community than were the male ascetics. There is reason for believing that there were organized convents for women before there were any for men, for when St. Anthony left the world in 270 to embrace the ascetic life, the *Vita* says he placed his sister in a nunnery.... We learn from Palladius that by the end of the 4th century nunneries were numerous all over Egypt, and they existed also in Palestine, in Italy and in Africa—in fact throughout the Christian world. In the West the Benedictine nuns played a great part in the Christian settlement of northwestern Europe. As the various monastic and mendicant orders arose, a female branch was in most cases formed alongside the order.

"Monasticism" (London/Chicago: Encyclopaedia Britannica, Ltd., 1964), v. 15, p. 690.

7. *Items:* FALL OF MAN (p. 466)

Why assail this obviously theological head under "Man/Woman/Sex"? Women themselves, more sensitive than men to the wide ranging implications of the "forbidden fruit" tale, furnish a convincing rationale:

> Something more than technology or reproduction must explain the kind of myths and attitudes which have devalued women. For example, many religions perpetuate abusive concepts: the myth that Eve caused the fall of man, or that the Orthodox Jew in a morning prayer thanks God that he was not born a woman.[1]

Of course, the library profession through its cataloging practice cannot by itself undo the pernicious "Fall of Man" concept. Further, it would be dishonest to cast the form, together with the works it describes, down an Orwellian "memory hole." Still, the abusive overtones can be somwhat reduced.

Remedy: Add a gloss: (JUDAEO-CHRISTIAN MYTHOLOGY) or (BIBLICAL MYTHOLOGY).

Note (Item 7)

1. "Editorial," *Women; A Journal of Liberation, op. cit.*

8. *Item:* CHILDBIRTH—PSYCHOLOGY (p. 218)

The scope note under CHILDBIRTH elucidates when this subhead is to be used:

> *Works on the system of psychological preparation for childbirth, referred to as "natural childbirth," are entered under the heading* Childbirth—Psychology.[1]

It's hard to believe that a woman created (or approved) this form, for most presumably know that "natural childbirth" is a system involving not only "psychological," but also *physical* "preparation," largely by means of special exercises. Even more seriously, perhaps, the LC form severely constricts the significance of "natural childbirth" for many women. The benefits derived may also be of a social and even economic and political order. "Psychology" most inadequately embraces these several dimensions, let along the obvious *physiological* aspect of probably-lessened pain.[2]

Remedy: Add to CHILDBIRTH the subhead —TRAINING or, preferably, elevate the unused form CHILDBIRTH, NATURAL to primary status, abandoning CHILDBIRTH—PSYCHOLOGY as the rubric for material on this multidimensional topic.[3]

Notes (Item 8)

1. P. 218.

2. Comments Vicki Pollard: "Natural childbirth training does help women do what doctors won't do. It teaches women to control their own bodies and how to help themselves in childbirth rather than depending on some man. Having a baby means using muscles that are otherwise rarely used. A woman doesn't know how to use these muscles unless she practices regularly before her labor. It's as ridiculous to expect a woman in modern, urban society to have a baby with no training as it would be to expect a person to run five miles without ever building up to it. But doctors will not tell you this because they see women as objects whose purpose is to produce babies, and they never question the fact that women should suffer in childbirth. Trained childbirth doesn't mean that all women will have a painless experience. Many women have been so badly frightened about childbirth and about their own bodies that they will always have a difficult time. But all women will have a much easier birth than they would have had without the training. They will be able to make any necessary decisions for themselves throughout the birth, and feel that they are in control." Cf. "Producing Society's Babies," *Women; A Journal of Liberation,*"v. 1, no. 1 (fall 1969), p. 20.

3. The scope note will require alteration, as well, most appropriately by removing the second sentence. The cross-references under —PSYCHOLOGY should then be expanded by adding both an *sa* and "××" for "Childbirth, Natural." The new form itself will need an "××" for "Natural childbirth."

Index Medicus, issued by the National Library of Medicine, employs NATURAL CHILDBIRTH as a primary head. Cf., e.g., v. 11, no. 4 (April 1970), p. 406.

9. *Item:* FREE LOVE
   sa **Concubinage**
   ×× **Concubinage (p. 514)**

Comstock, Bowdler, and other sin-obsessed guardians of public morals, convinced that sexual relations—at best—are "dirty" and chastity *ipso facto* virtuous,[1] would rejoice at the Free Love = Concubinage formula, while humbug-shattering libertarians like H. L. Mencken or Bertrand Russell would no doubt think it downright silly. What, essentially, does "free love"—or the more up-to-date term, "sexual freedom"—actually *mean*? Simply, according to Webster, "sexual intercourse or cohabitation without a legal wedding."[2] Even more importantly: sexual intercourse or cohabitation among *consenting* partners. *Without* consent, the "intercourse" is "rape," for which LC furnishes an independent head.[3] If *bought*, it becomes "Prostitution," also assigned a distinct rubric.[4] "Free love" or "sexual freedom" may surely involve extended cohabitation among unwedded partners, but the doctrine and its practitioners emphatically reject "guilt," "subserviency," "bondage," and "primitivism"—all usually associated with "concubinage"[5]—as elements or outgrowths of such a relationship. The "concubinage" referents, leftovers from an epoch demolished—literally, in any event—by *Ulysses, Lady Chatterley's Lover,* and *Tropic of Cancer,* both denigrate sexual activity and distort the historical, as well as post–Kinsey, significance of "free love."[6]

   Remedy: (a) Abolish "Concubinage" as an "××" and "*sa.*"

   (b) Establish "Sexual freedom" as an "×" under FREE LOVE, or—to fully modernize the treatment—replace FREE LOVE with SEXUAL FREEDOM, supplying an "×" for the former term.[7]

Notes (Item 9)

1. For a short, pungent discussion of the hackneyed notion that sexual pleasure satisfies one of the "lower instincts," and the resulting adulation of chastity or celibacy, cf. William Welsh, "Virginity Cult," *Freethinker,* v. 90, no. 19 (May 9, 1970), p. 148–49.
   2. P. 906.
   3. P. 1078.

4. P. 1038.

5. Cf. Webster, p. 472; *Shorter Oxford English Dictionary on Historical Principles*, 3d ed. (Oxford: Clarendon Press, 1964), v. 1, p. 363.

In a finite historical context, van den Berghe speaks of the "concubinage" practiced by Spanish men with "women of lower status" in colonial Mexico. The European laity, he notes, "condoned" such an interracial arrangement, this attitude being "congruent with the traditional *dual standard of Spanish sexual morality.*" *Race and Racism, op. cit.*, p. 46. Emphasis added. Later he tells of how the Portuguese planters in colonial Brazil engaged in "promiscuous concubinage with female slaves," a form of exploitation typical of "paternalistic" social structures. *Ibid.*, p. 65–6, 27–9.

6. The fact that Swiss Television in mid–1970 included a discussion of "Free Love" in a program dealing with "the emancipation of women" suggests a definite connection between sexual freedom and women's liberation. The show, however, was cancelled "at the last moment" when a former federal judge complained. Which also suggests the continuing strength of Comstockery. Cf. *IPI Report,* v. 18/19, no. 12/1 (April-May 1970), p. 12.

7. For an annotated list of "sexual freedom" magazines, cf. the section so-named in Muller, 2nd ed., *op. cit.*

10. *Item:* DIVORCE
×× **Woman—Social and moral questions (p. 378; Sears, p. 206)**

A double standard erupts once more in this head. Why divorce should qualify as a "social" or "moral" question for *women* and *not* for men is a conundrum answerable only in terms of masculine supremacy. And there are other problems, as well: (1) As Joan Marshall argues below, the subhead —SOCIAL AND MORAL QUESTIONS is misplaced under the "generic" WOMAN; and (2) As shown earlier with respect to "Negroes," the "moral" situation of women—particularly since it is not paralleled with any form covering the moral situation of *men*—represents an affront to womankind that reeks of paternalism.

Remedy: (a) Cancel —SOCIAL AND MORAL QUESTIONS as a subhead under WOMAN, creating in its stead the subdivision —SOCIAL CONDITIONS under WOMEN.

(b) Install under MEN the subhead —SOCIAL CONDITIONS.

(c) Under DIVORCE, either delete the new form "Women—Social conditions" as an "××," or complement it with "Men—Social conditions."

11. *Item:* LITERATURE, IMMORAL (p. 751; Sears, p. 368)

> Any adult should resent any other adult telling him what he may or may not read. When such a thing happens in the complete absence of any rational justification, it is time to say "Enough!!"[1]

It becomes abundantly clear from the *sa* referents, as well as the various works actually assigned this head, that LC has accepted whole-hog the Mrs. Grundy/"Nosey Parker" dictum that pleasureful sex or undisguised eroticism (as distinct from "soft" sex in TV commercials and magazine advertisements) is automatically tantamount to *im*morality.[2] By what authority, pray tell, does LC, or anyone else, determine that an erotic novel or volume of poetry is—purely *because* of its sex content—immoral?[3] The pornography/vice, obscenity/crime nexus is itself in no wise established. The very terms are presently subject to much legal and scientific dispute.[4] Moreover, given increasingly frank, "permissive," or—as some have suggested—"civilized" publishing and librarians consequently beleaguered by the censorious to keep ill-defined "smut" off their shelves, such a flagrantly puritanical, antediluvian head only donates ammunition to the "purity"-mongers and represents a clearcut form of professional suicide.[5] While "sex" *per se* undoubtedly offends some people, it remains the *sine qua non* for continued life and a source of real satisfaction—as liquor drinking, cigarette smoking, and watching football games may also be—for untold millions. This simple truism may upset the taboo-shackled Mrs. Grundy. But LC is under no obligation to pander to her, nor to besmirch a time-honored human pastime and procreative necessity.[6] In truth, it *is* time to say, "*Enough!!*"

Remedy: Cancel the head. Adequate alternatives already exist in EROTIC LITERATURE (p. 441), EROTIC POETRY (1967 ACS, p. 90), SEX IN THE BIBLE (July 1964–Dec. 1965 ACS, p. 203), LOVE IN LITERATURE (p. 760), SEX IN LITERATURE (p. 1166), OBSCENITY (LAW) (p. 908), LITERATURE AND MORALS (p. 751), SEXUAL PERVERSION IN LITERATURE (p. 1167), VULGARITY IN LITERATURE (p. 1382), and SEDUCTION IN LITERATURE (p. 1155).

Notes (Item 11)

1. G. L. Simons, "The Next Step," *Freethinker,* v. 90, no. 3 (Jan. 17, 1970), p. 19.

2. Among the four *sa*'s appear "Erotic Literature" and "Sex in Literature." The newly-created form, EROTICA (1969 ACS, p. 74), also features telltale *sa*'s to "Literature, Immoral" and "Obscenity (Law)."

Books catalogued under this head include Ralph Ginsburg, *An Unhurried View of Erotica;* with an introduction by Theodore Reik and preface by George Jean Nathan (New York: Heinemann, 1958); Eberhard Kronhausen, *Pornography and the Law; The Psychology of Erotic Realism and Pornography* (New York: Ballantine Books, 1959); and Henry Miller, *L'Obscenité et la Loi de Réflexion* (Paris: P. Seghers, 1949). Sources: *Library of Congress Catalog. Books: Subjects, 1955–1959* (Paterson, N.J.: Pageant Books, 1960), v. 12, p. 618–19; and *Library of Congress Catalog. Books: Subjects 1950–1954* (New York: Rowman & Littlefield, 1964), v. 12, p. 28.

3. Evidence from other times and places starkly illumines our peculiar monomania concerning "obscenity" and "immorality," disclosing its erotophobic, sex-denying essence and suggesting new, supracultural definitions. K. M. Munshi observes that in Sanskrit literature "we come across descriptions of love scenes which do not conform to the values of modern prudery. The *Gita-Govinda,* for instance, describes the amours of Radha and Krishna very frankly. The work became a classic in India, but was never censured on that account. Even our greatest poet, Kalidasa, than whom there has been no greater exponent of self-restraint, could invest sexual relations with classic brevity: 'Who, that has once tasted the joys will be able to abandon her who has bared her hips?' Here in a single verse Kalidasa voices the longings of that Yaksha *which is natural to man in all ages and in all countries.*" "Would any critic," he asks, "dare say that it is inartistic or unpoetic, because prudery is ashamed to read it?" Cf. "The Saga of Indian Sculpture," in A. Goswani, ed., *Indian Temple Sculpture* (Calcutta: Rupa & Co., 1959), p. 356. Emphasis added.

4. Cf., for example, Charles Rembar, *The End of Obscenity* (New York: Random House, 1968); the contributions by Ervin J. Gaines, Robert B.

Downs, Edward de Grazia, Henry Miller Madden, and Evelyn Geller to
Eric Moon's 1969 anthology, *Book Selection and Censorship in the Sixties*
(New York: Bowker); "Four-letter Words: A Symposium," *Humanist*
(Buffalo, N.Y.), v. 29, no. 5 (Sept.-Oct. 1969), p. 7–8+; G. L. Simons, *op.
cit.*, who declares that "no correlation has been found between an inclina-
tion to pornography and a tendency to sexual delinquency"; and "Inquest
on Pornography," the report by the Danish Forensic Medical Council to the
Danish Penal Code Council, which, having concluded that "no scientific
experiments exist which can lay a basis for the assumption that pornography
or 'obscene' pictures and films contribute to the committing of sexual
offences by normal adults or young people," proved instrumental in changing the pornography statutes in Denmark, *Humanist* (London), v. 85, no. 2
(Feb. 1970), p. 44–5.

5. The "lewd," "dirty" works assaulted by prudes or, more generously,
"decency-fighters" during recent years range from the D. H. Lawrence
classic, *Lady Chatterley's Lover*, Henry Miller's highly-influential *Tropic of
Cancer*, LeRoi Jones' short, provocative drama *The Slave*, William
Golding's *Lord of the Flies*, and Hubert Selby's grimly candid *Last Exit to
Brooklyn* to J. D. Salinger's "vulgar" *Catcher in the Rye*, Herman Hesse's *De-
mian* (assertedly part of a "worldwide plot by Satan"), James Baldwin's
Another Country (assailed as "obscene" in New Orleans and elsewhere),
William Burroughs' *Naked Lunch* (an opus of acknowledged "literary and
social importance"), Lorraine Hansberry's play *Raisin in the Sun*, Claude
Brown's much-recommended memoir of ghetto life, *Manchild in the Promised
Land*, and the "trashy" *Dictionary of American Slang*. Sources: Rembar, *op.
cit.; Newsletter on Intellectual Freedom*, v. 18, no. 1 (Jan. 1969), p. 15, 18; *Cen-
sorship Today*, v. 1, no. 3 (n.d.), p. 47–8; *ibid.*, v. 2, no. 2 (April/May 1969),
p. 30–1; Moon, *op. cit.*, p. 246–48, 290–91, 329; and John Holt, "To the
Rescue," *New York Review of Books*, v. 13, no. 6 (Oct. 9, 1969), p. 27–8.

6. Reviewing Rembar's opus in the Jan. 1969 *Newsletter on Intellectual
Freedom*, one librarian commented thusly upon our "national obsession
with sex-cum-sin": "Frankly, it appears baffling—in an age of napalm, mass
murder, concentration camps, and possible nuclear holocaust—that so
much anxiety and energy are expended on what, in this perspective, seems
relatively trivial. Further, the whole argument regarding the alleged pernicious effects of pornography on the moral fabric of society becomes increasingly ludicrous as more and more evidence arrives from little, Lutheran
Denmark, which last summer abolished obscenity laws altogether and thus
reduced the consumption of pornography." Cf. Sanford Berman, "No End
Yet," v. 18, no. 1, p. 19. Emphasis in original.

Analyzing the "change in the climate of opinion" that fomented the
Roth decision, Ervin J. Gaines notes that "Christian opposition to birth control, and indeed to any tampering with traditional sexual codes (masturbation,

abortion, homosexuality, adultery, fornication, etc.) in the name of higher law, began to seem irrelevant in the face of threat to human survival; at the same time there set in a strong tide of opinion favorable toward civil rights, privacy, and the sanctity of individual decisions with respect to self as distinct from society.... The 'pill' and the widespread publicity to it in the mass media increased the confidence of men and women to make their own decisions about their lives, whatever church or state might decree...." Cf. "Intellectual Freedom from *Roth* to the Presidential Commission on Obscenity and Pornography," in Moon, *op. cit.,* p. 238.

Anyone who chooses to defend the LC form should be prepared to rebut G. L. Simons' contention that "in general unless pleasure harms other people it is wrong to assess it in moral terms. There is no such thing as immoral pleasure *per se.* If a number of people go to see a nude painting for artistic reasons and enjoy it, then great! If people go for sexual titillation and get it, then great! Why should sexual titillation be frowned upon as a literary or artistic experience?... Of course, there are distinctions in the quality of literature—but are there *moral* distinctions? Human beings are capable ... of a wide range of pleasurable emotions. Why should it be right to try to evoke some of these by the written word and wrong to evoke others?" Cf. "In Praise of Pleasure," *Freethinker,* v. 89, no. 48 (Nov. 29, 1969), p. 381. Emphasis in original. The last word belongs to Supreme Court Justice William Douglas, who sagely observed that "A person without sex thoughts is abnormal. Sex thoughts may induce sex practices that make for better marital relations." Quoted by Irving Wallace, "A Problem Author Looks at Problem Librarians," in Moon, *op. cit.,* p. 262. From this viewpoint, LC—by linking sex with immorality—thereby endorses *ab*normality as a societal norm.

12. *Item:* NUDE IN ART
×× Art, Immoral (p. 903)

Among authorities on visual art, a debate has long flourished between the sex-arousal = dirt school and those who maintain that erotic feelings engendered by viewing a nude painting or sculpture ought not to produce guilt nor qualms in the beholder. An English philosopher, S. Alexander, most forthrightly propounded the anti-sex opinion. "If the nude is so treated," he said, "that it raises in the spectator ideas or desires appropriate to the material subject, it is false art, and bad morals."[1] It is this posture that LC implicitly endorses in ART, IMMORAL as both a primary head (p. 76) and "××" under NUDE IN ART. It is not, however, a position widely shared by critics or even by lay devotees, who may admire a Greek sculpture or Goya canvas as much for its elemental sex content as for its artistic execution. Kenneth Clark, a leading authority, has asked:

> Is there, after all, any reason why certain quasi-geometrical shapes should be satisfying except that they are simplified statements of the forms that please us in a woman's body? . . . This unexpected union of sex and geometry is a proof of how deeply the concept of the nude is linked with our most elementary notions of order and design.[2]

Mario Praz poses the further question: "Who can guarantee that even the least realistic representations of the nude are not capable of arousing the spectator?"[3] And then cites Clark's rebuttal to the Alexander thesis:

> In the mixture of memories and sensations aroused by the nudes of Rubens or Renoir are many which are 'appropriate to the material subject.' And since these words of a famous philosopher are often quoted, it is necessary to labour the obvious and say that no nude, however abstract, should fail to arouse in the spectator some vestige of erotic feeling, even although it be only the faintest shadow—and if it does not do so, it is bad art and false morals.[4]

The association of impropriety if not sin with entirely normal sex-reactions to nude art, a remnant of obsolete dowdyism, needs to be expurgated from the LC scheme.[5]

Remedy: Eliminate ART, IMMORAL as a primary head, with its consequent deletion under NUDE IN ART, SEX IN ART, and VICE. Two already existing forms, ART AND MORALS and OBSCENITY (LAW), should suffice as rubrics for material otherwise assigned this wonderfully prissy and outdated construction that for some time has wholly failed to reflect "contemporary community standards."

Notes (Item 12)

1. Quoted by Mario Praz, "Sex and Erotica," *Encyclopedia of World Art* (New York: McGraw-Hill, 1958), v. 12, p. 890.

2. Quoted by Praz, *ibid.*

3. *Ibid.*

4. Quoted in *ibid.*

5. The Indian example may again prove instructive. Munshi says of certain Mauryan sculptures, dating from about the 1st century B.C., that "voluptuousness and passion are as important as grace and spiritual calm." Much art, he claims, of the Andhra School in particular, was "dominated by the joy of life. Frankly sensuous, almost bursting with dynamism, the human figure represents its most brilliant phase." *Op. cit.,* p. 12–3. Speaking of a later period, he notes that the *Mithunas,* "the amorous lovers of Konarak, carved as they are in innumerable poses, and with unabashed realism have evoked considerable criticism." Regarding these criticisms of "amorous carvings," however, he enters "a caveat against people of one generation, brought up with its own standard of taste, sitting in judgment on the taste of another generation, a different age or a different social or aesthetic tradition. *There is no universal criterion,*" he emphasizes, "*of taste or delicacy for all things at all times.* Such critics are apt to forget that ascetics strictly pledged to life-long celibacy and ardent reformers preaching high moral principles have never, in the past, protested against what is now termed as 'obscene representation.'" He then states a few core questions, which to-day's censors, those so quick to brand sensuous art "immoral," should be compelled to answer:

> Is it not possible that these sculptures possess a significance which has been lost to us? Would it not be better to assume that the masters, who carved the sculptural wonders, did not realise that their masterpieces would be looked at *by those to whom the beauty of the human body would not be admirable; to whom universal creativeness could not be presented without evoking lewdness?*

Ibid., p. 34–5. Emphasis added. On the religious and philosophical tradition from which these specific sculptures emanated, a tradition accenting "the life-force pouring into the Universe . . . , manifesting itself no less in the gross matter of daily experience than in the divine beings of religious vision," cf. the extended remarks on p. 35.

13. *Item:* FRATERNITY SONGS
× Sorority songs (p. 513)

The male dominance inherent in this form needs no explication.

Remedy: Either establish another prime head, SORORITY SONGS, or convert FRATERNITY SONGS into an omnibus form: FRATERNITY AND SORORITY SONGS.[1]

Note (Item 13)

1. Time has wrought little improvement in this sphere. Cf. the new head, FRATERNITY LIBRARIES (1966 ACS, p. 61), which—like FRATERNITY SONGS—either requires a complementary form, SORORITY LIBRARIES, or may be expanded to FRATERNITY AND SORORITY LIBRARIES.

14. *Item:* WIFE BEATING
×× **Criminal law (p. 1403)**

Judging from the single "××," the (presumably) male author of this head didn't think the act worth much attention. The "beaten" wife, however, and her sisters may justly think otherwise.

Remedy: Add "××'s" for "Husband and wife" (p. 609), "Offenses against the person" (p. 912), "Wives" (p. 1410), and "Women—Social conditions."

15. *Items:* MAN   WOMAN

MAN	WOMAN
sa Anthropology	*sa* Charm
Anthropometry	Family
Color of man	Girls
Craniology	Mothers
Creation	Postage stamps—
Ethnology	Topics—Women
Heredity	Single women
Men	Teachers' wives
Men in literature	Young women
Persons	*also* Artists [Authors,
Philosophical	Musicians, etc.]
anthropology	Women; Women

×× **Anthropology**
Creation
Men
Primates (p. 773)

as artists [au-
thors, poets,
etc.]; Women in
art; Women in
charitable work;
and similar
headings

× **Female**
Feminism

×× **Anthropology**
Family
Girls
Sociology
Young women
(p. 1411)[1]

The term "Man" is used generically. *See also* references are made
from it to MEN and MEN IN LITERATURE, but not to WOMAN or WOMEN;
however, this is a minor and easily corrected fault. The term "Men"
refers to the male half of the generic "Man."[2] WOMAN, by logical
analogy, should also be a generic term. A comparison of the references
under the two heads, however, clearly indicates that LC's use of the
term WOMAN is extremely ambiguous. The "×" for "Female"
(although there is no such "×" for "Male" under MAN), and the
"××'s" for "Anthropology" and "Sociology" are the only referenced
terms that do not refer to attributes or aspects of particular women
or groups of women, rather than to the *universal* woman.

Remedy: (a) Add "Woman" and "Women" as *sa*'s under
MAN, together with an "×" for "Male."

(b) Excise all the present referents under WOMAN, except for
"Female," "Anthropology," and "Sociology." The deleted items
may be transferred to WOMEN.

Notes (Item 15)

1. The discussions and "remedies" for items 15 through 20 were largely
prepared by Joan K. Marshall, cataloger at Brooklyn College Library.

2. Although it may be wondered if MEN—MORTALITY (p. 805) should not be MAN—MORTALITY, since a comparable subdivision is not found under WOMAN or WOMEN.

16. *Item:* WOMAN—ANATOMY AND PHYSIOLOGY (p. 1411)

Since female "anatomy and physiology" certainly differ from the male varieties, this is a valid subdivision of the generic WOMAN. However, as the heading now stands, the reader interested in *female* anatomy and physiology must use *two* subject heads to get at the basic material in the collection, in that many works on *human* anatomy (unless females aren't "human") will deal with the anatomy of both sexes. This heading, as so many others in the list, illustrates the bias toward accepting the male as the norm: human = male.

Remedy: (a) Eliminate —ANATOMY AND PHYSIOLOGY as a subhead under WOMAN.

(b) Establish under ANATOMY, HUMAN (p. 50) two new subdivisions: —MALE and —FEMALE, with "×'s" for "Man—Anatomy" and "Woman—Anatomy."

(c) Presuming that PHYSIOLOGY (p. 981) is intended to cover both humans *and* animals (since no PHYSIOLOGY, HUMAN appears in the list), institute two new subdivisions under this head: —MALE and —FEMALE, with "×'s" for "Man—Physiology" and "Woman—Physiology."

(d) Institute under BODY, HUMAN (p. 143) two new subdivisions:

—MALE	—FEMALE
sa Anatomy, Human— Male	*sa* Anatomy, Human— Female
Physiology—Male	Physiology—Female
× Human body—Male	× Human body—Female
×× Anatomy, Human— Male	×× Anatomy, Human— Female
Physiology—Male	Physiology—Female

17. *Item:* WOMAN—BIOGRAPHY
× Heroines (p. 1411)

The "biography" of *generic* woman! And although it may be petty to quibble with an "×" referent from a subject head that is itself illogical, the "×" *does* show where the listmakers are at. For there is *no* "×" for HEROES (p. 587) to such a form as MAN—BIOGRAPHY, nor to WOMAN—BIOGRAPHY. This lopsided treatment can only reinforce the attitude of readers who have already accepted the implication as fact: that women who achieve are somehow extraordinary and peculiar, and whatever the denotation of the word, its connotation is of *fictitious* women.

Remedy: (a) Transfer the subhead —BIOGRAPHY to the primary head WOMEN.

(b) Either expand the HEROES form to HEROES AND HEROINES, with cross-references from and to WOMEN—BIOGRAPHY and MEN—BIOGRAPHY, or create a new head:

HEROINES
> *sa* Women—Biography
> ×× Women—Biography

18. *Item:* WOMAN—CHARITIES
sa Day nurseries
Fresh-air charity
Maternal and infant welfare
Milk depots
Women in charitable work (p. 1411)

"Charities," again, of *generic* woman. And even if it were WOMEN—CHARITIES, what does that mean (even to a cataloger)? The material to be found under the head is apparent only from the *sa*'s, which let the user in on the secret that the heading means charities whose object is to *aid* women. It would be *clearer* to say CHARITIES FOR WOMEN. It would be *better* not to say "Charities" at all in relation to any particular group of persons, for the word's connotation is, and has been for a very long time, derogatory to the recipient of the "charity."

Remedy: (a) Discard the subdivision — CHARITIES under all the primary heads where it now appears.

(b) Institute a new series of primary forms, beginning WELFARE WORK WITH . . . ; e.g., WELFARE WORK WITH MEN, WELFARE WORK WITH WOMEN, etc.[1]

Note (Item 18)

1. For an LC precedent, cf. WELFARE WORK IN INDUSTRY, p. 1400.

19. *Items:*

MAN (JEWISH THE-
OLOGY)
MAN (MOHAMMED-
ANISM)
MAN (THEOLOGY)
MAN (ZOROASTRIAN-
ISM)
(p. 744)

WOMEN IN BUDDHISM
WOMEN IN CHRISTIAN-
ITY
WOMEN IN HINDUISM
WOMEN IN MOHAM-
MEDANISM
WOMEN IN THE BIBLE
WOMEN IN THE KORAN
WOMEN IN THE TALMUD
(p. 1413–14)

WOMEN IN ART and WOMEN IN LITERATURE cover the representation of women in those fields. What, then, does WOMEN IN BUDDHISM mean? Does it mean the representation of women in Buddhist religious works, the theological position of women in Buddhism, or the day-to-day routine of women practicing the religion? And what does WOMEN IN THE BIBLE, etc., mean? Can the depiction of women in works such as these be separated from the theological position of women given in these books? If so, there should also be headings like MEN IN THE BIBLE, etc. Do the heads such as MAN (JEWISH THEOLOGY) and MAN (MOHAMMEDANISM), as the use of the generic term implies, cover the theological position of both men *and* women in these religions? It is sincerely to be doubted that any cataloger would interpret the choice of subject headings offered by the list that way; and further to be doubted that a user would so interpret the choice of heads without some reference guidance.

Remedy: Recast the WOMEN IN... entries to make them analogous to the MAN forms; e.g., WOMAN (JEWISH THEOLOGY), WOMAN (ISLAM), etc. If retained, the heads referring to the depiction of women in holy books should be complemented by MEN constructions; e.g., MEN IN THE BIBLE, MEN IN THE KORAN, etc.

20. *Items:* WOMEN IN AGRICULTURE [MISSIONARY WORK, THE CIVIL SERVICE, etc.] (p. 1413–14)

The objections made to WOMEN AS... apply with equal force to these "in" heads. For some incomprehensible reason, one sensible substitute form *has* been established: U.S. MARINE CORPS—WOMEN MARINES, equipped with "×'s" for "Women in the U.S. Marine Corps" and "Women Marines" (p. 1350).

Remedy: There are several possible alternatives; e.g., to create inverted adjectival forms like AGRICULTURISTS, WOMEN; CIVIL SERVANTS, WOMEN; and MISSIONARIES, WOMEN, with "×'s" for "Women agriculturists," "Women civil servants," and "Women missionaries"; or, in some cases (not, however, with "Missions"), to introduce — WOMEN as a direct subhead, resulting in such constructions as AGRICULTURE—WOMEN and CIVIL SERVICE—WOMEN.[1]

Note (Item 20)

1. Some flexibility and common sense will be required in order not to produce monstrosities like WOMEN BUSINESSMEN or BUSINESSMEN, WOMEN. In this particular instance, BUSINESSWOMEN should serve, all the more so since BUSINESSMEN already exists as a prime head (p. 172).

Section V

Children, Youth, "Idiots," and the "Underground"

1. *Item:* CHILDREN—MANAGEMENT (p. 220; Sears, p. 143–44)

> We live in a land which has declared war on its own children, on the future.... *To be young is a crime.*
> —Jerry Rubin[1]

It can hardly be denied that to adults, especially parents, children often seem difficult, intractable, an irritation. Yet they are *not* mere objects or barnyard animals. As the LC list itself admits in a long series of *sa* referents (p. 774–75), political campaigns, credit, factories, farms, offices, schools, and industries are fit *things* to be *managed.* Strangely, it does not also refer to "Children" although it elsewhere applies the self-same term to them. By now it should be commonly understood that, despite their age, children are *people.* Surely this is the cardinal conclusion to be distilled from the work and writing of pioneer psychologists, teachers, and educational reformers like Sylvia Ashton-Warner, A. S. Neill, Erich Fromm, John Holt, George Dennison, E. Z. Friedenberg, Herbert Kohl, Jonathan Kozol, Paul Goodman, and the groups associated with both *This Magazine Is About Schools* and the Teachers and Writers Collaborative.[2] It is a fundamental recognition that in recent years has produced the "free school" movement.[3] Of course, "children," by definition, are not as mature, independent, or fully-developed—biologically and otherwise—as grown-ups. Certainly, they require guidance and

171

special care. But "guidance" and "care" do not equal "management," a term dear to manipulators and repugnant to anyone who refuses to class *people*, including the young, with *things*.[4]

Remedy: (a) Cancel the subhead —MANAGEMENT.

(b) Establish a new subhead, —GUIDANCE AND DEVELOPMENT, with cross-references from and to CHILDREN—CARE AND HYGIENE and EDUCATION OF CHILDREN.[5]

Notes (Item 1)

1. *Do It! Scenarios of the Revolution* (New York: Simon & Schuster, 1970), p. 242. Emphasis in original.

2. For a cross-section of this literature, cf. Paul Goodman, *Growing Up Absurd* (New York: Random House, 1960) and *Compulsory Mis-Education* (New York: Horizon); Alexander Sutherland Neill, *Summerhill; A Radical Approach to Child Rearing* (with a foreword by Erich Fromm; New York: Hart, 1960); Sylvia Ashton-Warner, *Teacher* (New York: Simon & Schuster, 1963); Edgar Z. Friedenberg, *Dignity of Youth and Other Atavisms* (Boston: Beacon, 1965), *Coming of Age in America* (New York: Random House, 1965), and *Vanishing Adolescent* (Boston: Beacon, 1959); Herbert Kohl, *36 Children* (New York: New American Library, 1967), *Teaching the Unteachable; The Story of an Experiment in Children's Writing* (New York: New York Review, 1967), and "Up Against It," *New York Review of Books*, v. 13, no. 6 (Oct. 9, 1969), p. 57–9; Jonathan Kozol, *Death at an Early Age; The Destruction of the Heart and Minds of Negro Children in the Boston Public Schools* (New York: Houghton, 1967); George Dennison, *The Lives of Children* (New York: Random House, 1969); John Holt, *How Children Fail, How Children Learn*, and *The Underachieving School* (all New York: Pitman); and on children's legal status: David N. Ellhorn, "Kids Are People," *Civil Liberties*, no. 261 (April 1969), p. 1+. Also: the June 1969 issue of *Theory into Practice* (v. 8, no. 3), dedicated to "A fresh look at the child." *This Magazine* (56 Esplanade Street East, Suite 301, Toronto 215, Ontario, Canada) appears quarterly. The Collaborative issues an instructive, invigorating *Newsletter* from the Pratt Center for Community Improvement (244 Vanderbilt Avenue, Brooklyn, N.Y. 11205).

3. As a continuing source of data, cf. the *New Schools Exchange Newsletter*, issued by the New Schools Exchange (2840 Hidden Valley Lane, Santa Barbara, California 93103).

4. The *RG* form is CHILDREN—MANAGEMENT AND TRAINING, a marginal—if any—improvement over the LC head. Cf., e.g., v. 69, no. 4 (April 10, 1969), p. 30.

5. P. 219, 403.
Index Medicus uses CHILD GUIDANCE and CHILD REARING. Cf., e.g., v. 11, no. 4. (April 1970), p. 139.

2. *Item:* DISCIPLINE OF CHILDREN (p. 373)[1]

If any doubt lingers regarding the headmaster-, warden- or first sergeant–mentality that infuses the headings related to children, this form should end it. With whom are youngsters thus lumped as appropriate candidates for discipline? Industrial workers, soldiers, sailors, and prisoners.[2] Granted, they may frequently be disobedient, naughty, unruly. Still, the term—particularly in view of its other applications—reduces children as a class to something like a chain gang, a well drilled, spit-and-polish Army platoon, or rank of unthinking, unfeeling, instantly obedient automatons. Were that sort of image of our young translated into reality, it would not be hysteric in the least to speak of an impending dystopia, an unwanted but self-germinated "Brave New World."

Remedy: Delete, using the above recommended subhead —GUIDANCE AND DEVELOPMENT to encompass material formerly subsumed under the "Discipline" rubric.

Notes (Item 2)

1. Sears refers directly from "Children—Discipline" to CHILDREN—MANAGEMENT, p. 143.
2. Cf. the referents "Discipline, Industrial," "Discipline, Military," etc., p. 373.

3. *Items:* IDIOCY, IDIOT ASYLUMS (p. 618)

Were this a subject list published in the last century and never revised since, such terms might pass unremarked, the assumption being that at that distant time people didn't know any better and that on no account would any library still employ such a collection of antique absurdities as a cataloging tool. (Instead, it would be classed among "curiosa," a souvenir of a long-past folkways and follies.) It boggles the imagination to stumble upon them not in some dusty relic, but boldface-printed by LC in *1966*. To compound the puzzle: below the psychiatrically laughable term IDIOCY appears "Epilepsy" as an *sa* referent. Must these people, who suffer enough with the malady itself, be further burdened with stupid reproaches, with superstition rooted slander?[1]

Remedy: (a) Discard both "idiot" forms completely. If a work deals with "Mental deficiency," "Brain-damaged children," the "Mentally handicapped," "Psychiatric hospitals," or "Asylums," these terms already exist as primary heads, though "Mental retardation" might better express the ongoing *condition* of subnormality than "Mental deficiency," while INSTITUTIONS (FOR ALCOHOLICS, THE BLIND, DEAF, etc.) would mark an improvement over the Dickensian ASYLUMS.[2]

(b) It should be standard procedure once "a" is accomplished, but nonetheless worth underscoring, that "Idiocy" will be cleanly amputated from the "××'s" under EPILEPSY (p. 439).

Notes (Item 3)

1. It may be objected that "Idiocy" continues to figure in standard medical and psychiatric nomenclature, and that *Webster's Third* endows it with a fairly specific "scientific" meaning: "a feebleminded person that has a mental age not exceeding two years and accordingly requires complete custodial care" (p. 1224). There can be little doubt, however, that popular usage assigns the word an *un*scientific, derogatory significance. The very definition just cited is surrounded by two others: "*obs*: an ignorant or unschooled person: a simple unlearned person: CLOWN" and "a silly simple person: SIMPLETON, BLOCKHEAD...." Moreover, Karl F. Heiser and Benjamin B. Wolman attest that "In the history of man, there have always been individuals with a limited capacity for comprehending and reasoning, who fell behind intellectually and could not participate successfully in the economic, cultural, and social life. These individuals were labelled as dumb, stupid, imbeciles, and *idiots* and were utterly neglected, often ridiculed and exploited but never helped." Cf. their "Mental Deficiences," in Wolman, ed., *Handbook of Clinical Psychology* (New York: McGraw-Hill, 1965), p. 838.

Emphasis added. That the term has been recognized by specialists as laden with opprobrium as well as being inexact is implicit in the metamorphosis undergone by a leading professional association: In 1876, a number of institution officials formed the Association of Medical Officers of American Institutions for Idiots and Feebleminded Persons. In 1906 this society became the American Association for the Study of the Feebleminded, and in 1933 changed its name to the American Association on Mental Deficiency. Cf. Albert Deutsch, *The Mentally Ill in America*, 2nd ed. (New York: Columbia University Press, 1949), p. 347. Halbert B. and Nancy M. Robinson furnish even more conclusive evidence in their *Mentally Retarded Child: A Psychological Approach* (New York: McGraw-Hill, 1965):

> For many years, the terms, *idiot, imbecile,* and *moron* were used in the United States to denote abilities roughly in the IQ ranges 0 to 30, 30 to 50, and 50 to 70, respectively. In Great Britain, the term *feebleminded* replaced the term moron, and similar terms were used in other countries, but by and large all of these terms are now quite out of vogue. In 1954, a special subcommittee of WHO [the World Health Organization] proposed a system of nomenclature based on British, American, French, and German usage in which the terms *mild subnormality, moderate subnormality,* and *severe subnormality* were recommended. These terms do not carry the opprobrious connotations of the older nomenclature, and by their similarity to each other they accentuate the continuous nature of mental ability. . . .

Emphasis in original, p. 49. For a detailed discussion, cf. the whole chapter, "Problems of Definition and Current Status of the Field of Mental Retardation," p. 27–58.

Prof. Gunnar Dybwad, former Director of the Mental Retardation Project of the International Union for Child Welfare, reinforces the Robinsons' contention in his statement that "Twenty years ago, anybody who had taken a course in psychology 'knew' that the mentally retarded consisted of morons, imbeciles, and idiots. . . . Later, as increasing opposition was expressed in regard to these particular terms, 'mild,' 'moderate,' and 'severe' were substituted as more appropriate and were adopted by the WHO in its 1954 report." Cf. "Who Are the Mentally Retarded?," *Children*, v. 15, no. 2 (March-April 1968), p. 45. The WHO document itself, no. 75 in the organization's Technical Report Series, is titled *The Mentally Subnormal Child; Report of a Joint Expert Committee* (Geneva).

A leading academic publication in this field, it should be noted, does not bear the title *Journal of Idiocy, Moronity, and Imbecility,* but rather the title

Journal of Mental Subnormality. Cf. Dybwad, *op. cit.*, p. 46, and *Ulrich's International Periodicals Directory*, 12th ed. (New York: Bowker, 1967), v. 1, p. 290.

Sears wisely refers from "Idiocy" to MENTALLY HANDICAPPED (p. 318). The next edition, however, could well improve on this advance by canceling the referent altogether.

2. As LC precedents, cf. INSTITUTION LIBRARIES (p. 652), INMATES OF INSTITUTIONS (p. 648), and PUBLIC INSTITUTIONS (p. 1047).

The 1968 ACS on p. 212 finally canceled IDIOT ASYLUMS, now referring from the defunct form to MENTALLY HANDICAPPED — INSTITUTIONAL CARE. It did *not*, however, excise IDIOCY. If "idiots" are to be termed (properly) "Mentally handicapped," their *condition*, it follows, should be something like "Mental retardation" or "Mental subnormality." The same reasoning, in short, that produced MENTALLY HANDICAPPED — INSTITUTIONAL CARE as a substitute for IDIOT ASYLUMS should simultaneously have spawned a new rubric for IDIOCY. While welcome, the change is yet incomplete. And it may be further observed that "Asylums," as both a prime head and subdivision, elsewhere remains wholly intact (cf., e.g., 1968 ACS, p. 223). Indeed, "Idiot asylums" is itself still retained as a referent. One day, it is to be hoped, the scheme will be 100 percent "idiot"-free.

4. *Items:* CHILDREN AS ARTISTS; CHILDREN AS AUTHORS; etc. (p. 220–21; Sears, p. 144)

A few moments spent leafing through *I Never Saw Another Butterfly,* a collection of evocative, enduring verse and graphics produced by youngsters in the midst of torment and despair,[1] or *Children of the A-Bomb: The Testament of the Boys and Girls of Hiroshima,*[2] should devastate any lingering myths about children's incapacity to richly express themselves in word or picture. On the contrary, the overwhelming evidence suggests that *every* child, more so than *every* adult, is (at least potentially) a poet or artist.[3] LC, however, stands this postulate on its head, crediting only rare or "gifted" children with signal achievement as creators, implying that "ordinary" youths can't—or don't—cross the threshhold of *real* creativity. This is rank Adult Chauvinism and contributes mightily to widening the "Generation Gap."

Remedy: To conform with existing constructions like ARTISTS, AMERICAN and ARTISTS, BLIND (p. 81), revamp such forms into ART- ISTS, CHILD; AUTHORS, CHILD, etc., with "×'s" for "Child artists," "Child authors," etc.[4]

Notes (Item 4)

1. The State Jewish Museum in Prague assembled and published these "Children's drawings and poems from Theresienstadt concentration camp, 1942–1944." In the United States, McGraw-Hill assumed distribution in 1964. By May 1945, some 15,000 children had passed through the Terezin KZ. Only 100 survived.

2. (New York: Putnam, 1963). Arata Osada compiled these moving, vivid memoirs of the nuclear holocaust, written by eyewitnesses whose ages ranged from 4 to 16 at the time of the blast.

3. Cf., as further examples, random issues of the *Teachers and Writers Collaborative Newsletter, op. cit.,* each well-laden with compelling, child-authored prose and verse, much of it confected by "disadvantaged" young people; *Mother, These Are My Friends* (New York: Liberty House), a "collection of wishes of Harlem children in their own words," compiled by Mary Anne Gross (in Anne Sexton's opinion, "the speech of these children is true poetry," quoted in the Oct. 9, 1969, *New York Review of Books,* p. 58); and Daniel M. Mendelowitz, *Children Are Artists; An Introduction to Children's Art for Teachers and Parents.* 2nd ed. (Stanford, Calif.: Stanford University Press, 1963), including a chromatic portfolio of "Children's paintings from many lands," prefaced by the observation that "although each culture colors the way its children react to their environment, the visual language of childhood remains universal in its power to communicate ideas, experiences, and above all the intensity of feeling with which the growing child discovers the world."

Also: Kenneth Koch, "Wishes, Lies, and Dreams: Teaching Children to Write Poetry," *New York Review of Books,* v. 14, no. 7 (April 9, 1970), p. 17–29. Koch holds that "children have a great talent for writing poetry and love to do it." A sampling of "Poems from P.S. 61" appears on p. 29.

4. The 1967 ACS on p. 48 introduced CHILDREN'S WRITINGS as a prime head. That children *write* —indeed, voluminously—is thus admitted, but a scope note nonetheless explains that "*Discussions of such literature are entered under* Children as authors." The 1969 ACS likewise recognized the capacity of young people to draw and paint with a new form, CHILDREN'S ART (p. 38). It did not, however, revise CHILDREN AS ARTISTS.

5. *Item:* **Underground press**
See **Underground literature (p. 1339)**

> Our media, the underground press, both creates and reflects
> our new consciousness. The Establishment press reflects the
> irrelevant, dying and repressive institutions with which we are
> at war. . . . The underground press is the beating heart of the
> community.[1]

No, the "underground literature" treated by the referred-to head
is *not* the variously ribald, revolutionary, pro-pot, hard-rock, anti-
Establishment, psychedelic, "hip," four-letter-word-larded produce
of magazines and tabloids like *Oz, Georgia Straight, Great Speckled
Bird, Los Angeles Free Press, IT, Avatar, Kaleidoscope,* and the *East
Village Other.* It embraces, rather, the truly clandestine, officially
proscribed literature spawned by wartime resistance movements
such as the French Maquis. The calamity, especially from a youth
perspective, is that *no* head whatever encompasses the new genre—
labeled by its practitioners either the "underground" or "alternative" press—that dates from approxmiately 1964 and presently
numbers millions of young people (and others) among its reader-
ship. Standard indexes have simply subsumed material on this subject under "Newspapers" or "Periodicals," neither of which satisfactorily recognizes the extent, impact, or unparalleled nature of the
phenomenon.

    Remedy: (a) Establish UNDERGROUND PRESS, 1964–   as a
primary head, with an "×" for "Alternative press, 1964– ,"[2] and,
in recognition of the widespread harassment visited upon UG
hawkers and publishers, an "××" for "Censorship."[3]

    (b) Divide UNDERGROUND LITERATURE into two more precise,
realistic forms: UNDERGROUND LITERATURE (OCCUPIED COUNTRIES)
and UNDERGROUND LITERATURE (TOTALITARIAN STATES), changing the
present *See* roster to:

> *See* Underground literature (Occupied countries)
>   Underground literature (Totalitarian states)
>   Underground press, 1964–

The first head would encompass material now subsumed under UNDERGROUND LITERATURE, while the second may be applied to patently *illegal* literature confected or circulated *inside* essentially totalitarian, dictatorially-governed countries by nationals of those countries, whether in war or peacetime.[4]

(c) To differentiate the *civilian* "underground press" from its later, soldier-produced offshoot, create UNDERGROUND PRESS, U.S. MILITARY, 1966–　as a complementary form, with *See* references from "U.S.—Armed Forces—Underground press, 1966–　," "GI newspapers, Unofficial, 1966–　," "GI antiwar newspapers, 1966–　," "Antiwar newspapers, GI, 1966–　," and the unused heads, "Underground literature" and "Underground press."[5] Additionally, institute an "××" for "Censorship."

(d) Large collections of education, youth, and or radical material may wish to employ UNDERGROUND PRESS (SECONDARY SCHOOLS) to cover the High School Undergrounds (HSU), like *Options* (Sioux Falls, South Dakota) and *Smuff* (Chicago), which have been created variously to "voice student opinions . . . bring students together on the issues that affect them most . . . [and] check the hypocrisy and lies of administrators and the educational system in general."[6]

Notes (Item 5)

1. Jerry Rubin, *op. cit.*, p. 236–37.

2. *API* favors ALTERNATIVE PRESS, but since nearly all the publications so described have formed themselves into an "Underground Press Syndicate" (UPS), the latter term seems preferable. For bibliographic and evaluative data on the genre, cf. the several directories and commentaries cited by Sanford Berman in the *Assistant Librarian*, v. 63, no. 4 (April 1970), p. 58-9, as well as the listing that concludes Anne Leibl's contribution to the Jan.-Feb. 1970 *Canadian Library Journal*, *op. cit.*, p. 23. Also: Roger Lewis' discerning overview of "The American Underground Press," *Assistant Librarian*, v. 63, no. 8 (Aug. 1970), p. 122–24. Lewis, Research Assistant at the American Arts Documentation Centre, University of Exeter, organized the first British exhibition of American "underground" publications at the University Library in mid–1970.

The *BHI* has established UNDERGROUND PRESS as a primary head, with a "related heading" reference under NEWSPAPERS. Cf., e.g., no. 1 (Jan.-March 1970), p. 82, 119.

The "1964" refers to the year in which the *Los Angeles Free Press*, apparently the earliest UG organ, began publication. Cf. Katz, *Magazines for Libraries, op. cit.,* p. 353.

3. On the censorship aspects of UG publishing, particularly in Great Britain and America, cf. the extensive *API* citations under "Censorship" (e.g., v. 1, nos. 1/2, p. 12); consecutive issues of both *Censorship Today* and the *Newsletter on Intellectual Freedom* since mid–1969; and Sanford Berman's letter, "Underground Press," in the Jan. 22, 1970, *Times Literary Supplement* (no. 3543), p. 84.

4. For example: Franco Spain, post–April 1967 Greece, Nationalist-ruled South Africa, and the several "people's democracies," including the Soviet Union, where only literature embodying the prescribed orthodoxy is permitted. In this last connection, Wassily Leontief, reporting on a visit to Osaka's Expo 70, drily mentions that in the USSR pavilion "one does not see Solzhenitsyn's mournful face, nor does one find among the books displayed on endless shelves the underground publications of the 'Samizdat'..." Cf. "Mysterious Japan: A Diary," *New York Review of Books*, v. 14, no. 11 (June 4, 1970), p. 28. For continuing reportage on the worldwide press situation, accenting the repressive regimen in "totalitarian states," cf. the bimonthly *IPI Report* (International Press Institute, Münstergasse 9, 8001 Zürich, Switzerland). For a few firsthand observations on "intellectual freedom" in Greece at the time of the Colonels' coup and in Russia later that same year, cf. Sanford Berman, "Notes from Europe," *Newsletter on Intellectual Freedom,* v. 16 (Nov. 1967), p. 82–4.

5. Bill Katz, in his May 1, 1970, *Library Journal* column (v. 95, no. 9), lists the five principal titles published by (or for) GIs in Europe, describing these papers as "the chief raw material for documenting an almost incredible episode in military (if not publishing) history" (p. 1719). A full roster of all active "GI anti-war papers" usually occupies the last page of the bi-weekly *GI Press Service* (1029 Vermont Avenue, N.W., Room 907, Washington, D.C. 2005). Most of the European and many of the Stateside vehicles are produced under auspices of the American Servicemen's Union (ASU), Friends of Resisters Inside the Army (FRITA), and Resisters Inside the Army (RITA). Since Katz's note appeared, new GI "rags" have surfaced in Kaiserslautern, West Germany (*The Propergander*), Schwäbisch Gmünd (*Witness*), Hanau (*Speek Out*), Heidelberg (*About Face*, prepared by UBS: Unsatisfied Black Soldiers, and distributed by *Graffitti*, Schiffgasse 3, 6900 Heidelberg), Okinawa, Japan, and Vietnam (the last three are identically titled *We Got the BrAss* and available from R. Hobbit, 6-44 Ishii Bldg., Kagurazaka, Shinjuku-ku, Tokyo). Also, the European *We Got the BrAss* has in the meantime fused with *The Next Step* (P.O.B. 2441, Frankfurt-am-

Main) and Berlin's *Where It's At* amalgamated with *Up Against The Wall* (Postfach 65, 1 Berlin 12), while *Act* (10 Passage du Chantier, Paris 12) reports a mid–1970 per-issue press run of 25,000 copies. Source: personal communication from a "Frita" via the Politische Buchhandlung in Heidelberg. Cf. Also the section on "GI Antiwar Papers" in Muller, 2nd ed., *op. cit.*

The year "1966" indicates when the two issues of *Yin-yang*, in all likelihood first of the genre, appeared. Cf. Sanford Berman's annotation for *Vietnam GI* in Katz's April 15, 1970, *Library Journal* column (v. 95, no. 8), p. 1459. Copies of *Yin-yang*, incidentally, are archived at the UCLA Research Library's Department of Special Collections.

6. For a short history of HSU, plus a statement of purpose, cf. "Why High School Undergrounds Are Formed," *Los Angeles Free Press*, Jan. 22, 1971, p. 17.

6. *Item:* YOUTH AS CONSUMERS (1967 ACS, p. 295)

Adolescents thus join the ranks of Blacks, Jews, Amerindians, women and children for whom certain activities are considered extraordinary. Has no LC cataloger ever visited a record shop on a Saturday morning? Or peeked into a "psychedelic" emporium *any*time? Perhaps it ought to be made a regular staff activity, duly stipulated in job descriptions.

Remedy: Contract the form to YOUTH CONSUMERS.

7. *Items:* INSANE; INSANE, CRIMINAL AND DANGEROUS; INSANITY; and all inverted heads beginning with INSANITY, e.g., INSANITY, MORAL (p. 649)[1]

This series of principal headings implies a distinction between "insanity" and the related group of "mental" forms (e.g., MENTAL HEALTH LAWS, MENTAL ILLNESS, p. 807). Indeed, there *is* a very meaningful distinction, but it is one ignored in the LC list. "Insane" and "insanity" are *legal* terms used in such instances as: (a) when there is the need to prove criminal capacity, such as the near-universal

M'Naghten ruling,[2] or liability under contract[3]; or (b) when the question of commitment to a mental hospital comes before a tribunal.[4] In these and similar cases the need to prove insanity becomes an all-or-nothing matter.[5] This is a requirement made by the court, and medical specialists themselves would be very reluctant to give such a hard-and-fast ruling. In consequence, there is no such class of persons as the "insane," as suggested by the phrase: "*Works on the legal status of the insane are entered under the heading* Insanity—Jurisprudence" (p. 807). Insanity *is* a legal status—and nothing more. Further, the criteria of insanity operative in one legal context are rarely the same as in another.[6] When the term "insane" is not used in this very special and limited sense, when, for instance, it is interchanged with the term "mental illness" (e.g., "*Works on the law affecting the welfare of the insane are entered. . .,*" p. 649), then the label has very different connotations. It recalls the now discredited terms "lunatic" and "madness,"[7] which through an aura of mystification became no more than a moral insult carrying the accusation of permanent mental instability (as do the headings INSANE, KILLING OF THE and INSANITY, PERIODIC AND TRANSITORY).[8] There is the further implication that the insane are somehow a different species of human beings.[9] By far the most misleading and mischievous usage lies in the unthinking association with crime, as under INSANE, CRIMINAL AND DANGEROUS. Correctly used, this is a near tautology, since to be found "insane" must be in the context either of having committed an indictable offense, or being a danger to oneself, or a danger or menace to others.[10] Used loosely, as it is by LC, it reinforces the public stereotype that there is a positive and logical connection between mental illness and crime or—more specifically—unpredictable acts of violence.[11] Studies have shown that just the reverse is true.[12] *Sanity* is more a necessary prerequisite for violent, criminal and loathsome acts than "insanity," such crimes being lower among mental patients than among the general population.[13]

Remedy: (a) There are no grounds for retaining INSANE, INSANITY, and their various offshoots as prime heads. Instead, the two basic terms, since they have only *legal* import, should be reduced to unused forms which refer directly to appropriate *legal* headings. Both may thus be equipped with an omnibus *See* reference to

> Criminal liability
> Forensic psychiatry
> Liability (Law)
> Mental health laws

(b) "Lunacy," now a referent to INSANITY (p. 762), should be altogether eliminated: first, because the referred-to head will have been dismantled under "a" above; and second, inasmuch as it represents obsolescent, slipshod terminology, much like "Savages," "Idiocy," and "Asylums."

Notes (Item 7)

1. The discussion and "remedy" for Item 7 were prepared by Richard Bottomley, assistant lecturer in sociology at the University of Zambia and formerly a psychiatric social worker in England.

Sears, on p. 330, refers directly from "Insane" to INSANITY and MENTAL ILLNESS, from "Insane—Care and treatment" to MENTALLY ILL—CARE AND TREATMENT, from "Insane—Hospitals" to MENTALLY ILL—CARE AND TREATMENT, and from "Insane asylums" likewise to MENTALLY ILL—CARE AND TREATMENT. INSANITY, however, appears as a primary head, with *See also* entries for HALLUCINATIONS AND ILLUSIONS; MENTAL ILLNESS; MENTALLY HANDICAPPED; PERSONALITY, DISORDERS OF; PSYCHIATRY; PSYCHOLOGY, PATHOLOGICAL; and SUICIDE. It is further provided with "×'s' for "Dementia; Diseases, Mental; Insane; Lunacy; Madness; Mental diseases; Psychoses," as well as 7 "××'s": BRAIN—DISEASES; HALLUCINATIONS AND ILLUSIONS; MENTAL ILLNESS; NERVOUS SYSTEM—DISEASES; PERSONALITY, DISORDERS OF; PSYCHIATRY; and PSYCHOLOGY, PATHOLOGICAL.

2. Where the criteria are (a) the ability to understand the nature of the act, and (b) the ability to distinguish between right and wrong in respect of it. The defendant is entitled to acquittal on the grounds of insanity if he or she lacks the ability to do either. Cf. *21 Am Jur 2d Crim Law*, para. 34, and for Britain, *Halisbury's Laws, 10 Crim Law*, pt. 1, sec. 2, para. 530.

3. That he or she should be able to understand the character of transaction in a contract. Cf. for instance, *25 Am Jur Guardian and Ward*, para. 18 and 66 *et seq.*

4. As in *29 Am Jur Insane Pers.*, para. 35; also: Great Britain, *Mental Health Act* 1959.

5. "An offender is either wholly sane or wholly insane for a criminal offence." *21 Am Jur 2d Crim Law*, para. 40.

6. E.g., for hospitalization: "It has been generally recognized that the general test or criterion of insanity or unsoundness of mind, wanting commitment to a mental hospital or asylum, depends upon whether such insanity is of such a degree that if the persons so afflicted were allowed to be at large—would by reason of this be a danger to life, property, or person, or a menace to the public." An indigent insane may be committed without proof of dangerousness. *29 Am Jur Insane Pers.*, para. 35. The criteria for insanity just cited are so markedly different from those cited in the first three notes above that it is impossible to speak of the "insane" without specifying the legal context. In England, the term "insanity" is almost exclusively reserved in respect of criminal responsibility.

7. In England these terms have been superseded by the term "mental disorder," which is used in almost every instance excepting criminal responsibility. Cf. *Mental Health Act 1959* and *Halisbury's Laws 29 Mental Disorders,* pt. 1, sec. 1, para. 792.

8. Cf. J. C. Nunnally, Jr., *Popular Conceptions of Mental Health* (New York: Holt, Rinehart & Winston, 1961).

9. As "violent, immoral, criminal, filthy, idiosyncratic and worthless." Cf. L. H. Rogler and A. B. Hollingshead, *Trapped: Families and Schizophrenia* (New York: Wiley, 1965), p. 218.

10. *21* and *25 Am Jur., loc. cit.*

11. Cf. Rogler and Hollingshead, *op. cit.*; L. C. Hartlage, "Employer Receptivity to Former Mental Patients," *Social Casework,* v. 49, no. 10 (Dec. 1963), p. 587; and S. Star, *The Public's Ideas About Mental Illness* (Chicago: National Opinion Research Center, University of Chicago, 1955).

12. Cf., e.g., "Prisoners or Patients?," *Economist,* Jan. 28, 1967, p. 304. Of the orders made from courts to hospitals under Section 60 of the Mental Health Act 1959, 75 percent were for nonindictable offenses. Only 58 out of the 1,100 orders were made after offenses against persons. Cf. also: J. T. Scheff, *Being Mentally Ill* (London: Weidenfeld & Nicolson, 1967), p. 131. In his study of the behavior of patients at the time of admission, Scheff found that the psychiatrists responsible thought that 76 percent were unlikely to be violent. For similar indications from Cohen and Freeman, cf. their "How Dangerous to the Community Are State Hospital Patients?," *Connecticut State Medical Journal,* v. 9 (Sept. 1945), p. 697–700. Also: Hastings, "Follow Up Results in Psychiatric Illness," *American Journal of Psychiatry,* v. 114 (June 1958), p. 1057–66; Rappeport, and others, "Evaluation and Follow Up of State Hospital Patients Who Had Sanity Hearings," *ibid.,* v. 118 (June 1962), p. 1078–88; and, of course, the well-known argument that most patient violence on admission and within the hospital is situational, *viz* E. Goffman, *Asylums* (Harmondsworth: Penguin Books, 1968).

13. The problem of deciding what is "sane" or "insane" has been well discussed in Erich Fromm, *The Sane Society* (London: Routledge, 1956).

On the question of violence, R. D. Laing, representative of the "Liberation" movement in psychiatry, drily remarks: "Normal men have killed perhaps 1,000,000,000 of their fellow normal men in the last 50 years." Cf. *The Politics of Experience and the Bird of Paradise* (Harmondsworth: Penguin Books, 1967), p. 24. And for the normalization of violence on a world scale, cf. the discussion in David Copper, ed., *The Dialectics of Liberation* (Harmondsworth: Penguin Books, 1968).

Section VI

Do-It-Yourself

The foregoing exploration cannot be regarded as exhaustive. It was circumscribed by time, available resources, and the author's own blindspots. Beyond question, there remains much muck to rake within the LC list's 1,432 triple-columned pages. Here is an invitation, then, to the like-minded, to those unsatisfied with the scheme as it is and determined that such a basic tool should represent the best insights and information at our command: Locate, examine, and report—to library periodicals and LC itself—any further outlandish or unjustifiable forms, as well as recommending totally new heads required by our fast-changing times.

The novice may want to begin with a few "items" bypassed in this study, but nonetheless worth attention:

1. *Item:* INCORRIGIBLES (JUVENILE DELINQUENCY), p. 623

2. *Item:* LAW AND SOCIALISM
   x **Communism and law**
    Law and Communism (p. 725)

What political algebra, except of a super-simplistic, Leftophobic sort, could permit the equation: Socialism = Communism = Socialism?

3. *Item:* NON-CHURCH AFFILIATED PEOPLE (p. 897)

4. *Item:* PACIFIC COAST INDIANS, WARS WITH, 1847– (p. 934)

Wars with *whom*? The Black slaves on Southern plantations? The Asian laborers imported to lay rail? The East European Jews who flooded across the Atlantic at the turn of the century? The famine-haunted Irish, hoping to survive in the New World rather than starve in the Old? *Who* encroached on Indian lands? Shouldn't the burden be placed squarely upon the predators, instead of being diluted into a cosmic responsibility? And have these "wars" not yet ended?

5. *Item:* SABOTAGE
×× Socialism (p. 1124)

As a start, cf. the discussion concerning "Terrorism" as an "××" under ANARCHISM AND ANARCHISTS.

6. *Items:* SINGLE PEOPLE
×× Chastity
Virginity (p. 1183)

7. *Item:* FAMILY
sa Master and servant (p. 467)

Is this, perchance, an endorsement of St. Paul's injunction to "Let wives be subject to their husbands as to the Lord"?

8. *Item:* TEACHERS AS AUTHORS (1966 ACS, p. 153)

9. *Item:* FRIENDS AS SCIENTISTS (1967 ACS, p. 107)

The reference is to Quakers.

10. *Item:* PRISONERS OF WAR AS ARTISTS (1967 ACS, p. 207)

Regarding prisoners of *any sort* as artists or authors, cf., for example, Joseph A. Boissé's review of *Trial Poems: A Poet, a Painter—A Facsimile Edition of Their Prison Art,* by Daniel Berrigan and Thomas Lewis (Boston: Beacon Press, 1970), in the May 1, 1970, *Library Journal* (v. 95, no. 9), p. 1749.

11. *Item:* BANTUS AS CONSUMERS (1968 ACS, p. 41)

LC regards no less than 59 African peoples as "Bantu." Cf. 7th ed., p. 112. When assessing the head, consider—for example—that a member of one such "tribe," the Bemba, is vice-president of the Republic of Zambia, in which capacity he necessarily entertains considerably and, *ergo, consumes* considerably.

12. *Item:* SEXUAL PERVERSION
sa Cunnilingus
Fellatio (1968 ACS, p. 402)

Objective surveys of actual sexual practice, especially in "permissive" societies, might reveal that such acts are not in fact so "perverse"—statistically, at any rate.

13. *Item:* SPANISH AMERICANS AS CONSUMERS
× Spanish American consumers (1968 ACS, p. 422)

14. *Item:* **SUCCESS**
    sa **Business**
         Charm
         Saving and thrift
    ×× **Fortune**
         Wealth (p. 1246)

The four referents are extracted from a larger list, but well convey its tenor. The formulation poses several questions: Is this concept of "success" peculiar to the get-rich-quick, Madison Avenue–promulgated "American Dream"? Has the success-drive and "Protestant ethic," as Fromm, Horney, and others allege, perhaps produced as much *anxiety* as *personal satisfaction*? Might "success" also be founded on *other* values and means; e.g., "candor" instead of "charm," or "productive labor" rather than "fortune"?

Index

191

CHILDREN—MANAGEMENT 5, 171–73

Children of the A-Bomb (1963) 176–77

"Children, Youth, 'Idiots,' and the 'Underground'" 171–85

CHILDREN'S ART 177

CHILDREN'S SERMONS 56–7

CHILDREN'S SERMONS, CHRISTIAN, *proposed* 56

CHILDREN'S WRITINGS 177

CHINA—HISTORY—INVASIONS 93

CHINESE IN THE U.S. 31–5

Chivington, John 6

Chomsky, Noam 114, 119

CHRISTIAN CHURCH headings, *proposed* 48

CHRISTIAN DEVOTIONAL LITERATURE, *proposed* 59

CHRISTIAN MISSIONS TO headings, *proposed* 70

CHRISTIANITY AND OTHER RELIGIONS 41

CHRISTIANITY—HISTORY 48

CHRISTIANS AS SOLDIERS (hypothetical heading) 50

Christocentric headings 5, 12, 41–3, 48–51, 54, 56–9, 69–71, 72–3

CHURCH 48–9

CHURCH HISTORY 48–9

CIVIL RIGHTS 32, 140, 142

CIVIL SERVANTS, WOMEN, *proposed* 169

Civil society (term) 85–7, 103

CIVILIZATION, AFRICAN, *proposed* 102

CIVILIZATION AND CULTURE, *proposed subhead* 67

CIVILIZATION headings 41–3, 67, 102–04, 109

CIVILIZATION, OCCIDENTAL 109

CIVILIZATION, PAGAN 41–3

Civilized (term) 86

Clark, Kenneth 162

Clarke, John Henrik 40

Clarke, Marian 21

CLASSISM IN headings, *proposed* 11

CLASSISM, *proposed* 10–11

Classist cross-references 121–23, 125–26, 134–35

Classist headings 15, 132–33

CLOTHING AND DRESS, PRIMITIVE 85–7

COAL-MINERS—PENNSYLVANIA, *proposed cross-reference* 123

COAL MINES AND MINING 123

CO-DETERMINATION (INDUSTRIAL RELATIONS) 117

Cole, Sonia 81

Coles, Robert 20

COLLECTIVE SETTLEMENTS 121

Collier, Peter 52

COLONIAL PERIOD, *proposed subhead* 97, 100, 106

COLONIES (subhead) 83–5

COLONIZED PEOPLES, *proposed* 79

COLOR OF MAN 8

COLORED cross-reference 44–5, 47

Columbus, Christopher 52–3

COMMANDMENTS OF THE CHURCH 58

COMMANDMENTS OF THE CHURCH (ROMAN CATHOLIC), *proposed* 58

COMMUNES cross-references, *proposed* 121

COMMUNISM 111–12, 124, 134

COMMUNISM AND LAW (cross-reference) 187

COMMUNISM AND MOHAMMEDANISM 37–8